HIDDEN FAME

- Jancis Wiles -

An environmentally friendly book printed and bound in England by
www.printondemand-worldwide.com

Mixed Sources
Product group from well-managed
forests, and other controlled sources
www.fsc.org Cert no. TT-COC-002641
FSC © 1996 Forest Stewardship Council

PEFC Certified
This product is
from sustainably
managed forests
and controlled
sources
PEFC www.pefc.org
PEFC/16-33-415

This book is made entirely of chain-of-custody materials

www.fast-print.net/store.php

Hidden Fame
Copyright © Jancis Wiles 2012

A catalogue record for this book is available from the British Library

ISBN 978-178035-522-1

First published 2012 by
FASTPRINT PUBLISHING
Peterborough, England.

In memory of

Mabel and Ray

"And some there be which have no memorial; who are perished as though they had never been … Their bodies are buried in peace; but their name liveth for evermore."
Ecclesiasticus Ch 44 vv 9 & 14

CONTENTS

ACKNOWLEDGEMENTS

My sincerest thanks are due to the countless people and organisations who have helped me in connection with this book, in particular those who have so kindly given me permission to use copies of images in which they own the copyright, or which are in their custody but copyright-expired. These categories include many who have made images available through Wikipedia, and detailed acknowledgements regarding the use of all images are set out in Appendix 2. I am grateful also to the many people who have taken the time and trouble to reply to my enquiring emails, even if only to refer me elsewhere. I have made every effort in respect of each illustration to establish whether copyright still attaches to it and, if it does or might do so, to trace the copyright owner and obtain the necessary permission before using it. If I have inadvertently omitted to obtain permission from any copyright owner then I apologise.

This book contains the occasional anecdote to illustrate the discussion of a few of the words. I trust that those friends and family members who may recognise themselves in any of them will forgive me and, if necessary, find consolation in the fact that they remain anonymous.

I am indebted to the public library reference services for allowing me access to numerous books and publications, and to compilers of the wonderfully authoritative reference works that I have consulted including the Oxford English Dictionary, The Chambers Dictionary, Brewer's Dictionary of Phrase and Fable, Chambers Dictionary of Etymology, the Encyclopaedia

Britannica, the Dictionary of National Biography (1908) and its updated version the Oxford Dictionary of National Biography (2004).

Above all I thank my husband Mark, who has lived with this project for several years, provided illustrations and advice, and been a constant source of encouragement and support.

INTRODUCTION

For one's own name to have given rise to a word – to an extension, albeit tiny, of the English language – is undeniable proof that the world has changed as a result of one's time on earth. And there is hope for us all. There is no need to be rich or clever or famous: a surprising number of eponyms reflect the lives of people who are of no interest to the general historian. Even failure by subsequent generations to realise that there was a real person behind the word does nothing to diminish the memorial. Rather, the reverse. The less a word draws attention to itself as being derived from a name – for example, if it is no longer spelt with a capital letter – the more the word has become an integral part of the language and so the greater the achievement of the individual concerned.

This book is intended as a light-hearted stroll through the stories behind a limited number of eponymous words. Only those that I find particularly appealing have been selected. In some cases the interest lies in how the name, or part of it, became connected to the word. There may be some aspect of the life of the person (in one case animal) commemorated by the word that is of interest. There may be a personal context that gives it significance, or it may simply be that I enjoy the word itself. However, three discrete fields have been (almost) entirely excluded: geographical words, words derived from fictional characters, and words that are no more than the names of commercial products.

1

What this book most emphatically is <u>not</u>, is a dictionary. Those who want a source of reference may consult one of the suitably authoritative tomes already written by aficionados of the eponym. Such comprehensive works inevitably include large numbers of out-dated words, or technical words of little interest to the general reader, and are tied into presenting those words in alphabetical order.

Nor is it a biographical reference book. At most you will find a brief outline of the life of the person immortalised by the word. In the majority of cases there is considerably less than that: sometimes no more than the years of birth and death, and even these cannot always be established. My intention is to encourage the reader to flick through the pages and alight upon a word with the thought 'Who on earth was that?', or to spot something previously unknown about a familiar figure.

Language constantly has to respond to progress and come up with words for new concepts as and when they are needed. It may do so by burdening a word already in existence with a second meaning, but frequently language meets the challenge by creating new words. So eponyms naturally fall into groups according to those fields most subject to change: indeed part of their interest is that they lend themselves to division in this way. Many are found in scientific, technical and military fields – units of measurement are particularly popular. The same argument applies to fashion and food. The exception seems to be eponyms that are the result of someone having acted in such an extraordinary way that his (I could not find any women in this category) name has been coined to describe such behaviour. The reverse of the general rule is also true: creation of the new often renders the old obsolete, hence the plethora of abstruse eponyms found in dictionaries loath to allow the language to shrink.

In some cases a word is not directly eponymous: it is named after something else which itself happens to be an eponym. These words are rather unusual and can take some unravelling. They comprise a decidedly select group and can be thought of as secondary eponyms. 'Plimsolls' and 'Sloane Ranger' are good examples.

Every effort has been made not to make false claims and it is worth laying one or two of the most tempting of these to rest. 'Nosey Parker' sounded promising. After the dissolution of the monasteries under Henry VIII, Elizabeth I asked the Archbishop of Canterbury, Matthew Parker, to make a copy of all ancient documents and records that had escaped destruction. He thereupon made exhaustive searches and enquiries, tracking down books and manuscripts in order to carry out this enormous task. Since the phrase 'Nosey Parker' describes his activities so accurately it was perhaps inevitable that someone would claim the phrase originated with him. Sadly this has to be ruled out, as the Oxford English Dictionary tells us the earliest use of 'nosey', in the sense of inquisitive or prying, was not until 1910. Parker is therefore driven to relying on the seldom referred to 'Archbishop Parker's table' for his immortality – the list appearing in the book of Common Prayer of the prohibited degrees of relationship within which marriage is forbidden.

Similarly, 'Cabal' sounded hopeful. The word has been said to derive from the first letter of the names of each of the group of five who were close advisers to Charles II (Clifford, Arlington, Buckingham, Ashley and Lauderdale). Certainly that group was referred to as a cabal, but the dictionary again leads to disappointment: the word was already in use prior to that time.

The most famous false eponym of all, of course, has to be 'crap', widely stated to derive from the name of a Victorian manufacturer of lavatory cisterns. Unfortunately the word was in use long before then, but one is forced to wonder if Mr. Crapper felt compelled to consider a career in plumbing simply because of his name, just as one wonders whether Sir Frank Figgures, who held a very senior position in the Treasury some years ago, might have felt an equivalent compulsion.

But now it is time to turn to those real people hidden behind a word.

CHAPTER ONE

CLOTHING, ACCESSORIES AND TEXTILES

The ephemeral nature of fashion means that many words rapidly depart from general use: few such are addressed in this chapter. Others are not discussed because they are too technical (jacquard design, mercerised cotton). Eponyms from fiction such as trilby(i) and gamp(ii) are outside the scope of this book, but one word is included (knickers) which derives from the fictitious *nom de plume* of an author who was himself real enough.

Where words familiar only to those with long memories or with a specialist interest in clothes have been included, in each case this has been for a specific, sometimes personal, reason. Hence the inclusion of the Anthony Eden hat and raglan sleeve.

BLOOMERS

Amelia Bloomer (née Jenks) (1818-1894) was American and became editor and publisher of what was probably the first newspaper that addressed serious women's issues: 'The Lily'. Bloomer devoted her life to campaigning for temperance and women's rights, particularly in relation to employment, education and politics. Her crusading zeal was timely: married women had few rights, as can be seen from contemporary textbooks that usually discussed their legal status in a chapter entitled: 'Infants, Lunatics and Married Women'.

1.1: 'Bloomer' dress of the 1850s

As a young woman Bloomer would have worn the tight, whalebone corsets that were fashionable at the time. These restricted both movement and breathing, to such an extent that ladies exposed to even minor shock or stress were frequently subject to attacks of 'the vapours'. Smelling salts were routinely used as a restorative. By the mid nineteenth century the new Reform Dress, a comfortable outfit for women that allowed freedom of movement, was gaining some popularity in the women's rights movement. It consisted of a jacket and knee length skirt, worn over full-length baggy trousers gathered at the ankle. Bloomer wore it when campaigning at public meetings with the result that it became widely associated with her name and in time was referred to, in a distinctly derogatory way, as 'bloomers'. Since it covered the body from top to toe there can have been no question of indecency, but this did not prevent the fashion from being regarded as utterly scandalous. Those in the women's rights movement began to return to more conventional dress in order to stop their appearance attracting attention to the detriment of their message. Time has been unkind to Bloomer in remembering her for an item of clothing rather than for the causes she so determinedly promoted.

Bloomers were rescued from oblivion by the increased use of bicycles during the 1890s. The trousers, also known for a time as rationals, became shorter and were adopted as acceptable outerwear for female cyclists. They underwent various modifications of design and use, ultimately becoming bloomers in the modern sense: baggy knickers gathered with elastic both at the waist and just above the knee.

In these days of the thong it is hard to imagine how such heavy-duty underwear could ever have become transformed into such skimpy modern garments. The explanation is the miniskirt. In the mid 1960s skirts changed from mid-calf length to something so short there was really very little of them; they were on occasion referred to somewhat scathingly by older generations as pelmets. Hemlines were so high that sitting down could be rather too revealing and leaning forward when standing was definitely to be avoided.

Of necessity, the miniskirt had a dramatic effect on underwear. When hemlines initially began to rise, glimpses of stocking tops appeared. Suspenders became an unsightly barrier, limiting the upward trend. So tights suddenly appeared and hemlines responded by positively racing up the thigh, the requirement of decency alone preventing visible proof that the leg did not in fact extend as far as the armpit.

What is not as well-known is that earlier in the same decade the concept of bloomers for teenage girls, although old fashioned, had not been entirely laid to rest. At the beginning of the 1960s Harrods, as the school outfitters for at least one girls' boarding school, still supplied in fulfilment of a clothing list that stipulated 'knickers (3 prs., green)' an item undoubtedly well within the bloomers category, constructed of thick, dark green, knitted cotton and kept in place by the traditional elastic. Occasionally disaster would ensue when the waist elastic suddenly 'went' – the top end of the garment immediately descended inside out, towards the ankles, while the leg ends remained held in place by the knee elastic.

6

Nevertheless, in such circumstances there was no risk of immodesty, for worn beneath the garment was another item stipulated in the same clothing list as 'knicker linings (6 prs., white cotton)', resembling what are now termed full briefs and again held up with elastic at the waist. The green bloomers look-alikes were actually only essential for the school's gymnastics lessons, when tunics had to be removed before participation. Girls conscious of their appearance were driven to disguise the generous cut of the undergarment by rolling each leg up inside itself from the knee, the knee elastic serving to anchor in place the roll of excess material now collected round the top of the leg.

Trying to be positive, bloomers were effective in preventing draughts above the stocking top. They also covered suspenders and suspender belt completely, reinforcing absolute modesty at all times – not for nothing were they known as passion killers. In addition it was not unknown for bloomers, being sealed at the knee, to be used at meal times for the discreet transport of unappetising food away from the table for later disposal, though this was best avoided for sticky items unless absolutely desperate.

KNICKERS

A nodding acquaintance with some of the history of New York City is needed in order to understand the derivation of 'knickers'. In 1602 a Dutch company explored the area now known as New York and claimed ownership of it. It became known as New Netherland and was home to a thriving and lucrative fur trade. It was eventually colonised by the Dutch under the auspices of the Dutch West India Company, a director of the company buying the island of Manhattan from the native American Indians for 60 guilders' worth of 'trinkets' – in other words virtually nothing. Fort New Amsterdam was built there, trade expanded, and the city grew in wealth and importance. Such prosperity attracted the attention of the British government that, remembering the area had first been discovered by a British expedition led by the explorer John

Cabot in 1498, took the view that the province could not really be Dutch at all because it was already British. After much fighting, the British successfully seized the colony in 1664, New Netherland became New York and the city of New Amsterdam became the city of New York.

Drawing by F.O.C.Darley, 1849

1.2: 'Diedrich Knickerbocker'

It was not until the end of the American War of Independence that the British left New York City. In that same year one of the founders of American literature, Washington Irving (1783 – 1859), was born. Irving's satirical account of the early Dutch settlers in New York entitled "A History of New-York from the Beginning of the World to the End of the Dutch Dynasty" was written under the pseudonym Diedrich Knickerbocker. And the name was more than just a pseudonym - in an apparently factual preface headed 'Account of the Author', Knickerbocker is provided with a fictitious persona (complete with engraved portrait) as an eccentric Dutch-American historian who had suddenly disappeared from his lodging-house, leaving his manuscript

8

behind to be discovered by his erstwhile landlord. The book was tremendously popular and its influence was such that the word Knickerbocker came to mean any New Yorker descended from one of the original Dutch settlers.

The book's illustrations of Knickerbocker's alleged forebears, early immigrants to New Netherland, showed them wearing breeches fastened by a tie (instead of the usual cuff) just below the knee. When breeches tied or buckled at the knee began to become fashionable in the late 1860s as part of a casual outfit for men, the breeches were called knickerbockers. Some few years later both the garment and the name had been shortened and transported from the men's department to ladies' underwear.

PANTS

Untangling the origin of the word pants involves a fair amount of detective work and any discussion of it is well on the way to fulfilling the four essential elements in story writing as laid down by an apocryphal English teacher many years ago: sex, mystery, high society and religion. (Those familiar with the tale will know that a lazy but imaginative lad nevertheless succeeded in condensing his homework into a mere seven words: My God, the duchess is pregnant. Whodunnit?)

'Pants' is short for pantaloons, from the character Pantaloon, who was a rather pathetic old man in English pantomime of whom the other characters took advantage. His name was the anglicised version of Pantalone, a character from Commedia dell'Arte who was also a figure of fun, but more precisely defined. Pantalone was an old, rich, mean Venetian merchant, always on the lookout for sex. He was constantly being tricked into spending his gold, and his over-optimistic amorous hopes were time and again doomed to failure. Pantalone wore a cap, a close fitting red jacket, tight red trousers (which were a combination of breeches and stockings), slippers and a long loose black cloak. His mask had a hooked nose, moustache and pointed grey beard.

Drawing by Maurice Sand, 1860

1.3: Pantalone

Commedia dell'Arte dated from about 1600 and originated in Italy, providing a popular alternative to the otherwise rather formal theatre prevalent at that time. The comedies were improvised, rather boisterous shows, usually about romantic intrigues or tricks to obtain money. Although unscripted, they were far from random because there were certain stock characters and the plot for each show would be decided in advance. Other characters became anglicised as well as Pantalone, for example Arlecchino (Harlequin), and Pulcinello (Mr. Punch of the seaside Punch and Judy show).

The fact that the comedy character Pantalone was Venetian explains his name. Pantalone was a nickname widely given by those who did not come from Venice to those who did, but it is something of a mystery how the nickname originated. The flag of the republic of Venice depicts the lion of the patron saint of

Venice (St. Mark) and one view is that the name derived from Piantaleone (Planter of the Lion), in acknowledgement of the alleged custom by Venetian merchants of erecting the Venetian flag when establishing their business abroad. However, it is more likely that the name is derived from St. Pantaleon, a saint particularly popular among Venetians, as evidenced by their ancient church dedicated to him.

St. Pantaleon was martyred in about 305 AD. He was court physician to the emperor Maximian, and although much of what is known about his life and death is more legend than fact, nevertheless his martyrdom seems well established. He was very wealthy and a popular member of society at the emperor's court, but after embracing Christianity he gave all his wealth away and treated the poor without payment, sometimes effecting miraculous cures. Other doctors at court became jealous and denounced him as a Christian to the emperor, who condemned him to death.

The emperor can have had no idea what problems this sentence was going to create. The story goes that he began by trying to burn St. Pantaleon with torches, but Christ appeared to strengthen and heal the saint and to extinguish the torches. The next attempt was also a failure: the emperor had a cauldron of molten lead prepared, but when St. Pantaleon was about to step into it Christ again appeared and the lead suddenly cooled and solidified. The emperor must have been hoping for 'third time lucky' when St. Pantaleon was tied to a large stone and flung into the sea, but the stone miraculously floated. His next attempt was to throw St. Pantaleon to the lions, but – perhaps by now somewhat predictably – the animals became friendly and would not attack. Undeterred, the emperor decided to break St. Pantaleon on the wheel, but that, too, proved a disaster when the wheel itself broke. Yet still the emperor failed to realise that there was a message for him somewhere. He fell back on a more conventional method of execution with a proven track record of success: beheading. Again he ran into trouble. The sword bent and the executioners, showing a great deal more insight than the emperor, were converted to Christianity. The beheading did take place in the end, but only after St. Pantaleon agreed to allow it.

The word pantaloons has been with us for over two hundred years. On the other side of the Atlantic it became shortened to pants, but still retained its meaning of a type of leg covering, and so with changing fashions now refers to trousers. In Britain, by contrast, the word pants appears to have entered the language as a shortened version of underpants (for men) in the 1870s.

LEOTARD

The father of Jules Leotard apparently used to hold him upside down as a baby to stop him crying. Jules (1839 – 1870) claimed it was this unusual approach to parenting that gave him his love of gymnastics, but the fact that his father was a gymnastics teacher may also have had something to do with it.

It is said that when in the swimming pool one day the young Jules noticed some ropes hanging above it attached to the ventilator and had the idea of connecting a bar to them. He was then able to develop and practise various tricks on the bar above the pool in comparative safety: the concept of the flying trapeze had been born. Jules eventually became so adept on it that he joined the Cirque Napoleon in Paris and at the age of 21 undertook the first flying trapeze act performed in public. At that time it would have consisted of Leotard 'flying' from one trapeze to a second, stationary, one – the idea of having a person on the second trapeze to co-ordinate its swing and act as a catcher was introduced subsequently by other trapeze artists. As safety nets had not yet been invented Leotard would have performed his act over a pile of mattresses. The act was sensational – nothing like it had ever been seen before – and he performed in both Paris and London. He attracted so much publicity that he featured in a popular song, the chorus of which is still well-known:

"He'd fly through the air with the greatest of ease,
That daring young man on the flying trapeze."(iii)

1.4: Jules Leotard wearing his leotard

Specialist clothing was needed for Jules' performances, so he designed for himself a close fitting body suit with long arms and legs which allowed maximum ease of movement – and showed off his figure to its full advantage. Subsequently this type of suit was widely adopted by others and became known as a leotard, although Jules himself referred to it simply as 'un maillot'. His untimely death at the age of thirty-two was not the result of some dramatic acrobatic accident as might have been thought, but from smallpox.

SPENCER

Those of a certain age, particularly if they come from Scotland or the North of England, recollect that women of their parents' generation kept warm in winter by wearing a spencer - an item of underwear comprising a waist length, loosely fitted woollen jacket with short sleeves. Not glamorous, but glamour was not its purpose. A fashion conscious young woman would not dream of wearing such a thing, no matter how cold the weather. However, some 200 years ago the word meant a very different type of jacket - one that was then the height of fashion, best described as a short double-breasted man's overcoat without tails.

The first spencer – the one that set the fashion – was created and worn by the 2nd Earl Spencer (1758 – 1834). At first glance this seems astonishing, since he was reputed to be a rather dull traditionalist, far too busily absorbed in his work at the Admiralty and in collecting books for his outstanding library (which by the time he died was reputed to be the finest in Europe) to have the slightest interest in his appearance. It is not clear exactly why his statement of fashion came about, but it seems to be agreed that one day for whatever reason he appeared in society wearing a coat with tails that he himself had cut short. The fashion for short coats immediately became all the rage, with absolutely everyone who was anyone wanting to wear 'the spencer'.

The social standing of the Earl certainly makes the story plausible, since not only was he a member of the aristocracy, but his sister was the famously trend-setting society hostess Georgiana, Duchess of Devonshire. But why did the respectable, conservative Earl cut his own coat short in the first place? One story is that he was standing with his back to the fire when he accidentally burnt his coat tails, so he simply decided to cut them off and carry on about his business as usual. A more colourful version – which would be entirely in keeping with his reputation – is that he did it to prove his opinion that fashion was nothing but nonsense. That story has him deliberately cutting the tails off his coat and wearing it in the street in order to demonstrate that people of fashion were so easily led that they would follow any trend, no matter how ludicrous.

Initially, therefore, the spencer was a fashionable coat for men that completely broke with tradition by being short – it kept the wearer warm, but only down to his waist. Its essence still survives, with the addition of various decorations, in the short military mess jacket - unceremoniously referred to by some as a bum-freezer.

Photo © Marion May Designs UK

1.5: Spencer jacket

However, ladies were not to be left out of this exciting new trend and soon adopted the spencer jacket for themselves. In the early 1800s Empire line dresses (now so familiar from the rash of films based on the works of Jane Austen) were in fashion. Thus the first ladies' spencers, made in wool or velvet, were jackets comprising little more than a very short bodice with sleeves, corresponding to the high waistline of the time. Over the years, however, the word spencer became used for other types of short jacket for women until finally it has become merely an item of underwear, the only remaining resemblance to the original article being that it is a waist length jacket with sleeves worn for warmth.

Thus the story of the spencer is one of transformation from an ultrafashionable garment for men, to a dull but practical item of underclothing for women. The family behind it, however, provides a perfect contrast. The dull, traditional second Earl who created the spencer was the great, great, great grandfather of the ultimate fashion icon Diana, the late Princess of Wales, born Lady Diana Spencer.

15

CARDIGAN

The cardigan was named after James Thomas Brudenell, 7th Earl of Cardigan (1797-1868), who led the charge of the Light Brigade in the Crimean War. By all accounts he was an arrogant, vindictive and unreasonable man. As was common at that time he bought his way into the army and by his early thirties was a lieutenant colonel. Although he himself at that stage had still seen no active service, he was in command of experienced troops and quickly developed a reputation for falling out with the officers serving under him.

Cardigan was fanatical in his determination to ensure that the appearance of his troops was impeccable. The army provided everyday uniforms (less elaborate than the dress uniforms worn on formal occasions), which were replaced by the regiment every two years. Cardigan took the view that many of his troops' everyday uniforms needed urgent replacement because they no longer looked new. In such circumstances the new uniform had to be paid for by the soldier concerned and until he could do so the cost was charged as a debt to the troop account. In the case of one troop the number of new uniforms ordered was so high that the troop debt rose above the permitted maximum. Despite the fact that this breach of regulations was the direct result of Cardigan's own instructions, Cardigan victimised the officer in charge and ultimately had him court martialled. The officer was acquitted and the court was so critical of Cardigan's behaviour that he was removed from command. However, family influence was brought to bear and three years later Cardigan was back.

Within a few years Cardigan was again behaving true to form and had fallen out with one of his officers. The reason is revealing: the officer had been a member of a court martial that had refused to comply with Cardigan's demand that the court revise a sentence it had already passed. Then, during a formal mess dinner, the officer chose not to order one of the decanted wines, but to order a different wine served from the bottle. Cardigan was so cross to see a bottle on the table that he had the officer arrested. This time the military authorities considered that there was no justification even for holding a court martial and the officer was released.

1.6: James Brudenell, 7th Earl of Cardigan

Cardigan's tyrannical approach was not confined to his officers and men. In 1840 anonymous reports of his unreasonable behaviour began to appear in the press and when Cardigan found out who was responsible he challenged the man to a duel. Duelling pistols were normally bored in a way that made their aim rather erratic, but the one used by Cardigan on this occasion was bored differently and was so accurate that it would have been regarded as highly dishonourable to use such a weapon. Cardigan wounded his opponent and was arrested on a charge of intent to murder, but argued that he was not aware of his pistol's unusual quality. Being a member of the House of Lords, he was entitled to trial by his peers, with the whole of the House of Lords acting as jury. Cardigan exercised that right, and one cannot but think that his reason for doing so exemplified the principle so discreetly encapsulated by Messrs. Sellar and

Yeatman in their version of the provisions of Magna Carta: "... Barons should not be tried except by a special jury of other Barons who would <u>understand</u>."(iv). In the end Cardigan had no need to rely on their Lordships' 'understanding'. For political reasons the government very much wanted Cardigan to be acquitted and this no doubt explains why the prosecution (apparently deliberately) failed to produce enough evidence to prove their case.

Photo by Roger Fenton, courtesy U.S. Library of Congress

1.7: Assistant Surgeon of the 11th (Prince Albert's Own) Hussars, 1855

At about this time Cardigan's regiment was renamed 'Prince Albert's Own Hussars' by Queen Victoria. This involved the creation of a new uniform said to have been designed by Prince Albert personally and to have been made for the regiment by a Bond Street tailor, with Cardigan himself contributing a huge sum towards its considerable cost. It must be assumed that Cardigan was willing to contribute, given his obsession with appearance. The new uniform can only be described as

18

magnificent. It comprised a fur busby (with white plume), a blue jacket (profusely laced with yellow or gold braid), a short blue cloak worn over one shoulder (decorated with yellow or gold braid and trimmed with lambswool or fur) and crimson trousers (with yellow or gold stripe down the side). Small wonder that the regimental nickname became the 'Cherry Bums'.

Eventually Cardigan saw active service in the Crimean War and led the famously heroic but suicidal charge of the Light Brigade. On his return to England he was fêted as the conquering hero and the military style woollen jacket with buttons and braid that he had worn in Crimea as protection from the bitter cold was widely adopted and was named after him.

However, controversy was never far away and before long it was claimed that Cardigan had not actually led the famous charge. He brought a court action for libel that disproved the claim and established that he was amongst the first to reach the Russian guns. However, it also established that having done so, he did not stay to fight but was amongst the first, if not the first, to retire.

Given Cardigan's lifelong passion for immaculate, elegant clothing, today's reputation of the 'cardi' as an informal and frequently somewhat shapeless garment is, perhaps deservedly, the ultimate insult.

RAGLAN SLEEVE

The raglan coat was remarkable for having sleeves of a design never seen before. Traditionally, a coat sleeve was 'set in', that is, it was cut to cover just the arm, and ended where the arm meets the shoulder. By contrast, in a raglan coat the top of the sleeve is cut to cover not only the arm but the shoulder as well, and tapers gradually to a point, where it meets the collar. The result is a looser fit across the shoulder and although it is unusual now to find a coat with raglan sleeves, they are widely used in knitwear and sportswear.

Drawing © C.M. Wiles

1.8: Casual 'top' with raglan sleeves

The coat, and thus the design of sleeve, was named after Fitzroy James Henry Somerset, later 1st Baron of Raglan (1788-1855). Raglan was a younger son of the Duke of Beaufort and, as a result of being wounded at Waterloo, had to have his right arm amputated above the elbow. Subsequently he remained closely linked with Wellington but saw no further active service until the Crimean war, when he was put in general command of the British forces.

Whilst Raglan's military career is well documented, the reason for his sartorial fame remains obscure. One story is that he designed the coat for his forces in Crimea, but this does seem rather unlikely bearing in mind that during that war the British army was particularly badly equipped. In those circumstances the chance of anyone in high command (except possibly Cardigan) taking time to design a new coat when there were so many more pressing problems, let alone the chance that the new coat would have been supplied, seems extremely thin. A more likely reason must be that Raglan was the first person to wear a coat cut in this way, possibly

20

because his tailor had specifically designed the sleeve to make the coat easier for a man missing most of one arm to put it on.

Raglan is notorious for being the military commander whose ambiguous order to the Light Brigade at Balaclava resulted in the heroic charge from which so few returned. Initially he was made the scapegoat for the disaster, but it does seem that the misunderstanding over his order arose because of pre-existing ill-feeling between Captain Nolan who delivered the order, Lord Lucan who was in overall command of the cavalry, and Lord Lucan's brother-in-law Lord Cardigan who commanded the Light Brigade. Raglan appears to have been more at home with diplomacy than with military strategy but he must be given credit for being a reasonable, honourable man who had had the insight to advise most strongly that Lords Lucan and Cardigan should not be appointed to positions of command where they would be in contact with each other. His advice had been ignored.

MACKINTOSH

Scotland is traditionally known for, amongst other things, the wetness of its weather and the thrift of its inhabitants. The production of the first waterproof clothing by the Glaswegian chemist Charles Macintosh (1766 – 1843), by means of a process invented by him as a result of trying to find a use for a waste product, is therefore satisfyingly apposite.

To some extent Macintosh must have inherited an interest in both chemistry and textiles from his father, who owned a factory making purple dye extracted from various lichens. Macintosh undertook several lines of research using innovative chemical processes, and one of them involved experiments to find a use for waste tar from the local coal gas works. Distillation of the tar produced naphtha and he discovered that naphtha would dissolve india-rubber. He used this discovery to make a thick waterproof cloth by spreading the rubber solution on one side of a piece of wool cloth and sticking another layer of the cloth on top. The whole thing was then used to make the original Mackintosh (with the curious addition of the letter 'k') cloak.

There were teething problems. To make the cloak it was necessary to stitch through the cloth and this inevitably made holes, and therefore leaks, in the layer of rubber. The rubber deteriorated from being in contact with wool and the cloth was unstable, going stiff in winter and sticky in summer. Ultimately these problems were resolved (the discovery of vulcanisation – see 'Plimsolls' below - helped) and Macintosh's name became permanently linked not only to waterproof material but also to almost any type of waterproof coat, when his name is usually shortened to just 'mac(k)'. The nylon 'pack-a-mac' of the 1950s and the PVC mac of the 1960s both refer to his name even though made from totally different fabrics.

PLIMSOLLS

We now call rubber-soled sports shoes 'trainers'. These are often miracles of modern design and engineering and priced accordingly, although there has been a recent recrudescence of plainer ones described as 'old school retro'. Trainers are so fashionable, comfortable and practical that many people seldom wear any other footwear. Indeed, this has had such a widespread effect on modern feet that the British army has restructured its training programme to allow feet accustomed only to trainers adequate time to adjust to army boots.

Step back some 50 years and the real 'old school retros' have no high tech construction, returning to the humble plimsolls, also known as sand shoes, gumshoes or, in the South West of England, daps (possibly in imitation of the sound made when walking in them). Plimsolls were cheap, with a plain canvas top (lace-up or elasticated), bonded to a thin rubber sole. They were almost always black. White was available, but the colour could only be maintained by regular painting with a thick coat of something resembling whitewash. White plimsolls tended to be regarded as rather grand because they were mainly associated with tennis clubs. Black plimsolls

22

were worn by those who could not afford leather shoes and they were also universally worn for school sporting activities. Step even further back in time to the late 1800s when rubber soled canvas shoes were first produced and they return to being rather expensive and decidedly up-market.

Photo © User Alansplodge/
Wikimedia Commons

Photo courtesy Shaun Labluk

1.9:

(a) Traditional child's plim-solls with elasticated top

(b) Basketball trainers

How plimsolls acquired their name is not straightforward. They would more logically have been called 'Goodyears' after Charles Goodyear, who spent his life working with rubber and was clearly a man with an obsession. Raw rubber is unsuitable for use in manufacturing because it is either sticky or brittle, depending upon weather conditions. Goodyear carried out research for some years, mainly in his kitchen, trying to find a way round these problems. The key to success was the vulcanisation process discovered in 1839. Although the story of his discovery has various versions, it is clear that it happened by accident, although Goodyear must be given credit for having the knowledge and insight to recognise its significance. He had for some considerable time been experimenting without success, trying the addition of various chemicals to raw rubber. One day, he was waving around - in frustration or fury - his latest effort, this time rubber mixed with sulphur, when a blob flew off and landed on a hot stove.

On cleaning the blob off, he found that the rubber had been transformed into something that was strong, flexible and above all no longer sticky. This chemical transformation enabled rubber to be bonded permanently to materials such as canvas and could also be used for a variety of other manufacturing processes such as production of rubber tyres, with which Goodyear's name is still associated.

Samuel Plimsoll (1824-1898) had no connection at all with rubber. He was a social reformer famous for improving the plight of merchant seamen. In particular, he publicised the scandal of coffin ships – ships that were unseaworthy and/or overloaded and over-insured. The ship would set sail in the owner's hope and expectation that it would sink. The law at that time made it an offence for a crew member to refuse to sail with a ship once he had contracted to do so, even if it became clear that the ship was dangerously unsafe. As a Member of Parliament, Plimsoll pressed for the introduction of 'load line' legislation, a statutory requirement that every ship should have a safety line painted on its side which, if underwater, would demonstrate that the ship was overloaded. After considerable opposition – ship-owners had powerful connections in Parliament – Plimsoll eventually succeeded. The Merchant Shipping (Plimsoll) Act was passed in 1876 and the line became known as the Plimsoll line. That should have been the end of the matter but unfortunately the legislation did not specify where the line was to be painted. This loophole was abused to such an extent that before amending legislation was passed one ship-owner even painted the line on his ship's funnel.

Plimsoll had been born in Bristol and after he became famous the City hosted a banquet in his honour. Plimsoll was met on his arrival at the station by various important members of the council and the official party then embarked on a small boat to take them across the harbour to Brunel's ship, the Great Western, where dinner had been arranged for them. Many of the dignitaries were somewhat portly and the boat rode perilously low in the water due to their combined weight (even before the dinner). At the time loan lines were a hot topic and an old sailor nearby found the sight of the small boat wallowing about full of important people very amusing. The boat's passengers must have been even more amused when he, ignorant of their identity, shouted across that he would "complain to Plimsoll" about them.

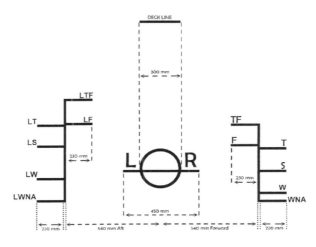

LR – Lloyd's Register
LTF – Lumber Tropical Fresh Water
LT – Lumber Tropical Seawater
LF – Lumber Fresh Water
LS – Lumber Summer Seawater
LW- Lumber Winter Seawater
LWNA – Lumber Winter North Atlantic
TF – Tropical Fresh Water
F – Fresh Water
T – Tropical Seawater
S – Summer Temperate Seawater
W – Winter Temperate Seawater
WNA – Winter North Atlantic

1.10: The Modern Plimsoll Load Line

To return to shoes, rubber soled canvas shoes did not acquire the name plimsolls until the 1920s. This is surprising, given that the introduction of load line legislation had been so controversial and very much in the public awareness for some fifty years. The most likely reason seems to be that it was not until a new design for canvas rubber soled shoes appeared, a design that incorporated a strip of rubber stuck round them on the outside covering where the sole was bonded to the upper, that the shoes became popularly known as plimsolls. Some bright spark thought the strip analogous to the Plimsoll line – feet remained dry only for as long as the surrounding water level remained below the top of the line – and the name 'Plimsolls' stuck.

WELLINGTONS

Everyone knows the modern rubber wellies. Not fashionable, but essential for a muddy country walk. By contrast, when Wellington boots first appeared they were for military use and made of leather, quickly developing into highly fashionable footwear for the smartest of social occasions. The boot and shoe collection at the Northampton Museum exhibits a pair of dress Wellington boots from the 1830s in black patent leather with a bow on each toe, tan leather legs covered in knitted silk, and green leather tops.

Exactly why Wellingtons are named after the first Duke of Wellington (1769-1852) (born Arthur Wellesley) is not clear. One suggestion is that the Duke personally designed the boots for the benefit of the troops under his command, but it is perhaps unlikely that a commander (other than Cardigan again) would concern himself with the minutiae of troops' footwear. Another suggestion is that the boots were designed specifically for him by his boot-maker, but that argument is inconsistent with reports that the style was already in use by mounted troops at the Battle of Waterloo in 1815 before it ever attracted the name of wellingtons. The most likely probability is that the Duke liked the style and wore it, and that since he was fêted as the hero of the day following his spectacular triumph at Waterloo, whatever he chose to wear became popular amongst those in society.

Photo © Peter J. Ashman

1.11: Wellington Boots worn by the Household Cavalry (other ranks)

The Duke had a successful political career and was prime minister for a time, but is principally remembered for his success in defeating Napoleon at Waterloo. However, that success was very nearly a disaster. Wellington engaged battle knowing that his allies the Prussians under Field Marshal Blucher were marching to join him. Wellington was relying on their timely arrival, but they were delayed. The battle was reaching a decisive point late in the afternoon, Wellington's forces were exhausted and the French were on the point of victory before Blucher's eventual arrival saved the day.

Apart from Wellington, the names of the two other main commanders at the battle of Waterloo also endured for some years as the name of a boot. Specialists in the history of costume take the view that the Wellington boot extended up to the knee and was characterised by a flat top, whereas a Napoleon boot covered the knee in front but was cut away at the back to allow the knee to bend comfortably, particularly when on horseback. Blucher boots by contrast did not extend as far as the knee and, although they too were developed into footwear of high fashion for a time, were also the forerunner of the modern army boot.

27

BOWLER HAT

Stories abound as to how the bowler hat acquired its name, but most agree that the impetus for its design came from William Coke (pronounced 'Cook'), owner of the Holkham Estate in Norfolk. In 1850 Coke asked the long established and exclusive hatters, James Lock & Co. of St. James's, to design a practical hat for his gamekeepers that would protect the head and remain securely in place.

Photo © Holkham Estate

1.12: Gamekeepers' Lunch, Holkham, circa 1910

Precisely why it was to have the qualities stipulated by Coke is a matter of disagreement. One theory is that Coke was infuriated at the money wasted from having to provide numerous replacements for hats knocked off or entangled in branches and lost when the wearer was out riding. Another is that his gamekeepers needed something reliable to protect the head when searching for, pursuing and confronting poachers. Whatever the reason, the resulting design fitted the head closely enough to stay on and was hard enough to protect the head against accidental (or perhaps deliberate) knocks. The original version was also strong enough to provide additional height for peering over walls – this quality was tested by Coke who stood on the hat in the shop before completing his purchase. Having designed the hat, it seems that Lock's sent the design to Thomas and William Bowler, felt-makers in Southwark, who made it for them in accordance with Lock's specifications.

A positive plethora of eponyms surrounds the bowler hat. Lock's themselves always prefer to call it a coke, after the name of their client who commissioned it. In the USA it is known as a derby, a reference to the Earl of Derby, although there is debate as to exactly which Earl. One candidate is the 14th Earl (1799 – 1869), a famous politician of his day, who habitually wore a bowler when attending horse races. The other candidate is the 12th Earl (1752 - 1834), because of the bowler's popularity among the racing fraternity at Epsom on Derby Day, the famous race itself being a reference to the 12th Earl who, with his friend Sir Charles Bunbury, instituted it in 1780 and who won the toss as to which of the two of them should feature in its name. In contrast, the French ignore all personal references and simply use the somewhat picturesque 'un melon'.

The status of the Bowler hat is such that it has also become incorporated into a phrase with a specialised meaning, reflecting the widespread use of bowler hats by civilians of almost any description. In the RAF to be 'bowler-hatted' or 'given a bowler hat' meant being thrown out of uniformed service.

ANTHONY EDEN HAT

Robert Anthony Eden (1897 – 1977) (created earl of Avon in 1961) went to Eton, gained a first in oriental languages from Oxford and was awarded the military cross during World War I. Subsequently he went into politics and gained a reputation as a politician with strong diplomatic skills. Unfortunately, these did not keep him immune from major criticism and despite his many achievements he is most remembered for being the prime minister in charge of the unsatisfactory handling of the Suez crisis in 1956.

1.13: Traditional 'Anthony Eden' Felt

Eden was not only a high profile politician but was good looking and a snappy dresser, sporting a black homburg with a tapered crown dented along the top from front to back, and a rolled brim with a bound edge. This popularised the style in the 1950s to such an extent that the hat became known generally as an Anthony Eden. So widely worn was it that when men attending professional meetings had all deposited their virtually indistinguishable hats in the cloakroom on arrival, the last to leave the meeting afterwards would have no option but to return home with the last hat left unclaimed, invariably the wrong size and suitable only for covert exchange at a subsequent meeting.

STETSON

To most people in the UK the word 'Stetson' means a cowboy hat, regardless of which company manufactured it, so it no longer has the commercial connection that once it had. Such a hat is also called a ten gallon hat, but you can forget the comforting idea that its capacity would allow a cowboy to scoop up enough water to refresh both himself and his exhausted horse after riding around all day in the intense heat of the Wild West. The truth is more prosaic. The hats were decorated with braid – 'gallon' in Spanish, sounding like 'gallon' to English speakers. Why ten, though, is anybody's guess.

Photo © User -oo0(Gold Trader)0oo-/ Wikimedia Commons

1.14: Stetson from the 1920s

The name of the hat derives from its maker John Batterson Stetson (1830- 1906) who, when he first marketed the hat, called it 'Boss of the Plains'. Stetson was brought up in New Jersey and as a young man went west in the gold rush. He did not strike gold, but while prospecting he wore a wide brimmed, high crowned hat – shady and cool. A fellow prospector wanted to buy it from him. Recognising a business opportunity, Stetson abandoned the uncertain search for gold and concentrated instead on using the skills he had learnt from his father, a master hatter, to set up his own hat company. That company prospered and still has a reputation for hats of quality in numerous different designs.

Stetson apparently designed the Boss of the Plains himself, but it seems that a felt hat incorporating a wide brim and high crown had already been designed and patented by Christy's,

31

then one of the largest hat makers in England. Stetson lost the resulting legal battle: the court held that it was Christy's who had invented the hat and Stetson could therefore only market his Boss of the Plains after payment of a licence fee. Stetson of course had the last laugh: Christy's golden days are over, despite its former fame and its spectacularly wide range of specialist hats such as police helmets, mortar boards, Tudor hats for the Yeomen of the Guard, tricorne hats for the Chelsea Pensioners and embroidered cocked hats for the doorkeepers at the Bank of England.

Photo © User -oo0(Gold Trader)0oo-/ Wikimedia Commons

1.15: 'Boss of the Plains' original design

Hat-making had its insalubrious side. Urine was used to speed up the making of felt and at first this would simply have been supplied personally by each hat-maker in the obvious way, probably assisted by large quantities of beer when demand for hats was strong. But as business expanded extra supplies needed to be bought in. At least one of Christy's factories was located in a road called Penny Lane, its name originating from the time when the factory bought buckets of urine for a penny each. The process of making felt also used a solution of mercury, the fumes from which caused brain damage to those working in poorly ventilated rooms, hence the phrase 'mad as a hatter'.

One may be forgiven for wondering how anyone could ever have thought of using a solution of mercury in the first place. An explanation is provided by a traditional, and certainly plausible, story from within the industry. It is said that in the early days it was found that one particular hatter was able to complete the felt-making process faster than anyone else – his urine was simply more effective. It transpired that the man was undergoing mercury treatment for venereal disease, probably syphilis.

GLADSTONE BAG

William Ewert Gladstone (1809-1898) – yet another prime minister – was an outstanding statesman. He was also impressively intelligent, graduating from Oxford at the age of 21 with a first not only in Greats (classics) but also in mathematics. A colleague said of him that Gladstone could achieve in four hours what would take any other man 16 hours, and that he worked 16 hours a day. It is widely agreed that the Gladstone bag was named after this 'Grand Old Man' of politics, but no-one seems prepared to offer an explanation as to why. One is therefore forced to the conclusion that he must have used one himself.

The Gladstone bag is one of the most practical designs invented. Because the top opens on hinges positioned well down the sides of the bag, it combines good storage space with easy access. The bag is therefore highly versatile. In the professional world it used to be renowned as the doctor's little black bag and was commodious enough to lend credibility to the explanation given to children in a more prudish age that Mama's new baby had been brought in the doctor's bag. In business, Henry John Heinz (of 57 varieties fame) used a Gladstone bag when he came to England in 1886 to bring samples of his finest products to Fortnum & Mason's (which agreed to stock them). In a criminal context the bag also achieved fame in connection with Jack the Ripper – a man carrying a Gladstone bag was seen hurrying away from the scene of the crime shortly after one of the murders was committed.

1.16: A much used leather Gladstone bag

Gladstone's own attitude towards prostitutes could not have been more of a contrast to Jack's. In his private life he devoted a considerable amount of time and money to helping those who wanted to lead a different way of life to do so. He regularly used to walk home in the late evening after the House of Commons had risen and would accost any prostitute he came across, offering her a meal and a bed for the night at his home under the care of his wife. The following day the woman would be given the opportunity to move into a hostel (financed in part by Gladstone), with food and medical attention provided, while a new job was found for her. As can be imagined, Gladstone's motives for such activities were misconstrued by some, and his diaries show that his actions clearly caused arousal and consequent remorse, allayed by punishment through self-flagellation. But there is nothing to suggest that he ever behaved improperly towards the women concerned.

SIDEBURNS

Bradley Wiggins' triumph in the 2012 Tour de France, followed three weeks later by a gold medal at the London Olympics, make him one of the most popular and well-known British cyclists. His sideburns (sideboards) sparked a new fashion trend and fans took to wearing exaggerated lookalike stick-on ones to demonstrate their support. Even those, however, pale into insignificance when compared with the facial decoration of Ambrose Everett Burnside (1824-1881), whose luxurious whiskers first gave rise to the term 'burnsides', later known as 'sideburns'.

Photo by Mathew B. Brady. Courtesy U.S. Library of Congress

1.17: Maj. Gen. Ambrose E. Burnside, circa 1860

Burnside was an officer in the American Civil War, but is generally regarded as having been promoted to a level beyond his ability, earning him a reputation for being decidedly incompetent. His later career as a manufacturer of rifles was more successful and ultimately he turned to politics, becoming governor of Rhode Island and later a senator.

GEORGETTE

Paris traditionally had a reputation as the centre for both glamour and risqué entertainment, epitomised by the Moulin Rouge. So it is highly appropriate that it is a Parisian – Madame Georgette de la Plante, living in the early part of the twentieth century and described variously as a designer or a dressmaker – who created georgette. First, the glamour. Georgette is strong, extremely fine and, although made of silk, is not shiny. It drapes beautifully. Lined with a thicker silk as necessary, it is ideal for elegant evening gowns, provided it is actually silk georgette and not a cheap, artificial imitation. Secondly, the risqué. Georgette chiffon is advertised as veiling for belly dancers and others, since it covers the body as though discreetly, but at the same time its diaphanous quality reveals more than a hint of what is beneath.

PETERSHAM

There is no obvious reason why the thick ribbed ribbon used for hatbands came to be named after Charles Stanhope, Viscount Petersham (1780-1851) so perhaps his hats may have popularised its use. As a young man Petersham had quite a reputation, being part of the smart, and distinctly wild, set of friends surrounding the Prince Regent, later George IV. Petersham did not do anything by halves. He took an exaggerated interest in his personal appearance, designing many of his own clothes and setting new fashions. He had a passion for snuff and it was said of him that he had a different snuffbox for every day of the year. At one time he was passionate about the colour brown as well: brown clothes, brown horses, brown carriage and brown uniforms for his servants. Rumour has it that the reason was an even greater passion for a certain Ms. Brown.

Petersham had an affair with an actress seventeen years younger than himself, who had already had two illegitimate children from one affair followed by a broken engagement to somebody else. As was to be expected, his family disapproved strongly, but once his father had died they married and by all accounts remained happily together until Petersham, now 4th Earl of Harrington, died some twenty years later. Following marriage they lived at the family seat of Elvaston Castle and Harrington's new interest, shared by his wife, was developing the gardens there into a Gothic extravaganza. The social mores of the time meant that although it was acceptable for the couple to appear in society whilst known to be conducting an affair, once married the unsuitability of the match resulted in their total exclusion from social events.

DOILY

Photo © C.M. Wiles

1.18: A Modern Doily

Mr. Doyley ran a drapery shop in the Strand at some time in the late seventeenth century, a shop that remained in business until about 1850. Not much else is known about him, except that his business was said to have thrived from dealing in cheap materials that were nevertheless 'genteel'.

At that time genteel was a rather complimentary word and meant fashionable or well-bred, whereas now, like the doily itself, it bears a somewhat derogatory implication of snobbish false refinement, brutally illustrated by Sir John Betjeman:

"Milk and then just as it comes dear?
I'm afraid the preserve's full of stones;
Beg pardon, I'm soiling the doilies
With afternoon tea-cakes and scones."(v)

CHAPTER TWO

FOOD and DRINK

There is a steady need for new vocabulary to reflect changes in eating habits so it is not surprising that the kitchen abounds with eponyms. Some are so amusing that they seem too good to be true. Unfortunately that is because sometimes they are too good to be true, being merely inventions that have gained credibility with each repetition.

Take 'curry', for example. There is a persuasive story about a certain George Curry, a British officer in the Indian Army during the 1800s. He was said to have been extremely partial to the local spiced food, although despite his best efforts he failed to popularise it with the troops. But the word is derived from Tamil and appeared in the English language in 1598. There is even an English recipe for making curry that dates from a century before George came on the scene.

'Marmalade' is another. One wonderful tale features a Portuguese innkeeper called Joao Marmelado, born in 1450, who was once sent so many Seville oranges in settlement of a debt that he boiled them up with sugar in an effort to find a use for them. He allegedly left dishes of the resulting stuff on the tables for his guests, but the Portuguese were not interested – perhaps because, so the story goes, they tried it with sardines. (Portuguese? Sardines? Already a hint that the story's credentials are suspect.) By contrast a group of British travellers, who found the leftovers on the tables at breakfast the following morning, tried it on toast and were so impressed that they bought a large quantity to take home. This story has actually been thought up quite carefully as both the period and country of origin are correct, but the word 'marmalade' is based on a pre-existing Portuguese word for quince (*marmelo*) from which marmalade was originally made. Nevertheless the story has proved so compelling that there is a strikingly similar rival version in which the Portuguese innkeeper is replaced by a canny Scottish grocer and the consignment of oranges came from a Spanish ship stranded near Dundee.

Similarly 'ketchup'. Some would have us believe that a certain Noah Ketchup moved to the USA from India in about 1700 and made a successful living out of selling the tomato and mushroom relishes traditional in his country of origin. However, the word derives from Chinese.

There are plenty of other fakes: Jorge-Luis Avocado, Sir Oswald Binge, Pierre-Alphonse Buffet, Gottfried and Siegmund Lager. People with these names are widely quoted as examples of eponyms, with suitably amusing biographical details, but it cannot be claimed that any of them has become part of the English language and even the names themselves are probably fictitious.

But there are plenty of real people to consider.

BEEF STROGANOFF

Beef stroganoff abounds with confusion, not only as to exactly how to make it but also as to when it was created, who is commemorated by the name and even how to spell it – strogonov, stroganov, strogonoff or stroganoff are all acceptable. Its fundamental elements are thin strips of top quality steak fried with a little onion and served in a mushroom and soured cream sauce.

The dish came to fame as the prize-winning entry in a competition held in St. Petersburg in the 1890s, submitted by the chef working for Count Paul (Pavel) Stroganoff, who was a well-known gourmet of the time. But beef stroganoff was being eaten long before then. Many sources quote an earlier member of the family, Count Pavel Alexandrovich Stroganoff (1772-1817), as 'the man of the dish'. Others say it was Count Gregori Alexandrovich Stroganov (1770-1857), an exceptionally well regarded Russian ambassador with a love of entertaining. Larousse(i) goes even earlier and suggests the name might derive from Gregori Dimitri Strogonov (1650-1715) who apparently employed a French cook, but it does just cross the mind that perhaps the story's French connection might have encouraged the French editor to seize upon it somewhat over-hastily. Whoever is correct it does seem that the prize-winning entry in the 1890s was merely submitted under the already well-established name of beef stroganoff, although the exact recipe may have been a refined version of one used previously. One can at least be sure that whatever the argument about which particular member of the family is commemorated, the consistent point is the family itself.

2.1: View of the Strogonov Palace from the Nevsky Prospekt

A particular feature of strogonoff is that the meat is cut into strips. Various explanations have been put forward as to why. It has been suggested somewhat unkindly that the relevant Count was elderly and having lost his teeth could no longer chew a whole piece of steak. Alternatively it has been claimed that when the relevant Count was in Siberia and needed to eat at short notice, the meat was so cold that it was only possible to deal with it by shaving thin slivers off the frozen block.

The Stroganov family goes back several centuries and in the 16th century was composed of wealthy and influential merchants, who were largely responsible for the Russian annexation of Siberia and shortly afterwards were instrumental in bringing the Romanovs to the tsardom. Gregori Dimitri was raised to the nobility by Peter the Great and many years after Gregori's death his heirs were raised to the inherited dignity of Count.

WOOLTON PIE

Think World War II. Think food shortages. Submarine attacks meant that only goods essential for the war effort were worth the risk of transport and the expense of naval protection, so imported food was practically non-existent. Children grew up without even seeing a banana until the war ended. Meat, cheese and eggs were severely rationed. If you were lucky you might be able set up a pig club with your neighbours and share in the pig's purchase, care and finally meat, provided you could find somewhere to keep it. But most people were not as fortunate as that and had to rely heavily on fruit and vegetables that were not rationed. Many followed the government's exhortation to 'Dig for Victory' by converting their gardens into vegetable plots. Families had to do creative things with vegetables to have enough to eat.

Food supplies during the war were the responsibility of the Minister of Food, Frederick James Marquis, Earl of Woolton (1883-1964). Before the war he had been managing director of the John Lewis Partnership and his talent and success were such that he had been awarded a peerage for his services to British business. He brought similar energy and success to his ministerial post. His organization of food rationing not only ensured that people did not actually starve but also resulted in children brought up during the war being generally healthier than those brought up either before or since.

As well as tackling rationing, Lord Woolton set about advertising the advantages of those foods that were available through posters and rhymes, using two cartoon characters:

Potato Pete and Dr. Carrot.

The Song of Potato Pete(ii)
Potatoes new, potatoes old,
Potato (in a salad) cold.
Potatoes baked or mashed or fried,
Potatoes whole, potato pied.
Enjoy them all including chips,
Remembering spuds don't come in ships.

Photos © Imperial War Museums

2.2: Government posters from the Second World War

Potato Pete inspired other popular rhymes promoting a similar message(iii):

> Those who have the will to win
> Cook potatoes in their skin,
> Knowing that the sight of peelings
> Deeply hurts Lord Woolton's feelings.

Even well-known nursery rhymes were hijacked in the interests of increasing the potato's use and appeal(iv):

> There was an old woman who lived in a shoe.
> Who had so many children she didn't know what to do.
> She gave them potatoes instead of some bread,
> And the children were happy and very well fed.

The advertising campaign also suggested recipes. One such was known as Woolton Pie which, although created at his request by a chef at the Savoy Hotel, never really achieved popularity. Its ingredients were little more than potatoes, cauliflower, swedes and carrots flavoured with a teaspoonful of Marmite. Those old enough to remember eating Woolton Pie still refer to it somewhat ruefully.

CHATEAUBRIAND STEAK

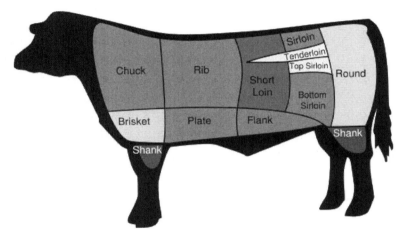

Courtesy User JoeSmack/Wikimedia Commons

2.3: Beef cut chart showing position of the relevant cut, labelled 'tenderloin'

The mere thought of Woolton pie demands immediate rescue by something meaty, and what better than a chateaubriand steak, the main feature of which is its size. Cooking it is therefore something of a culinary challenge. The steak has to be cooked long enough to prevent the inside from being completely raw, without ending up with a thick, overcooked crust on the outside. This problem was initially solved by protecting each of the two sides with an extra, inferior steak so that during cooking the outside steaks could be overcooked with impunity before being thrown away.

Somewhat predictably this was found to be so wasteful that the practice was soon changed.

The man to whom the steak was dedicated is Francois Rene de Chateaubriand (1768-1848), also known as the Vicomte de Chateaubriand. He was something of an idle aristocrat until the French Revolution led him to depart somewhat hurriedly for England where he took up writing in order to earn a living. On his return to post-revolutionary France he continued to write successfully and subsequently went into politics.

Some say that the dish was invented by Chateaubriand's own chef, who named it in recognition of his employer. But there is a reputable and more compelling story(v) of how the steak came to be 'christened' – and the word is used somewhat advisedly. This story claims that the new dish was created at the Parisian restaurant Champeaux, probably in 1822. An employee there with a blasphemous turn of mind said that the top quality steak, cooked between two such inferior pieces, put him in mind of the crucifixion of Christ between two robbers, as discussed in Chateaubriand's book *Genie de Christianisme.*

In France chateaubriand quickly became regarded as the ultimate steak experience and was very much in vogue. The British were also impressed by it, but not by the name. The members of a well-known gentleman's club in London, on being presented with a menu featuring chateaubriand, complained that they did not know what it meant. When all was explained they insisted that, since the steak was cut from the fillet, it should simply be presented under the tried and tested name of filet de boeuf.

BEEF WELLINGTON

In case thoughts of Lord Woolton and his pie are still lingering, the carnivorous theme continues with Beef Wellington – essentially a complete fillet of beef seared at a high temperature then smothered in mushroom and liver pâté, wrapped in puff pastry and baked in the oven. It was named after the Duke of Wellington (the Waterloo one), though it is not nearly as familiar as the waterproof boots. Some have even gone so far as to suggest that Beef Wellington gained its name from its similarity to the boots (hopefully in shape rather than texture or taste). The dish itself is comparatively recent, despite a much-quoted story that it was created in an effort to impress the notoriously undiscerning palette of the Duke himself.

PARMENTIER POTATOES

Back to potatoes: dice them into small cubes, fry them in butter, sprinkle them with a little chopped parsley and you have parmentier potatoes.

2.4: Antoine-Augustin Parmentier

Forget Maris Piper and King Edward, whoever they were. And even forget Agincourt, because when it comes to potatoes the man to remember is French: Antoine-Auguste Parmentier (1737-1813). The French find this easy as in France it goes without saying that any recipe invoking his name involves potatoes in one form or another. By contrast, to most British people Monsieur Parmentier is unheard of, yet dictionaries assure us of his part in potato history and it has to be said that in the potato world his story eclipses all others.

46

So what did he do for the potato? Was he an explorer who introduced it into France? No – the potato was already in Europe, brought back to Spain from South America even before it was introduced to England. Was he perhaps a great horticulturalist who developed different types of potato or better ways of growing them? No again. Could he have been a chef, famous for devising tempting new ways of cooking the potato? Still no. Was he then a chemist who found improved methods of fertilising or pest control? Well, he was a chemist but that is not what links him to potatoes. Essentially Parmentier did no more for the potato than eat it. But then he persuaded others to eat it by putting into action what must be the world's most strategic and successful advertising campaign, founded on a brilliant understanding of human psychology. Saatchi and Saatchi would have taken their hats off to him. Lord Woolton's efforts with Potato Pete pale into insignificance.

A glimpse of Parmentier's world is needed to appreciate his achievement. He lived at a time when the potato was abhorred in France. It was widely regarded as poisonous (its flowers do closely resemble those of the poisonous woody nightshade) and was considered by some to spread the plague or even leprosy. The French thought of it as suitable only for animals and the English. Initially Parmentier himself was forced into eating potatoes to avoid starvation – he was a prisoner-of-war in Germany during the Seven Year War and the prison diet consisted of potatoes and little else. He eventually returned to France at a time of famine and learnt that a prize was being offered for the best idea for overcoming the crisis. Parmentier won the prize by suggesting potatoes. However, prejudice dies hard and it seemed that people really were prepared to starve rather than risk eating one. Potatoes desperately needed a new image and in order to bring about a change in attitude Parmentier started at the top. He succeeded in persuading the king to try them and getting the queen to wear potato flowers as an accessory. This was at a time when the French royal family eating dinner was regarded as a public event with onlookers free to come and watch. Once royalty was seen to be eating potatoes the rest of the nobility were keen to follow suit. The tiers état, however, still remained to be convinced, so Parmentier devised a plan. He planted two large fields of potatoes on the outskirts of Paris and placed them under a twenty-four hour guard. Local people understandably concluded that whatever was in the field was valuable and highly desirable. However – and this is the cunning bit – the guards had been instructed not to be too vigilant at night. Local people were able to find an opportunity to sneak in and steal some of the crop. Consumption of the potato never looked back.

BÉCHAMEL SAUCE

Béchamel sauce is the basic white savoury sauce made with butter, flour and milk, seasoned with salt and pepper and sometimes grated nutmeg. It forms a basis to which flavourings can be added to create other sauces. Béchamel sauce appeared during the reign of Louis XIV and at that time was made not with milk but with stock. The resulting velouté was reduced over heat until it was thick, then egg yolks and double cream added.

The sauce is named after Louis de Béchameil (1630-1703), steward of Louis XIV. Béchameil was a wealthy gourmet in charge of running the King's household. There are numerous stories as to who invented the sauce and as to exactly how it was named, but the status of Béchameil's position makes it unlikely that he invented the sauce himself. It is more probable that one of the cooks under his command produced it when trying to improve on an existing recipe. The cook may then have named it in honour of Béchameil, which would have been a good move from the point of view of his future career prospects. Or one can imagine that if the important Béchameil asked for the new sauce to be served on several occasions, then the instructions in the kitchen to 'make that new sauce again for Béchameil' would quickly have contracted into 'make Béchameil's sauce' with the result that the name just stuck.

MORNAY SAUCE

Add cream and grated cheese, preferably gruyère, to béchamel sauce and you have mornay sauce. More than one reputable dictionary tells us that it was named after Philippe de Mornay (1529-1623), a writer and politician. He was also known to be a very discreet diplomat and in 1572 was sent on a confidential mission to William the Silent, Prince of Orange. One cannot help wondering, in a moment of unseemly frivolity, how history ever found out about it.

Other sources, including Larousse, contradict the dictionary's conjecture as to the origin of the name, telling us that a chef by the name of Joseph Voiron created the sauce and named it after his eldest son Mornay Voiron. Given that Philippe de Mornay died before the middle of the seventeenth century, that Voiron was a well-known chef at the end of the nineteenth century and that the earliest recorded reference to mornay sauce (in English at least) was not until the beginning of the twentieth century, it does seem – with the utmost respect to the dedicated and erudite dictionary compilers – that the chef's son is the more likely candidate.

Not a great deal is known about either Joseph Voiron or his son. However, the Restaurant Durand at which Joseph worked during the 1890s was popular with the Parisian literary monde, including Emile Zola. It is believed to be there that in 1898 Zola drafted his letter 'J'accuse' addressed to the French President, in which he supported an appeal by the French army officer Dreyfus against his conviction for treason, a conviction which had more to do with Dreyfus being Jewish than with any factual evidence.

In it Zola named those he considered responsible for this grave miscarriage of justice and accused each in turn of incompetence, dishonesty or corruption. He then sent a copy to the newspapers and its publication resulted in Zola himself being convicted of libel and sentenced to prison for a year. It was only many years later that the court held on appeal that much of the evidence against Dreyfus was fabricated and his name was cleared.

2.5: Front page of the newspaper 'L'Aurore', 13th January 1898

SANDWICH

The word sandwich originated with John Montague (1718 – 1792), 4th Earl of Sandwich. Although in terms of a lunchtime snack Sandwich comes from the same place as the humble ploughman, when it comes to lifestyle he was at the opposite end of the spectrum. The image of the common or garden sandwich has drawn an unwarranted and misleading veil of respectability over a most unsavoury character.

So what was the connection between the 4th Earl and sandwiches? He was certainly not in the business of providing food for the poor and hungry. Being a member of the aristocracy he was not in business at all, although over the years things have now changed and the current Earl has set up a business selling top quality sandwiches using his family name and crest in an astute marketing strategy.

Returning to the 4th Earl, it was his request – demand – that a piece of beef be brought to him between two pieces of bread, that established his name as part of our language. There is more than one version of the story and it has been suggested, perhaps in deference to the fact that he was a member of the government, that the poor man was hungry because he was so hard at work and did not have time to leave his desk. But it is unbelievable that no-one had ever thought of using bread to enclose a piece of cold meat before, so there must have been something peculiarly memorable about his particular request. A snack while seated at the office desk hardly fits the bill. The more likely version is that Sandwich, who was an inveterate gambler, had been sitting at the gaming table all night and wanted something to keep him going that could be eaten without interrupting his play and that wouldn't make the cards too greasy.

The 4th Earl was known not only for gambling. He was a leading member of the notorious Hell Fire Club, also called the Order of the Knights of St Francis of Wycombe, or The Monks of Medmenham Abbey. The purpose of the club was to promote drinking and immorality, and its activities included fancy dress 'monks and nuns' orgies and blasphemous rituals. On one occasion another member, John Wilkes (the well-known politician), played a practical joke during celebration of a Black Mass. He dressed a baboon up as the devil, hid it in a cupboard behind the altar of the candlelit chapel and rigged up a remote control mechanism so that he could open the cupboard door without going near it. At the point in the proceedings where the devil was invoked he released the baboon, which by then was understandably extremely cross.

Sandwich and some others were too shocked to recognise the creature for what it was and jumped to the conclusion that it was indeed the devil incarnate, thereby causing immense amusement to all the others. Sandwich never forgave Wilkes.

Photo © Bjørn Christian Tørrissen

2.6: Baboon

Sandwich was unfortunate in his long-term relationships. His wife suffered from mental illness. He then at the age of forty-four took up with a teenage seamstress and they lived together, apparently happily, for sixteen years until she was murdered in Covent Garden by a jealous would-be lover.

His career was equally blighted. As First Lord of the Admiralty his performance was disastrous. A Parliamentary Report of the time made it clear that although administration within the Admiralty had left much to be desired before Sandwich took over, under his leadership it fell to an all time low with gross misuse of funds and widespread bribery. The state of the dockyards under his supervision was appalling. His one redeeming feature was his interest in exploration. He used his influence to provide Admiralty funding for Captain

Cook who, on discovering a hitherto unknown group of islands, named them the Sandwich Islands. That tribute to his benefactor has faded into the mists of time – they are now called Hawaii (but the remote South Sandwich Islands, also named by Cook, still retain his name).

Sandwich's lasting fame is therefore almost entirely etymological, but in that field he has scored a resounding success. The word sandwich is such an integral part of the language that no-one would dream of writing it with a capital letter. Not only that, but the noun turned out to be so useful that some one hundred years after it entered the language it became pressed into use as a verb – to find oneself sandwiched between a rock and a hard place, for example – and this was well before the recent trend of 'verbification'.

FRANGIPANE

Frangipane: think almonds – either an almond flavoured pastry or an almond flavoured confectioner's cream used in making pastries and desserts. The word appears in a French recipe as early as 1674 but took nearly two hundred years to come across the Channel. Despite the word being seldom used in English, frangipane is included here because of its interesting derivation.

Dictionaries explain that the man from whose name frangipane is derived was a sixteenth century Italian nobleman who invented a glove perfume. His exact name is not entirely clear – some say it was Muzio, others Cesare, Frangipani. The details of how the perfume came to be made are also a bit vague. It is said that Frangipani was a botanist who on his travels abroad discovered a tree with exceptionally fragrant flowers that he later used to make a perfume. The perfume was almond scented and the almond flavoured pastry was named after it.

Nowadays we are well used to the idea of perfumes everywhere, from air fresheners through cleaning products and cosmetics to 'scratch 'n' sniff' books. Yet the idea of scented gloves does seem a bit extreme. However, it needs to be borne in mind that in the sixteenth and seventeenth centuries personal hygiene was a low priority and sewage disposal rudimentary to say the least. In England it was common to carry a nosegay – a small posy of scented flowers to reduce the wearer's awareness of the surrounding stink and in the hope of reducing the risk of infection. Judges at the Old Bailey, ever anxious to avoid jail fever (typhus), were regularly using them in Victorian times and the custom has not entirely died out: they still carry flowers as they walk in formal procession to reconvene the court at the beginning of each legal year.

Scented gloves would have served a similar purpose. The first such gloves, with a perfume so heavy that it served almost as much as a disinfectant as for pleasure, were introduced to England from Spain. Their use was not necessarily restricted to those in high society – a reference in county archives has been found to a pair of scented gloves being exchanged for a pig(vi).

Italian gloves by contrast, lightly scented with the essence of natural flower oils, imbued during a process lasting several days, were such a refined luxury item that they were supplied to royalty. The perfume invented by Frangipani was used to scent the gloves of Louis XIII and when the Earl of Oxford returned from his travels to Italy and presented a pair to Queen Elizabeth I, the fashion for 'Oxford gloves' as they came to be called was quickly established. Scented gloves even merit a mention by Shakespeare(vii). Napoleon was said to wear them when going into battle, but the ingredients he used (two-thirds peppermint with added apple, lily of the valley and heliotrope) suggest that he may have carried them as a restorative rather than a fashion accessory.

CRÊPES SUZETTES

Mention 'pudding' and what comes to mind is likely to be a substantial, quintessentially English 'pud' which lands in the stomach with a satisfying thump, can be guaranteed to keep out the cold, and is usually eaten with custard. This image is totally at variance with the exotic, frivolous nature of crêpes suzettes, yet there are some to whom the word 'dessert' is anathema and 'sweet' even worse. These members of the old guard still firmly refer even to crêpes suzettes as 'pudding'.

During the early part of the last century crêpes suzettes were regarded as the pinnacle of gastronomic sophistication in both Europe and the United States, with competing schools of thought as to whether the crêpes should be flambéed or not. But the identity of Suzette is as uncertain as the identity of the inventor of the dish. There are no less than four contenders for the recipe, all French. It is almost as if any fame as a chef would be fatally flawed without a concomitant claim to have created this dessert. If the correct chef could be established, Suzette herself would fall into place.

The first candidate is Jean Redoux, who dates from the seventeenth century. It is said that he named the dish for Suzette, Princesse de Carignan, who lived near Fontainebleau. The accuracy of the story and details of the Princesse are unfortunately both obscured by the mists of time. It seems intuitive that, as he lived ages before any of the other candidates, he must have been the first to have made the crêpes, but there is little convincing evidence that crêpes suzettes as such were in existence before the 1890s.

The second candidate, the renowned Auguste Escoffier, was king pin in the kitchens of the Savoy during the years 1890-98, when crêpes suzettes first appeared there on the menu. He makes no direct claim to have come up with the idea, but he was certainly responsible for being the first to publish the recipe. Perhaps he developed an old recipe of his fellow-countryman Redoux, with a little magic of his own, to create crêpes suzettes in the form that became all the rage, but if he did, the Suzette after whom he named it is not known.

This brings us to the third candidate, Henri Charpentier, who did claim the idea was his. In his autobiography[viii] he records that, as an apprentice chef at the Café de Paris in Monte Carlo in 1896, he had nearly finished preparing crêpes for the Prince of Wales (later Edward VII) when the alcoholic mixture prepared for the sauce accidentally caught fire. Disaster! There was no time to start again, but on tasting the result he was relieved to find the flavour was enhanced and so served it as it was, claiming it was a new creation made for the Prince. He continues that the Prince was delighted and asked that as Suzette, the small daughter of one of his friends, was present, the dish should be named after her. Despite the appeal of the story and the wealth of detail, it is to be noted that Charpentier would have been only 16 years old at the time. Is it really possible that such a junior trainee would have been given the responsibility of not only preparing but also serving a dish for such an important diner? The story is widely claimed to be true but the authoritative Larousse now regards it as not so. Perhaps Charpentier was simply making the most of the fact that his name was already associated with crêpes suzettes because he was manager at the Savoy Restaurant when they were a feature of the menu there.

The final candidate is a Monsieur Joseph. In the 1890s Joseph was proprietor of the restaurant Marivaux in Paris, which was the nearest restaurant to the Comédie Française. The story goes that the script of a play being performed there in 1897 required a plate of crêpes to be eaten on stage by a famous actress of the time, Suzanne Reichenberg (1853-1924), nicknamed Suzette. The crêpes were provided by Joseph, who thought up the idea of pouring brandy over the crêpes and igniting them in order to lend interest to the performance. Unfortunately the Joseph claim is also likely to be incorrect. To be fair to him it seems to have been put forward on his behalf rather than by he himself, and indeed only seems to have surfaced as a means of discrediting the Charpentier claim. By then Joseph was not around to comment on the accuracy or otherwise of his part in it.

PAVLOVA

Pavlova proudly remains the veritable crème de la crème of desserts, despite the affectionate but somewhat demeaning nickname of 'pav' imposed upon it Down Under. For those unlucky enough not to have come across one, a pavlova is whipped cream and summer fruits arranged on a meringue base. It has been claimed by one mistaken source that the 'man of the pav' was the Pavlov of dogs fame. Given that Pavlov's research involved eliciting salivation from dogs in anticipation of eating, the idea seems quite inspired and conjures up any number of improbable images featuring basset hounds looking smug.

2.7: Anna Pavlova as 'The Dying Swan', St. Petersburg 1905

Other sources agree, however, that pavlova originated in the Antipodes and was named in honour of the Russian ballerina Anna Pavlova (1881 – 1931). But there the agreement ends. A fierce battle rages over whether or not the meringue has to be made with cornflour and vinegar and whether the fruit used must be passionfruit. For years an even more heartfelt battle used to rage about exactly where the dessert originated. Anna Pavlova toured in both Australia and New Zealand in 1926 and again in Australia in 1929. Both countries claimed to have invented the dessert and both regard it as their own national dish. Whole forests have been endangered by the pages used up over the argument.

The Australians claimed that the pavlova originated in Perth in 1935, some six years after Anna Pavlova had stayed there on tour. The story goes that when the chef presented it a diner commented that the dessert was 'as light as Pavlova' and the name stuck.

The New Zealand claim had several possibilities, none really convincing. A book of local recipes(ix) was published in 1927 containing instructions for making 'meringue cake' using pavlova ingredients but cooked in two sandwich cake tins, so it would not have looked like a pavlova and was not called pavlova. In the same year a booklet(x) appeared containing a recipe using the name pavlova, but made with gelatine, so it would not have tasted like a pavlova. Shortly afterwards a book(xi) with a recipe for 'pavlova cakes' was published, but these were made into a large number of little meringues with nuts, so still not really a pavlova.

Some ten years ago, however, the argument appears to have been laid to rest with New Zealand declared the absolute winner. A cookbook dating from 1933(xii) produced by the Mother's Union from a rural town in New Zealand has been unearthed and this contains both the correct recipe and the correct name.

With so much argument it is all too easy to lose sight of Anna Pavlova herself. She was born into a poor family, but from the age of eight always wanted to be a ballerina. Innate talent coupled with extremely hard work made her the most famous and successful dancer of her day. From the age of ten she trained at the Imperial Ballet School in St. Petersburg and gained the status of prima ballerina by the age of twenty-five. She settled in London, established a ballet school and organized her own ballet company, but spent most of her life on tour. The role particularly associated with her was 'The Dying Swan', choreographed for her by Fokine to the music of

'The Swan', a short piece from 'Carnival of the Animals' by Saint-Saëns. She died while on tour and the subsequent night, when the time came for her to have performed 'The Dying Swan', the music was played in tribute to her and the curtains were opened as usual, but to an empty stage.

PEACH MELBA and MELBA TOAST

The opera singer Helen Mitchell (1861-1931) was a superstar, a soprano with an extraordinarily extensive vocal range. She was born near Melbourne, Australia and took the stage name of Nellie Melba – Nellie for Helen and Melba for Melbourne. While appearing at Covent Garden in 1894 she lived at the Savoy Hotel, at the time when Escoffier was in charge. She apparently gave him two tickets to see her perform in Wagner's Lohengrin, an opera in which the hero is a mysterious knight who appears from the other side of a lake in a boat drawn by a swan. This gave Escoffier the idea of presenting Melba with an impressive new dessert consisting of poached peaches served on hand-made vanilla ice cream dusted with icing sugar. Its ingredients were not so very unusual but its presentation was unsurpassed. A swan was carved out of a block of ice and the silver dish containing the dessert set between its wings. It was not until a few years later that raspberry purée was added, to produce peach melba as we know it. More recently it has become associated with tinned peaches and a sugary raspberry sauce with little fruit content, giving it an undeserved reputation as a quick, second rate dessert.

Turning to melba toast is to move from the luxurious to the spartan. It was originally created for Marie Ritz, wife of the famous hotelier with whom Escoffier worked, but was served to Melba either when she was unwell or when she was following a diet that specified toast. It includes no unusual ingredients – it is in fact nothing more than pieces of toast – but again the presentation is all. The toast is extraordinarily thin, crisp and curly. To make it, start with a normal slice of thin toast and cut off the crusts. Then put it down flat and cut it horizontally in half, to produce two slices with the same 'footprint' as the original, but half the thickness. Finally cut each piece diagonally into two or four and grill, or bake in a hot oven.

Photo © gastronomydomine

2.8: Melba toast

Dame Nellie Melba was famous not only for her voice but also for a large number of 'final' appearances. The first of these took place in 1926 and they continued until her final final appearance in 1928. The circumstances surrounding her death some three years later suggest that she must have found life difficult once she had left behind the applause and adoration that had followed her stage performances. She had undergone risky, and what was then still very experimental, surgery for a facelift. Infection developed and, with antibiotics not yet discovered, she died of blood poisoning.

GROG
Admiral Edward Vernon (1684 – 1757) was a high-ranking naval commander of considerable fame, but his name is now virtually unknown. In contrast, we are assured by no less an authority than the Royal Navy that his nickname of Old Grog –

a reference to his habit of wearing a coat made of a thick, stiff silk and wool material called grogram – has survived the centuries by giving us the word grog.

For hundreds of years the provision of alcohol played a vital role in the smooth running of the Royal Navy and did much to prevent mutiny. Drinking water stored on board ship for any length of time became foul and in the early days of the navy the problem was addressed by issuing each seaman with a daily ration of one gallon of beer. Later this was replaced by a ration of spirits if beer was not available. Brandy was tried for a short time but in 1687 – following the British capture of Jamaica from the Spanish – this was changed to rum. A seaman's daily allowance was settled at half a pint of rum, issued part in the morning and part in the evening. Nowadays this ration seems on the generous side to say the least – even allowing for the fact that one pint was measured as one eighth of a purser's one gallon measure, which only contained seven, not eight, pints.

Vernon was in command of the Royal Navy in the West Indies in 1740 and the hot climate there meant that beer would not keep for any length of time. He therefore became the first person to order the issue of watered down rum to his seamen – the rum presumably took away the taste of foul water and acted to some extent as a disinfectant. This practice spread throughout the navy, often with the addition of lemon or lime juice as well as water in order to protect against scurvy, and the drink quickly became known as grog. Think of Vernon if you wake up one morning feeling a bit the worse for wear, as Old Grog also has the distinction of being able to claim the adjective 'groggy'.

On exceptional occasions an extra issue of grog might be issued to all the ship's company following an order to 'splice the mainbrace'. The wording is now obscure since it derives from the days of sail. Conjure up an image of a stately ship with three tall masts, each of which has several yards, or crossbeams, with a huge sail suspended from each yard. The mainbrace was the rope that kept the main yard (which carried the biggest sail) in position in relation to the wind and it took a huge strain whenever the ship changed course. It therefore had to be extremely strong and could be as thick as five inches in diameter. If the mainbrace was broken the ship could not be steered properly and even (or especially) if weather conditions were bad, repair was a matter of utmost urgency. This meant going up into the rigging to remove the damaged section and while still up there to splice the remaining pieces of rope back together into a continuous length by untwisting the individual strands of both ends and interweaving them with each other. This was not only arduous and dangerous but had to be done as fast as possible because until it was completed the ship could not change tack. The best members of the crew would be picked for the task and on its completion were deservedly rewarded with an extra ration of rum. With the disappearance of sail, the job itself disappeared and the order now only refers to the customary reward that used to follow its performance.

Serving in the navy was hard and, as can be imagined from the size of the rum ration, drunkenness was an ever-present problem. Especially at risk were boys on their fourteenth birthday because they then qualified for the whole ration of rum instead of only half. The floggings administered as a punishment for drunkenness were remarkably unsuccessful in controlling it and so other approaches were tried. Admiral Vernon, as we have seen, took the precaution of ordering that the seamen (though not officers) should have their rum ration served ready watered down. His order was that it should be diluted in the proportions 3:1 water to rum (referred to as three water grog). Occasional attempts by others to water it down further to, say, five water grog created threats of mutiny and had to be abandoned. During the nineteenth century the ration was considerably reduced and a minimum age of 20 years introduced. It was finally abolished altogether in 1970. But naval tradition dies hard. Both the Admiralty and members of the royal family can still order the mainbrace to be spliced. The most recent occasion on which Her Majesty the

Queen did so was in June 2012, as part of her diamond jubilee celebrations.

EARL GREY TEA

What does the name Charles Grey, second Earl Grey of Howick (1764 - 1845), mean to most of us? Nothing, but one could do a great deal worse than find immortality in a tea bag. Earl Grey is regarded as a superior tea and is one of the earliest blended teas in Britain. For many, a cup of tea will be the first thought on waking, will soothe away the stresses of the day last thing at night, as well as refresh the tired and thirsty several times during the hours in between. It will be the priority at times of crisis or sudden disaster. In fact for millions of us Earl Grey has become a trusted friend.

The irony is that Grey himself was not directly connected to the tea and the fact that he came into the equation at all is an illustration of cultural differences. When Prime Minister, he sent a diplomatic mission to China, during the course of which one of the British envoys saved the life of a Chinese Mandarin. As a token of thanks the Mandarin sent some specially blended tea together with the recipe for it, not to the man who carried out the rescue but to the man responsible for the mission itself – Earl Grey.

Do not assume that Grey's political career was a reflection of his name. He was the Prime Minister responsible for forcing the first great Parliamentary Reform Bill through Parliament in the teeth of tremendous opposition in 1832. Twice the Bill was thrown out by the House of Lords and Grey was unable to persuade the King to create some fifty new peers who could have been relied upon to vote the Bill through on a third attempt. Grey therefore resigned, but this led to so much unrest across the country that a week later the King was left with no alternative but to reinstate him and agree to the new peers. In the event the threat alone was enough to silence the opposition and the Bill was passed.

Parliamentary reform had been desperately needed – the risks of dishonest manipulation of postal voting about which we now concern ourselves are as peanuts compared with the dishonesty inherent in the system as it was then. Corruption and trickery were endemic and bribery widespread. It was comparatively easy to influence the result of an election because often there were very few people in a constituency who were entitled to vote. The rules as to who had the right to vote were uncertain due to their inordinate complexity and many areas had no representation in Parliament at all. There was no such thing as a secret ballot: following an election, constituencies published a printed list both of the names of voters and of the candidate for whom they voted.

ANNO VICESIMO SECUNDO

Georgii III. Regis.

∗∗∗∗∗∗∗∗∗∗∗∗∗∗∗∗∗∗∗∗∗∗∗∗∗∗∗∗∗

CAP. XXXI.

An Act for the preventing of Bribery and Corruption in the Election of Members to serve in Parliament for the Borough of *Cricklade*, in the County of *Wilts*.

 WHEREAS there was the most no- Preamble. torious Bribery and Corruption at the last Election of Burgesses to serve in Parliament for the Borough of Cricklade in the County of Wilts: And whereas such Bribery and Corruption is likely to continue and be practised in the said Borough in future, unless some Means are taken to prevent the same; in order therefore to prevent such unlawful Practices for the future, and that the said Borough may from henceforth be duly represented in Parliament; be it enacted by the King's most Excellent Majesty, by and with the Advice and Consent of the Lords Spiritual and Temporal, and

6 Q 2   Com-

Courtesy Wiltshire & Swindon Archives

2.9: First page of an Act of Parliament passed in 1782 to prevent corruption in Parliamentary elections in Cricklade

Even by the standards of the time, however, the goings-on in the small town of Cricklade in Wiltshire were scandalous. When the result of the 1774 election there was challenged, an enquiry found that one candidate had persuaded his supporters to vote early in the day and arranged for the bailiff to close the poll early whilst he was still in the lead. That election was held to be void and the result of the subsequent one was reversed after discounting the votes of those who had voted without any right to do so. In 1780 things there were even worse, with the election of one candidate eventually declared void because 160 out of the total of 172 who had voted for him were proved to have accepted bribes – the going rate being the huge sum, for those days, of five guineas per vote. Things were so bad that an Act of Parliament was passed shortly afterwards in an attempt to deal with the problem.

Intriguingly, the Act only applied to Cricklade and there were many objections raised before it was passed. The unavoidable conclusion is that the right to vote was regarded by many as conferring a perfectly proper right to be paid for exercising it in favour of the highest bidder.

SALLY LUNN

A Sally Lunn, with its close connection to regency Bath, conjures up an image of genteel, well-dressed ladies sipping tea from china cups and eating slices of cake. But those who find the image of such refinement unappealing need not despair. The first written reference to a Sally Lunn was in 1780 and records that a fiddler in Bath dropped down dead "after drinking a large quantity of Bath Waters, and eating a hearty breakfast of spungy hot rolls, or Sally Luns"(xiii).

The accepted story goes that a young woman called Sally Lunn arrived in Bath towards the end of the seventeenth century and set up a bakery there, selling a new type of rich brioche bun, or teacake containing no dried fruit, that became very popular and was referred to by her name. The house where she apparently lived and worked currently houses a tea-shop and small museum, and the Sally Lunns sold there today are claimed to be made to her original secret recipe.

Courtesy Sally Lunn's

2.10: Ground floor of Sally Lunn's tea shop in Bath

Investigations from further afield suggest a possible doubt regarding the story. A somewhat similar teacake is found in France where it is known as a 'solimemne' or 'solilem' and one version of the traditional tale says that the young woman who arrived in Bath was a Huguenot refugee who had brought the recipe for teacakes with her and called them by their French name, which to English ears would have sounded very like Sally Lunn. However, experts who have researched the topic of French teacakes failed to find any evidence of their presence there earlier than 1815.

The tourist industry in Bath remains firmly convinced by the traditional story that is given at least some authority – albeit guarded – by dictionaries. Add to that the lack of evidence regarding the prior existence of the French rival and it seems reasonable to regard the traditional story as likely to be authentic.

VICTORIA SPONGE

Alexandrina Victoria Hanover (1819-1901), Queen Victoria and Empress of India, reigned for some sixty-four years at a time when the Britain Empire was at its height, so perhaps it is not surprising that innumerable places and things were named in her honour. These include that integral part of the traditional English afternoon tea: the cake known as a Victoria sponge.

© H.M. Queen Elizabeth II 2012

2.11: Self portrait sketch by Princess Victoria of Kent (later Queen Victoria)

Drinking tea became fashionable in the seventeenth century but it was not until Victorian times that afternoon tea as a light meal came into vogue, apparently instigated by the Duchess of Bedford who insisted that she needed something to sustain her during the long gap between lunch and dinner. She arranged for a member of her staff to bring a tray of tea, bread and butter to her room and it was not long before she was inviting friends to join her. Leisured ladies quickly adopted the habit and the bread and butter extended to dainty sandwiches, scones and cakes. To be really smart, ever more elaborate accessories were needed and producers of china, napiery and silver tea services responded to the demand. A complete new etiquette developed and it was not long before ladies were changing into the latest fashion for the occasion – a loose and flowing tea-gown, which was feminine and above all comfortable, in sharp contrast to the formal gown worn over tightly laced corsets to be donned when dressing for dinner.

The widowed Queen Victoria joined the trend for holding tea parties and was apparently so fond of sponge cake, split in half and filled with jam, that slices of such cake became known as Victoria sandwiches and thus the cake from which they were made became Victoria sandwich cake, then simply Victoria sponge.

The ceremony formerly associated with afternoon tea is no longer widespread and has generally lapsed into what is often no more than a mug of tea (and a biscuit if you are lucky) swallowed at a desk in front of the computer screen. But it can still be found by those who yearn for a touch of leisured elegance. For the complete works there is nothing to beat Palm Court Afternoon Tea at the Ritz, where the attentive yet discreet service makes those partaking feel like royalty, and the sandwiches really do arrive without crusts. But be warned! This is no spur of the moment decision. A table has to be booked weeks in advance (unless, perhaps, you are very well-known and/or influential) and the cost is breathtaking. If you are lucky enough to have a really indulgent relative, you might mention in passing your surprise at discovering that you can now find gift vouchers for nearly anything, even for afternoon tea for two at the Ritz. And keep your fingers crossed...

MADELEINES

There is a culture clash here. A French madeleine is a small, rich, sponge cake without icing, cooked in a tray of ribbed, oval moulds so that when cooked each resembles a sea shell. By contrast the English madeleine is made from a plainer mixture but is shaped like a flowerpot, covered with coconut and jam, and topped with a glacé cherry.

Photo © User MrDarcy/ Wikimedia Commons

2.12: Baking tray for cooking petites Madeleines de Commercy

Madeleines originated in France and do seem to have been named after a real person, but there are three possibilities – all of whom are associated with the town of Commercy. Reference books are reluctant to commit themselves but suggest that the relevant Madeleine was probably Madeleine Paulmier, a nineteenth century pastry cook employed by a wealthy resident there. However, Larousse opts for a peasant girl who is said to have made the cakes in 1755 on the occasion of a visit to Commercy castle by Stanislaw Leszczynski, one time ruler of the area. The story goes that he was so impressed that he gave some of the cakes to his daughter Marie, who happened to be the wife of Louis XV, who was equally impressed and set a fashion for them at Versailles. Or the reference could just possibly be to Mary Magdalene, to whom the local convent was dedicated, because the nuns there used to bake the cakes before being forced to sell the recipe during the French Revolution.

For some people madeleines equal Proust and vice versa. Even if you have never read a word of Proust you may well know that he wrote of an intensely vivid childhood memory that came back to him when, years later, he took a mouthful of a madeleine. The memory of going to see his aunt on

Sunday mornings and being given a morsel of her madeleine, dipped in tea, was so distant that he had been unaware of its existence. Even when it was triggered by the identical taste many years later he only had at first an intense feeling of joy. It took him some time to pinpoint the childhood experience responsible, but once he had done so he vividly recalled not just the moment of eating the cake but also the house, town and people living there, by then all long gone. On a more humble scale, a three-year old child, on starting to eat a plain Bath Oliver biscuit, was once similarly transported back to a forgotten day some six months earlier, commenting after the first bite (with a faraway look in his eyes): "It's long ages since I ate this biscuit. It was outside and the sun was shining ...". The curious thing is that in both cases the thing tasted was not of itself something that you would expect to be all that important to a young person – a madeleine is not the most luxurious of cakes and a dry cracker distinctly dull. And in both cases the taste itself was trivial compared with the overwhelming memory of the context in which the taste had first been experienced.

SACHERTORTE

This famously rich chocolate cake, decorated with chocolate icing and apricot jam, was created by Franz Sacher (1816-1907), pastry cook to the Austrian statesman Metternich, probably for the Congress of Vienna in 1814-15. The cake became hugely popular but its recipe remained a closely guarded secret. Some sixty years later Franz' son and daughter-in-law established the grand Sacher Hotel where they served, amongst other things, the by now renowned sachertorte.

Time passed and the cake fell out of fashion but underwent a renaissance following the 1939-45 war. Austrians take their pastries very seriously indeed and sachertorte became a feature of Vienna. There was therefore much status, as well as considerable financial advantage, to be gained by the patisserie that could establish that the cake sold by them was the authentic one. For years a bitter – no, in deference to the cake's ingredients such an adjective must be deleted – fierce battle was waged between the Hotel Sacher and the Viennese patisserie Demel's as to which of them was selling the genuine article. The Hotel's claim was based on the obvious family connection but Demel's claim had more substance than might initially be imagined, since they had been sold the right to produce sachertorte, from a true recipe, by Franz Sacher's grandson. Eventually the parties ended up in court and after some six years judgement was given in favour of the Hotel. For all practical purposes the court case appears to the outsider to have been about little more than where to put the apricot jam. The Hotel's approach was to split the cake in half horizontally and spread the jam between the two layers. Demel's, by contrast, favoured glazing the cake with jam on top and then icing over it.

Photo © User Simfan34/ Wikimedia Commons

2.13: Sachertorte from the Hotel Sacher, Vienna

In order to comply with the court order allowing only the Hotel to call its cake 'genuine' sachertorte, Demel's took to marketing theirs as the 'original' sachertorte. Many other versions are also now sold throughout Vienna. All are cracked up to be exceedingly indulgent, wicked cake. However, some find it a little dry and in need of the substantial helping of cream and cup of coffee with which it is traditionally served.

GARIBALDI BISCUITS

Garibaldis are the biscuits shown on a doily at the end of Chapter 1. The biscuit part is quite plain but serves as a foil to the layer of currant paste sandwiched between the two biscuit layers, the whole thing having then been firmly squashed as flat as possible with a rolling pin before baking. Various commercial brands are widely available and the name conveniently lends itself as an apt description of their comparative qualities. An economy biscuit with only a small amount of currant paste is definitely 'less gari-, more –baldi'.

Courtesy U.S. Library of Congress

2.14: Guiseppe Garibaldi, 1861

Guiseppe Garibaldi (1807-1882) was an expert in guerrilla warfare and it was largely due to his efforts that Italy, which had comprised a number of small independent states each with its own army, was unified into a single country. What seems odd is that in Britain the name should have caught on for a biscuit. Garibaldi was really nothing to do with the UK and neither Italy nor any of the states comprising it were ever part of the British Empire. But he was immensely popular with Victorian society. Money was raised here for his cause, he visited Britain and the Prince of Wales attended a reception held for him.

The thought of garibaldi as a name for a biscuit summons up the inviting image of exhausted guerrilla fighters staggering back to camp in the safety of the woods, laden with backpacks and rifles, restoring their energies on arrival with a handful of well-travelled and hence rather battered garibaldi biscuits fished out from their pockets. No such luck. That story – or something like it – is told by some, but Brewer(xiv) tells us firmly that the biscuits gained their name because Garibaldi was very fond of them, eating them at home and sending them as presents to friends. So no picturesque image, but that is more than compensated for by two picturesque nicknames for them: 'squashed flies' or, if you live in Scotland, 'flies' graveyards'.

CHAPTER THREE

VEHICLES and TRAVEL

There is a striking contrast between the derivation of the names of horse-drawn vehicles and motorised vehicles. This is well illustrated at the humblest level by the old ubiquitous cart, lacking the status of any specific name, in comparison with its modern equivalent, the Ford Transit van.

Drawing © C.E.Wiles

3.1: A cart carrying pottery, 1897

When the horse ruled the road, a vehicle was usually distinctly upmarket before it attracted a name. If a man was wealthy and could not find a carriage that met his particular requirements, he would simply ask his coachbuilder to make one that did. Once out on the roads the unfamiliar vehicle would attract attention and tended to be referred to by the name of its owner. If it looked fashionable, or even just useful, others would ask their coachbuilders to make something similar and what started as a 'one-off' became an established type.

Production of motorised vehicles is altogether different: investment in expensive machinery is needed well before a single car (or van) can roll off the production line. And having once got the operation up and running, sale of a large number of vehicles is essential if the initial outlay is to be recouped. Therefore those who manufacture motor vehicles usually do so through a limited company, the name of the company frequently reflecting the name of the entrepreneur: Ford, Ferrari and Lamborghini for example, or even Mercedes where the maker adopted his daughter's name. However, when something turns out to be so exceptional that use of its name is no longer restricted solely to the thing itself, it moves beyond the commercial into the dictionary. Rolls-Royce springs to mind.

The Sopwith Camel is an exception which should not be here at all, but the name is intriguing and was the inspiration for this book. So although Sopwith set up his own company, thus putting his name into the world of commerce, there could be no question of leaving his Camel out.

BROUGHAM

The first brougham, built in 1838, was designed by Henry Peter Brougham (1778-1868). He wanted a smart, light, one horse four-wheeled closed carriage for his own use when travelling about in London in all weathers. The design clearly identified a hole in the market because before long several different coachbuilders were producing similar vehicles and they became a familiar sight. Some de luxe models had quite an advanced "spec", featuring brocade curtains, silver handles, fitted reading lamps, mirrors and clocks; some had ventilation slots for tobacco smoke and a speaking tube for communicating with the coachman. Double broughams were made – these were larger vehicles accommodating four passengers instead of two.

In his day Brougham was well-known for both his legal and political careers. He was born in Edinburgh into a family of modest means without social connections, and as a young man studied science at university before being called to the bar. Brougham achieved success (but not popularity) in his legal career by his steadfast and able support of the Queen, Caroline. She has now been obscured by the mists of time but make no mistake, as the wife of George IV she is not just some dull figure from the past.

© *User Morburre/ Wikimedia Commons*

3.2: The Brougham

George's marital track record was a mess from the beginning. He was notoriously dissolute, but after numerous affairs had secretly married Mrs. Fitzherbert. Mrs. Fitzherbert was Roman Catholic and George was heir to the throne, so the marriage was illegal. It seems to have been felt by all (except the happy couple) that it was also invalid. Over the next ten years George, as Prince Regent or 'Prinny', continued an extravagant life style and ran up such an enormous level of debt that he could not hope to repay it. A deal was reached: Parliament would vote him the money to cover his debts provided he left Mrs. Fitzherbert and married his suitably royal cousin Caroline of Brunswick. This would clear the way for him to perform his duty and produce a legitimate heir. George had no real option and reluctantly agreed.

The deal backfired because the marriage with Caroline was disastrous. She was coarse, dowdy and, not to put too fine a point on it, she smelled. With the help of enough stiff drinks to render him beyond caring, George was able to last out the honeymoon and do what was required. Nine months later a daughter was born, but within the year the couple were legally separated. Caroline returned to Brunswick where, it was rumoured, she had numerous lovers. When George became king some twenty-five years later, Caroline came back to England determined to take her place as queen.

Both George and the government were horrified and tried to buy her off with the offer of a generous annuity, payable on condition that she remained abroad. She refused. Divorce would have required an Act of Parliament but this was considered too risky since it would have involved production of explicit evidence against Caroline, with the consequent danger that she would then produce evidence of George's even worse behaviour. So a Bill of Pains and Penalties was introduced instead, intended to dissolve the marriage and deny Caroline the status of queen. Caroline had few supporters inside Parliament, but when the Bill was being debated the case on her behalf was presented so persuasively by Brougham – who had been one of her advisers for a number of years – that the Bill had to be withdrawn. Caroline remained queen, but despite Brougham's arguments was not given the right of coronation. Indeed, when she went she went to Westminster Abbey to attend her husband's coronation ceremony she was prevented from entering and the door was shut in her face. Although in perfect health at that stage, she conveniently died less than three weeks later.

Even more important than Brougham's legal career was his political career. Although brought up in an ultra-conservative society, he joined the Whig party and passionately supported progressive causes such as Parliamentary reform, public education and the abolition of the slave trade – causes which upset many vested interests. Brougham was regarded by party leaders as something of a loose cannon. They needed his powers of oratory and persuasion in order to push through their policies, but his eccentricity and tactlessness made them reluctant to allow him any more power than absolutely necessary. This stunted his political career and ultimately he was persuaded to become Lord Chancellor – an appointment designed to get him out of the House of Commons. Thus Brougham became responsible for the safe keeping of the great seal – essential for the sealing of state documents of the utmost importance. Unfortunately he lost it during a visit to a country house in Scotland, eventually finding it during a game of blindman's buff. Both the loss and the circumstances of its recovery did little to promote confidence in his continuing suitability for the Lord Chancellorship and when his party next returned to government his appointment was not renewed.

HANSOM CAB

The hansom cab was the forerunner of the modern taxi, but the idea of vehicles available for private hire was far from new. The earliest example of a taxi-rank in London appeared in the Strand in 1634. At that time the vehicles standing in line available for hire were hackney coaches – old, cumbersome carriages past their best and no longer required by their original aristocratic owners. Their presence, hanging around on busy corners to attract business, soon caused such an obstruction that they were banned from waiting in the street and were required to operate out of private yards. As jams became an ever-increasing problem – Pepys' diary records his frustrations at getting stuck in traffic – it was not long before hackney coaches were controlled by a licensing system with a limitation on the number of licences issued.

By early Victorian times the dilapidated hackney coaches were being replaced by hackney cabriolets (hence hackney cabs). The most widespread of these was the clarence, named in honour of King William IV (previously Duke of Clarence). Another was the victoria – named in honour of the reigning Queen.

Photo © Catherine Lassesen

3.3: The Victoria

Things changed dramatically with the invention of the two-wheeled hansom cab, first designed by Joseph Aloysius Hansom (1803-1882) in 1834. It did away with the need for two of the usual four wheels, without sacrificing stability. Originally this was achieved using a very low-slung cab between wheels so large that the tops of them came up as high as the cab's roof. Within a couple of years one John Chapman had extensively refined the design to produce the hansom as we know it: stable, manoeuvrable, fast and above all smart, with such accessories as polished brass fittings and silk blinds at the windows. The driver sat perched on a high seat behind the cab, the long reins extending over the top of the cab to the horse's head. A lever arrangement enabled him to open the door for passengers without having to leave his seat, and driver and passenger could communicate through a trap door in the roof. In 1903 it was estimated that there were some

7,500 licensed hansom cabs on the streets of London, but with the coming of the motorcar the number of hansoms plying their trade dwindled rapidly and eleven years later only 200 remained in business.

© *The Sherlock Holmes Museum*

3.4: The Sherlock Holmes Museum's 1899 Forder Hansom cab

Hansom was an architect who went bankrupt over the building of Birmingham town hall, but carried on to have a successful career specialising in ecclesiastical buildings. Apart from his 'Patent Safety Cab' he seems to have had little interest in designing anything other than buildings. Quite how or why he chose to keep a golden eagle in his back yard is anybody's guess.

Chapman's name was never reflected in the name of the vehicles produced to his design because he had sold his rights at an early stage. Hansom achieved the fame but not the fortune. Although he sold the patent for £10,000 to the Hansom Cab Company set up to build and market the cabs, the company ran into financial difficulties and he was never paid.

BLACK MARIA

Courtesy Kent Police Museum Photo Archive

3.5: Black Maria used in the TV series 'Foyle's War', set during World War II

Although the term 'black Maria' is comparatively recent, the Maria responsible for it is obscure. It has been claimed that the reference is to Marie Manning, a seamstress and lady's maid, who was hanged for murder at the end of 1849 after a sensational trial. When she had to appear in court – transported there from prison in a suitable conveyance – she attended dressed most attractively in black. It has been estimated that as many as fifty thousand people attended her hanging, one of whom was Charles Dickens who used her character as the basis for Lady Dedlock's maid in Bleak House. Marie took care over her appearance to the last: The Times reported that at her hanging she wore a handsome black satin gown and a black lace veil obscuring the whole of her face. It is said that black satin went out of fashion for many years afterwards as a result. Dickens was so appalled by the behaviour of those attending the execution that he wrote to The Times(i), expressing his horror that from midnight he could see "boys and girls already assembled in the best places", and commenting that a "sight so inconceivably awful as the wickedness and levity of the immense crowd collected at that execution this morning could be imagined by no man".

However, reputable dictionaries indicate that the first use of the term 'black Maria' in Britain was not until twenty-five years after these events, which does not support the idea of a close link with Manning. Further research shows that it was actually in use in the United States some years before the Manning trial - in the 1830s in New York and by the 1840s in Boston. American sources indicate that the original Maria was Maria Lee, a black woman of formidable size and strength, who kept a lodging house. The tale goes that if the police had to deal with a difficult and aggressive wrongdoer, they would ask for her help in arresting him and taking him to jail. Certainly the story has been around for a long time and there can be little doubt that such a woman existed. Although picturesque, the link to a vehicle for the conveyance of prisoners is hardly authoritative. However, it is mentioned by Brewer(ii) as a possibility.

TAR MACADAM

In England the familiar blackish road surface consisting of small stones mixed with tar is formally referred to as tar macadam but more commonly shortened simply to tarmac. John Loudon McAdam (1756 – 1836) was a Scot, the youngest of ten children. At the age of fourteen his father died and he was sent to New York to be brought up by a wealthy uncle. In time John developed his own successful business interests, but because he fought on the British side in the American War of Independence the bulk of his fortune was confiscated and, being understandably no longer welcome in the USA, he returned to Scotland. There he was able to buy a modest estate and set up in business with a lease of some tar kilns to produce coke from coal, tar being a valuable by-product.

Until the eighteenth century roadways in Britain had been in a dire state. There had been no proper surfacing and most were little more than mud, worn into deep ruts during wet weather that then set solid when the weather was dry. The passing of the Turnpike Acts allowed local landowners to get together to form turnpike trusts in order to finance the construction and maintenance of proper roads. The costs were then recovered through a system of tolls levied at gateways, known as turnpikes. The tolls were calculated according to the numbers and kinds of animals using the road and, for vehicles, the size and type of wheels. McAdam became a trustee of one such trust near his Scottish estate but does not at that stage seem to have been involved in the nitty-gritty of road building. It appears that he merely participated financially in a venture that he hoped would, amongst other things, improve communications to and from his estate.

Unfortunately the business acumen that had served McAdam so well in New York had by now deserted him and eventually he was in such financial straits that he had to sell his house. He took a government appointment for provisioning the Navy – Britain was again at war with France – which required him to move to the South West of England. Shortly after taking up this post he was appointed surveyor to the trustees of several turnpikes and the career for which he is now remembered was launched.

The new method of road building developed by McAdam was based firstly on his realisation that the underlying ground had to remain dry in order for it to be strong enough to support the road surface. To achieve this he not only adopted the principle established by Telford of having a road surface higher in the centre than at the sides in order to encourage surface drainage, but he also required that the road surface be raised above that of the immediately surrounding land, if necessary by digging drainage ditches beside it. Further, he noticed that if an even surface comprised of small stones is laid over a foundation layer of large stones, before long the small ones work their way to the bottom leaving the large ones on top, resulting in a lumpy surface unsuitable for vehicles. He realised that if, by contrast, the stones used were all small chippings, when spread in layers and rolled flat they compacted together providing an even, strong, waterproof surface. He therefore stipulated that all the stones in the roads he built had to be no more than one and a half inches long, with a maximum specified weight. And just when his orders created a demand in the South West for huge supplies of small stones, there happened to be a convenient source of cheap labour for stone breaking nearby: French prisoners from the Napoleonic Wars held in the new prison at Dartmoor.

From Illustrated London News, 1843

3.6: Rebecca Rioters

Turnpike tolls were unpopular and put an especially heavy burden on farmers taking animals to market. The improvement in road surfaces had made travel easier but dramatically increased the cost of using them. In Wales poverty exacerbated the resentment felt towards the tolls and led to the Rebecca Riots. A number of groups calling themselves 'the hosts of Rebecca', probably a reference to the Old Testament blessing on Rebecca that her offspring "possess the gate of those that hate them"(iii), attacked and destroyed many of the tollgates. Each group was led by a local farmworker wearing a bonnet and petticoats over his usual

84

clothing: others among the rioters also often adopted similar garb.

McAdam is frequently given the credit for being the first to use tar in road construction. His business involvement with tar kilns in Scotland might be seen to confirm this, but it is almost certainly a misapprehension. Strictly speaking a 'macadamised' road was one that merely incorporated his design features as to drainage and layers of compacted stones of a specified size. Although the first patent for use of a tar-like substance for roads in Britain was granted some two years before McAdam died it was not taken out by him or by anyone in the South West or Scotland, but by someone in the London area. And the idea did not get very far: it was not until the early twentieth century that tarmacadam – stones suitable for a macadamised road but spread with or mixed with tar to stick them together and provide greater resistance to the wear and tear of increased motorised traffic – became widely established.

McAdam's contribution to the roadway network was never properly rewarded. Despite his patent rights his ideas were widely copied across Britain. The government did eventually offer a knighthood, which he turned down. The government also made him a modest financial award towards meeting part of his costs, but this was less than half the figure that had originally been considered. There is an implication that the downward adjustment was the result of animosity from some turnpike trustees, landowners with Parliamentary influence, created by McAdam's exposure of the corruption and inadequacies of many such trusts.

DIESEL

The word diesel has been around since the late 1800s and is such an integral part of our daily language that it feels like a genuinely English word. This impression is confirmed by the terror one feels, when facing an array of motorway service station pumps in France, that just maybe the English-French dictionary might be wrong and the pump labelled 'gazole' might not actually deliver diesel at all. With not merely a fuel to his name but also the use of 'diesel' to refer to a type of engine as well as to vehicles using such engines, Diesel has the rare distinction of having scored an etymological hat trick – without a capital letter in sight.

Rudolf Diesel (1858-1913) was the son of Bavarian parents but was born and lived in France. At the age of eleven his childhood was disrupted when France declared war on Prussia and he and his family were deported as enemy aliens. They went to England, but after a year Rudolf left and went on his own to Bavaria where he stayed with his cousin. He must have found school difficult, given that he was first taught in France in French, then in England in English and finally in Bavaria in German, and he suffered attacks of migraine. Despite these problems, at the age of eighteen he achieved brilliant exam results and won a scholarship to the prestigious institution now known as Technische Universitat München.

Whilst there, Diesel learned that steam engines were only 10% efficient and this made him determined to design something that would be less wasteful. Initially he took a job with an engineering firm producing refrigeration machinery and worked there for some ten years before leaving to concentrate on designing his new engine. After various difficulties he was granted a patent but commercial development of the engine took some five more years to get going, because the technology of the time could not reliably meet the demands of his design.

During this time Diesel was under great stress, in financial difficulties and working all hours, and his childhood migraines began again. When at last the engine achieved success, Diesel became a wealthy man, but financial security did nothing to restore his health. Attacks of migraine worsened, then disastrous investments resulted in near-bankruptcy. Diesel put his affairs in order, selected the date of September 29th marking it with a cross in his diary and, when travelling to England on a cross channel ferry, disappeared overboard on that date leaving his hat and coat folded up on the deck.

Drawing © C.M. Wiles

3.7: Cross Channel ferry from the early 1900s

ZEPPELIN

Photo © User Omnibus/Wikimedia Commons

3.8: Cluster ballooning

A child leaving a party, clutching the string of a helium balloon, dreams of being attached to so many one day that he or she could take off and fly. In 1982 that dream came true for a man who tied forty-two giant reinforced plastic balloons firmly to his garden chair and floated up, up and away into the blue yonder to a height of some three miles. He had taken the practical precaution of arming himself with a pistol in order to shoot holes in an appropriate number of balloons when he was ready to return to land. And when he did so, he was in trouble with the police for being a potential danger to air traffic. But the seed had been sown for a whole new sport: cluster ballooning.

Count Ferdinand Adolf August Heinrich, Graf von Zeppelin (1838-1917), had already retired from a career in the army so he was no child when he started to design a lighter-than-air aircraft. He had been inspired by his experience of hot air ballooning and his ambition was to design something that not only went up in the air but which could also be steered. His approach was closer to the child's dream than would at first appear because he had the idea of using not one large balloon but a whole lot of small ones. He organised these 'balloons' (bags filled with hydrogen) and anchored them in place within a vast cigar-shaped fabric shell. Suspended beneath the shell along its length was a long thin gondola containing a motor and controls as well as space for passengers. The French had already been working along similar lines but Zeppelin was the first to think of adding a rigid metal framework between the fabric shell and bags of gas to help the airship keep its shape. After some ten years' work and many setbacks, which won him a great deal of scorn and the nickname 'The Foolish Count', the end result was an airship so advanced and so large that it was buoyant enough to carry travellers in some comfort. The first Zeppelin made its successful maiden flight in 1900. By 1910 Zeppelin had become a national hero and the first commercial passenger air service had been set up.

Zeppelins were used during the 1914-18 war to bomb London. As they flew at 20,000 feet, higher than the aeroplanes of the time, they were extremely difficult to shoot down. By 1916 an improved version of the Sopwith Camel at the very limit of its abilities could get close enough to have a chance. From the ground it could hardly have looked like a fair contest – a little midget of an aeroplane less than 7 metres long against an airship of some 200 metres. However, Zeppelins only flew at a very gentle pace and their extreme weakness was inflammability – once one caught fire that was the end of it.

Photo courtesy U.S. Library of Congress

3.9: UK Government Poster 1915

After the 1914-18 war the airship industry continued to develop. Design improved and passengers travelled in a space inside the airship instead of suspended in a gondola beneath. Luxury transatlantic and even round the world passenger services were established. The alternative mode of travel was the ocean liner, so airships were built to incorporate the standard of amenities needed to compete with the level of comfort offered to a liner's first class passengers. Airships became vastly bigger.

Photo by Gus Pasquerella, courtesy U.S. Navy

3.10: The Hindenburg catching fire on May 6, 1937

The biggest and most famous Zeppelin of all, the Hindenburg, was built to carry seventy passengers in ultimate luxury and had to be nearly as long as the Titanic in order to include a dining room, cocktail lounge, library and sitting room complete with grant piano, plus the extra gas needed to lift all that weight into the air. Fares were commensurate with the cost of providing such an advanced level of comfort and only the wealthy could afford to travel in this way. Although the non-inflammable gas helium had by now become available it was not used in the Hindenburg because it was not as light as hydrogen and so could not provide enough lift, unless the Hindenburg was to be made even bigger. When the Hindenburg crashed in 1937 it burst into flames causing such a terrible loss of life that commercial airship travel came to an end.

ROLLS-ROYCE®

An elderly gentleman who had been a motoring enthusiast throughout his life was one day reversing his car, his pride and joy, out of the garage. It had an automatic gear change so he needed to brake to control the reverse. Despite a light touch on the brake pedal he found the car was still going too fast and the need for braking became no longer a matter of cautious control. He braked harder, then as hard as he could, with his foot down to the floor. Previously he had always driven cars with manual gearboxes, so perhaps he was not fully at ease with an automatic. But whatever the reason, he found that it was not the brake he was pressing but the accelerator. The car's powerful engine responded accordingly and it shot back into the brick wall on the opposite side of the yard. Most cars would have stopped there, but this was a Rolls-Royce, and to a Rolls-Royce an obstacle such as a garden wall is trivial. Its weight and solid construction took it straight through. In the few moments it took for the driver to correct his mistake and find the brake pedal, the car kept going, leaving impressive tyre tracks as it went, across the perfectly manicured lawn beyond, knocking over the model heron that had been peacefully surveying a pond of koi carp and finally coming to rest amongst a great deal of broken glass in the greenhouse. The neighbour was not well pleased and did not seem to appreciate his great good fortune: although the garden had been devastated neither he nor his family had been out there at the time.

These events make one reconsider for a moment what one expects from a Rolls-Royce (if not necessarily from the driver). Rolls and Royce: two names which taken together have become so widely used to symbolise the ultimate in quality and reliability that they have moved beyond their commercial meaning, beyond even the world of engineering, and can be used to refer to almost anything. A Dyson vacuum cleaner, for example, might be described by an enthusiastic owner who had no qualms about mixing eponyms as 'the Rolls-Royce of hoovers'.

Rolls and Royce could not have come from two more contrasting backgrounds. The Honourable Charles Stewart Rolls (1877-1910) went to Eton and graduated from Cambridge with a degree in engineering. He was in the fortunate position of having the money to pursue his passion for cycling, motor cycling, flying and driving cars. He took part in a number of long distance classic European races and in 1903 established the world land speed record of 93 m.p.h. He helped to found the Aero Club (later the Royal Aero Club) and in 1910 was awarded his Aviator's Certificate by the Club – only the second ever issued. In the same year he was the first person to fly across the English Channel and back without stopping. He also achieved another 'first' in that year: he died in the first fatal flying accident in Britain.

Photo © Belinda Bailey

3.11: 1937 Rolls-Royce Phantom III in Ivory

Henry Royce (later Sir Henry Royce) (1863-1933) was the son of a far from prosperous miller. Royce's father died when he was still a child and the family struggled to survive. He was only able to go to school for two years because of the family's need for him to earn an income. He began by selling newspapers and after various other jobs was by the age of nineteen employed as an electrician. By the time Royce was twenty-one he had saved enough money to enable him to set up in partnership with a colleague in Manchester, making simple electrical goods. By working long hours, living frugally and producing goods that were better designed, better made and more reliable than those of their competitors, the partners were able to expand their business. Throughout his life Royce was famed for his attention to detail, outstanding workmanship and insistence on the best, both in materials and in design. He was an exceptional craftsman who loved making things that worked. Even after he had achieved fame and fortune he still always described himself as a mechanic.

Rolls and Royce were both involved in their different ways with French cars. By 1903 Royce was able to buy a small, second hand French car. He found it to be unreliable and worked on improving it, using the best of modern engineering. He designed, made and fitted new parts as necessary and his unusual skills in doing so resulted in a car that was quieter, smoother and a great deal more reliable than any other at the time. Meanwhile Rolls had recently set up in business in London selling expensive French cars. A friend, who knew that Rolls would prefer to sell high quality British cars if he could find them, had heard about Royce's car in Manchester and in 1904 he persuaded Rolls to go to Manchester to meet Royce. Each immediately recognised in the other a similar dedication to the achievement of the best. And the rest, as they say, is history.

SOPWITH CAMEL

What is a Sopwith Camel? Sir Thomas Octave Murdoch Sopwith (1888 – 1989) was by all accounts a modest, charming, humorous man who was instrumental in the development of aircraft design, technology and production from almost the earliest days of powered flight. The single-seater Sopwith Camel is the most well-known fighter aeroplane of the First World War and was so named because of a pronounced hump in its outline at the front of the fuselage.

Tommy Sopwith was born into a moderately wealthy family and was the eighth child, hence his second name. At the age of ten he faced tragedy: when out shooting with his father the gun lying across Tommy's knees went off accidentally and his father was killed. When Tommy left school he failed to get a place at the Royal Naval College – he always said he wasn't clever enough – and instead trained as an engineer. He bought his first aeroplane in October 1910 and taught himself to fly, not being deterred by a crash on the first attempt. His determination was such that within a few weeks he passed the Royal Aero Club's tests and was awarded his Aviator's Certificate.

The following year British official observers sent to a flying show in France were amazed to realise the extent to which the governments of both France and Germany were financing aircraft research and the development of aeronautics. This fired the British government into somewhat belated action and military trials were held the following year to select aircraft suitable for pilot training. Sopwith, one of the very few experienced pilots at the time, acted as test pilot and found that the standard of aeroplanes entered for the trials was so poor that he felt he could design something better himself.

In those days aeroplanes were small, built merely from a sketched design, made out of wood and covered with fabric. So Sopwith set up Sopwith Aviation Company Ltd. and teamed up with his mechanic and an outstanding trainee pilot, Harry Hawker. Their first effort was built in a shed and the fabric covering was made by one of Sopwith's sisters on her sewing machine. The enterprise grew and the first major design to emerge was the Sopwith Pup.

Next came the Sopwith Camel. This was very successful: during the First World War pilots flying them shot down a total of 1,294 enemy aircraft, including that flown by Baron von Richthofen – the famous 'Red Baron' who alone had accounted for some 80 allied aircraft. It was designed to be astonishingly manoeuvrable but the very qualities which made it so, also meant that the gyroscopic effect of the propeller rendered it notoriously difficult to fly. Unless appropriate counter-measures were taken by the pilot any attempt to turn left would at the same time result in the plane climbing to such an extent that it would end up looping the loop. Conversely, any attempt to turn right would send it into a dive. Pilots who were skilled enough to fly it were impressed by its abilities and held it in great affection, but many never got the chance. The number of pilots lost in accidents involving the Camel was not far short of the number of Camels that were shot down by the enemy.

Photo © Imperial War Museums (Q 67556)

3.12: Sopwith F1 Camel, single-seat scout, 1917

After the war the Sopwith Aviation Company was wound up and the Sopwith team set up Hawker Engineering (later Hawker Siddeley) which went on to develop the Hurricane. As 1939 approached Sopwith realised that war was inevitable, but the Government remained reluctant to commit itself to the purchase of aircraft. He therefore took an enormous risk and began work on 1,000 Hurricanes without knowing if the Government would order any at all. When the order finally did come through, time was of the essence: in 1940 Germany began the Battle of Britain with 3,300 aircraft as opposed to the RAF's 871, and that number would have been considerably lower without Sopwith's early start.

Sopwith remained with Hawker Siddeley and, as chairman, oversaw the development of the Harrier jump jet. He was widely held in high regard, not merely for his achievements but also at a personal level and his hundredth birthday was celebrated in style. A fly past of aeroplanes with which he had been involved was arranged, including a Sopwith Pup, a

Hurricane and a Harrier jump jet. Sopwith could no longer see, but was able to recognise each from its sound.

BELISHA BEACON

The Minster of Transport during the 1930s was Leslie Hore-Belisha (1893 – 1957). His determination to reduce the number of road traffic accidents resulted in the introduction of what became known as Belisha beacons: amber coloured lights on top of tall poles painted with black and white stripes that drew motorists' attention to the presence of a pedestrian crossing. His road safety measures also included the introduction of driving tests and the Highway Code.

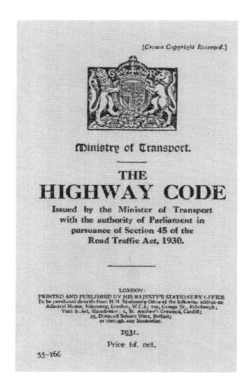

**3.13: Front page of the first edition
of the Highway Code, 1931**

During the early 1950s the message conveyed by Belisha beacons was emphasised by making the amber lights flash and by painting black and white stripes across the road: zebra crossings had arrived. The number of these is now dwindling as they are replaced by the more high-tech pelican crossings with traffic lights and diagrammatic figures in red and green. Plain ordinary zebras will no doubt eventually disappear altogether and Hore-Belisha's name will be forgotten by the general public.

The irony is that during his lifetime neither his record as Minister of Transport nor his valuable contributions to road safety were what made him famous. He hit the headlines by virtue of his activities as Secretary of State for War, to which position he had been appointed by Neville Chamberlain in 1937. Chamberlain wanted someone to introduce drastic changes to reform the army, despite the fact that any attempt to change the status quo in such a powerful organisation, steeped in tradition, would inevitably upset its upper echelons.

In many ways Hore-Belisha was a good choice to tackle army reform. He was young, energetic and ambitious. During the 1914-1918 War he had served in the Royal Army Service Corps, so he had considerable insight into the practicalities needed to enable an army to function effectively. He had no difficulty in talking as an equal to people of any social standing and when thinking about reform would not confine himself to seeking the views from those of high rank. He was popular with the press. He was also a man who had the courage of his convictions, even where these clashed with the views of senior advisers. From the point of view of the establishment, however, he was never 'one of us'; his flamboyant and abrasive behaviour was not that of a gentleman. He was also Jewish, at a time when anti-Semitism was not only widespread but also socially acceptable – there were those among the upper classes who sympathised with some of Hitler's views and a number went so far as actively to campaign for the exclusion of Jews from government.

Hore-Belisha began his reforms by taking steps to improve recruitment. These included better pay, better promotion prospects, better living conditions (such as provision of modernised heated barracks), better catering, and the scrapping of unnecessary petty regulations. Hore-Belisha also fought to achieve a more effective distribution of resources through prioritising mechanisation and anti-aircraft defence, in preference to the existing huge military commitment in India. Top ranks in the army were not happy: three senior members of the Army Council who could not accept the changes were forced out and replaced.

Thus far Chamberlain was pleased with the reforms, but Hore-Belisha wanted to take them further. He wanted officer training to be available to those who were most able, regardless of social background. He wanted to transform cavalry regiments, those very regiments that carried the highest social status, into new armoured divisions equipped with tanks. The army and navy, both steeped in the traditions of centuries, had a notoriously snobbish attitude towards the recently formed RAF, a service characterised by what they considered to be an improper level of informality. Hore-Belisha wanted to get rid of the divisions that arose from this attitude and to create close co-operation between all three services.

These policies were anathema to the top brass. Without Chamberlain's support Hore-Belisha could not force them through, and by now Chamberlain had returned from Munich with Hitler's assurance that he had no intention of attacking Britain. "Peace for our time"(iv) meant that Chamberlain's priorities for the armed services remained the defence of Britain and the Empire, with no involvement in Europe and therefore no preparation for a possible war in Europe. Hore-Belisha must have been fully aware of the very real menace posed by Hitler and infuriated Chamberlain by pressing for conscription and for money for rearmament, but was unable to convince the Cabinet of its necessity until only shortly before war was declared. He was by then in a vulnerable position, having become unpopular not only among senior army personnel but also among his political colleagues.

Despite his best efforts in the face of a complete lack of support Hore-Belisha, as Secretary of State for War, inevitably attracted criticism for the inadequacy of preparation of the armed services when war was declared. He then fuelled the fire by questioning the army's tactics in the field and by criticising their construction of the pillboxes built to extend the defences of the French Maginot line. This was the last straw for the top ranks. Through personal contacts they were able to involve the King, who persuaded Chamberlain to remove Hore-Belisha from office. Hore-Belisha was offered the Board of Trade as a sop but refused to accept it. His career was ruined.

JCB

Photo © Anthony Appleyard

3.14: JCB Backhoe Loader

JCB is an exciting word that breaks all the usual rules. For a start, it is not written in lower case like a normal word but only ever appears as three capital letters. So it looks like an acronym, but it isn't one. Acronyms are often manipulated in order to produce pronounceable words, to avoid the inelegance of spelling out their constituent letters – ISAs or NATO for example. Not so JCB. JCB has a mind of its own, defying any temptation to call it something frivolous like Jay-c'b. Perhaps this is inherent in the size and power of the thing itself. The word positively requires one to approach it with respect: it demands the full 'jay-cee-bee' treatment (not that anyone would ever dream of writing it like that) and appears in the vocabulary of small children at an extraordinarily young age.

Photo © Anthony Appleyard

3.15: Farm trailer, believed to be the first vehicle made by J.C. Bamford

On the face of it JCB appears to be merely a commercial name, but it is an exception that proves the rule. It is admittedly the logo of a company manufacturing a wide variety of heavy construction equipment, its products easily identified by their distinctive appearance: bright yellow with JCB written on them in prominent black letters. But so innovative and so popular has been the equipment designed and produced by the company that the name is now out on its own. Although presumably no competing manufacturer could or would endorse its own products with the name of its rival, nevertheless JCB is widely used in everyday speech to refer to any heavy earth moving equipment of a similar size and shape, even if manufactured by an entirely different company.

Joseph Cyril Bamford (1916 – 2001) – who became known as Mr. JCB - was an engineer with a flair for design, coining the phrase "don't complicate, simplicate". He set up his own company and began business in 1945 in a rented garage measuring 4 by 5 metres, using army surplus stock and second hand tools. From the very beginning he reinvested all the profits and eventually built the business up into a multi-million pound company, using innovative design and up-to-date technology. The company achieved fame with the design and production of its backhoe loader, which is the classic JCB with a hydraulic shovel in the front and a digging arm at the back.

CHAPTER FOUR

MEASUREMENT

Units of measurement, like hymns, fall into two groups: ancient and modern. Virtually none of the ancient ones reflects a name because the need for measurement of such things as distance, area, volume and weight was so fundamental that the vocabulary for it developed as part of the general language. But do not equate fundamental with simple: a quick gallop round some of these ancient units should be enough to make even the most die-hard traditionalist grateful for the metric system.

4.1: Medieval ploughmen with oxen

Distance was comparatively straightforward, but even the familiar miles, yards, feet and inches degenerate into furlongs, rods (or poles or perches), chains, links and barleycorns, not

102

to mention hands and fingers if your hobby is horses, or cubits if you are interested in arks. Area takes us to oxgangs, acres, roods and back to rods again.

We can still cope with at least the idea, if not the arithmetic, of some avoirdupois weight - tons, hundredweights, stones, pounds, ounces, drams and grains. And despite metrication babies steadfastly continue to arrive in pounds and ounces. Apothecaries' weight (pounds, ounces, drachms, scruples and grains) sounds temptingly similar but is not the same: suddenly a pound contains twelve ounces instead of sixteen, presenting a particular challenge to dispensing chemists in the days when they used to make up medicines in apothecaries' weight but buy drugs in avoirdupois. Precious metals had a separate system all to themselves, Troy weight – pounds, ounces, pennyweights, carats and grains – but don't mistake these carats for those relating to diamonds. And various individual items had their own esoteric scales: wool came in weys, tods, stones and cloves; butter in tubs, firkins and closes.

Dry measure (volume) starts off innocently with pints, quarts and gallons (which explains why some fishmongers still sell prawns by the pint) but when it launches into pecks, bushels and coombs is definitely best left alone. However, if sheer complexity is what you are looking for then the victor's crown must go to liquid measure. Your imperial gallon is not the same as your wine gallon and there was absolutely no agreement on the standard size of a pig, since hogsheads of spirits, beer, wine and claret all contained different quantities. And so on, into the lost world of firkins, kilderkins, and butts, plus the Methuselahs and jeroboams so beloved of crossword setters and then back to the teacupful, ounce, drachm and minim (or drop) of the apothecary.

One gains respect for the forgotten armies of schoolchildren who had to know how at least some of these various units related to each other and to cope with their addition and subtraction, all calculated on different bases, none of which was ten (those of a certain age will remember forever the chant 'sixteen ounces one pound, fourteen pounds one stone'), so calculators would not have been much help even if they had been in existence.

4.2: Interior of a Flemish apothecary's shop

But that is enough of the ancient. In the last few hundred years advances in technology have been dramatic. Discoveries and new concepts have led to an urgent need for new measurements and, in contrast to the ancient units, most of the modern ones are based on the name of someone who worked in the relevant scientific field. Many are now such an integral part of the language that those using them are hardly aware that the words started off as a name. When viewed as a whole, modern units provide an impressive tribute to European scientific achievement. And looking at the lives of these scientists, the tendency is for a man to do it in a laboratory, but for the occasional husband and wife team to do it in a garden shed, so to speak.

One word of warning. The litre (the symbol for which is the letter l) has sometimes caused confusion owing to the fact that a lower case letter l appears very like the number 1. It was therefore mooted that the symbol should be written as a capital letter, although such use of the upper case had hitherto been strictly reserved for eponymous units. This suggestion somewhat predictably tempted some joker to invent a scientist to justify the change, choosing the name and dates Claude Emile Jean-Baptiste Litre (1716 – 1778), allegedly a glass manufacturer from a family of wine bottle makers. The hoax began in 1978 and convinced many for several years. Others were unable to resist adding to the story by suggesting he had a daughter Millicent, responsible for the millilitre. The bigwigs of the Système Internationale or SI, the internationally recognised system of units for scientific measurements, were not amused and the symbol remains firmly unchanged in the lower case.

TEMPERATURE

FAHRENHEIT

To appreciate the achievement of Fahrenheit some idea of the historical context in which he lived is needed. Measurement of changes in temperature had been around for a long time. More than two thousand years ago Philo of Byzantium had set out to measure changes in air temperature by fitting a tube into a hollow sphere and putting the other end of the tube into a jug of water. When the sphere was moved into a hot spot, bubbles came out of the tube as the air in the sphere expanded. Conversely, when the sphere was moved into the shade, the level of water in the tube rose as the air contracted.

In the early seventeenth century Robert Fludd developed this simple experiment by rearranging the three bits of kit involved and adding marks on the tube to show how far the level of water in the tube had changed. Neither experiment, however, did anything to calibrate what the levels of temperature actually were, nor to enable the changes in temperature to be compared with anything else. By about 1700 some progress was being made: thermometers filled with alcohol and even with red wine had been made, but there was still no standard system of calibration.

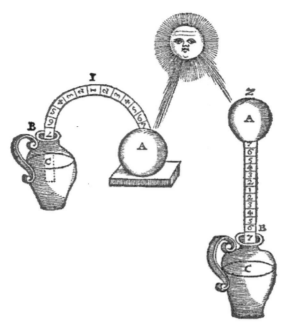

From 'Philosophia Moysaica', courtesy Wellcome Library, London

4.3: Fludd's illustration of:
'X' Philo's thermometer   'Z' Fludd's rearrangement of it

Daniel Gabriel Fahrenheit (1686 – 1736), therefore, appeared on the scene at a critical time. The son of a merchant, he was born in Danzig (Gdansk) and earned his living by making scientific instruments, including thermometers, which at that time consisted of a long, thin, sealed glass tube with a bulb at one end, usually filled with alcohol.

It must have occurred to anyone who has used Fahrenheit's temperature scale that it is very odd how he ended up with two numbers so apparently random as 32° for the freezing point of water and 212° for its boiling point. The simplicity of the reason dramatically illustrates just how much we now take for granted. 'Ended up' says it all: he had to create a standard, consistent temperature scale before he could use it to show what the boiling and freezing points of water actually were.

106

Fahrenheit was interested in the study of heat, but at that time there was no way in which temperature could be accurately measured because no exact fixed temperatures were known. Even the freezing point of pure water was regarded as variable because water can be cooled down so quickly that before it has had time to freeze right through it reaches a temperature below its normal freezing point. So Fahrenheit, who was exceptionally skilled at glass blowing, set about making his own accurately calibrated thermometer.

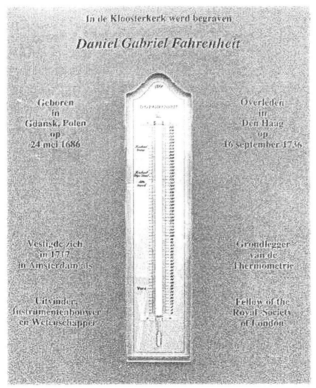

4.4: Memorial plaque at Fahrenheit's burial site in The Hague

He wanted to start his scale at the lowest reliable temperature he was likely to come across. He decided to use the coldest temperature at which he could get a mixture of water and salt to begin to freeze, which he called 0°. He could not use the boiling point of water since no-one yet knew very much about it: thermometers filled with alcohol would simply explode if any attempt were made to measure a temperature as high as, let alone higher than, the boiling point of alcohol (now known to be 172°F). So for his upper fixed temperature he chose the body heat of a healthy person. He decided to call it 12° but soon realised that the size of degree thus produced was inconveniently large. In order to get degrees of a more useful size he looked at suitable multiples of twelve and plumped for the multiple eight, producing 96°. By continuing his degree marks along the thermometer beyond the upper fixed point (keeping the length of each degree constant), he could use it to measure a wide range of temperatures.

It was only after Fahrenheit had calibrated his thermometer that he went on to use it in experimental work and to find out that the temperature at which pure water begins to freeze is constant, and that this happened to take place at 32° on his scale. In order to study the boiling point of water he invented the mercury-in-glass thermometer by filling the bulb with mercury instead of alcohol, calibrating it with the 0° and 96° that he already now knew and then extending the calibration in degrees of equal steps upwards. He found that water boiled at 212°.

CELSIUS

The Swedish scientist Anders Celsius (1701 – 1744) was a professor of astronomy, following in the footsteps of his father and two grandfathers, who had been professors in astronomy or mathematics. Celsius calibrated his thermometer for use in meteorological investigations, using the freezing and boiling points of water that, thanks to Fahrenheit, were now two fixed temperatures that could be accurately determined. To keep it simple Celsius used the numbers 0 and 100 and thus created the centigrade scale (degrees centigrade and degrees Celsius are one and the same), so it seems strangely illogical that he allocated 0° to boiling and 100° to freezing. Almost as soon as he died these were reversed by Linnaeus, a fellow professor at the same university (who classified plants).

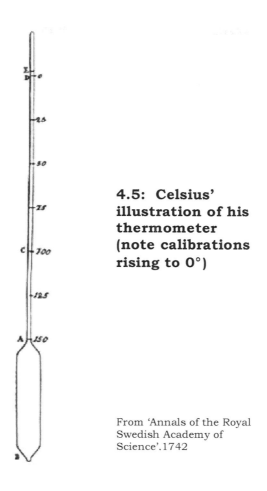

4.5: Celsius' illustration of his thermometer (note calibrations rising to 0°)

From 'Annals of the Royal Swedish Academy of Science'.1742

Celsius was an ardent supporter of Sweden's change from the Julian to the Gregorian calendar. This seems of little significance now as it would never occur to us that, apart from the inevitable minor difference created by the date line, the date might be different in another country. The very idea would reduce those responsible for international travel timetables to a jelly. But in the eighteenth century the situation across Europe can only be described as chaotic. The problem began with the Papal Bull of 1582 when Pope Gregory XIII, advised by his astronomers, decreed that in order to bring the civil calendar back into line with the astronomical year a new civil calendar should be adopted in place of the existing Julian calendar. He specified that ten days were to be dropped out of October for the year in which the change was made.

Gregorian range	Julian range	Difference
From 15 October 1582 to 10 March 1700	From 5 October 1582 to 28 February 1700	10 days
From 11 March 1700 to 11 March 1800	From 29 February 1700 to 28 February 1800	11 days
From 12 March 1800 to 12 March 1900	From 29 February 1800 to 28 February 1900	12 days
From 13 March 1900 to 13 March 2100	From 29 February 1900 to 28 February 2100	13 days

Table showing how the difference in the date between the Gregorian calendar and the Julian calendar keeps increasing(i)

Catholic countries like Italy, Spain, Poland and most of France complied fairly promptly, but Protestant countries took more time to make up their minds. Switzerland took a piecemeal approach. Norway and Denmark changed in 1700. Great Britain left it until 1752 and at the same time took the opportunity of starting the New Year in January instead of the middle of March (so that February came shortly after the beginning of the year instead of near the end), making 1751 a short year of less than nine months. Russia, Greece and Turkey came way behind the rest of Europe, not adopting the new calendar until 1918, 1924 and 1927 respectively.

But in the midst of all this Sweden decided to go it alone and really made a complete pig's ear of the whole thing. To get a glimpse of the extent of the mess, it is important to be aware that adoption of the Gregorian calendar did not just involve losing ten days. To prevent the civil and astronomical calendars drifting 'out of sync' in the future, the Papal Bull also decreed that the turn of the century, which being divisible by four had previously always been a leap year, was to be a leap year only if the century was divisible by four hundred. Sweden decided to adopt the Gregorian calendar in 1700 but did not want to lose all the days at once, so decided to phase it in by abolishing leap years altogether until they were in line with the new calendar. They accordingly cancelled their leap year in 1700, thereby putting themselves one day ahead of countries still using the Julian calendar, but they were of course still ten days behind those who had moved over to the new calendar. Then by mistake they made 1704 and 1708 leap years as usual. After this unsatisfactory start they gave up and decided to get back into line with other Julian calendar users. This was achieved by awarding themselves a double leap year (in order to compensate for the day lost in 1700), giving February 1712 thirty days in Sweden. It was not until 1753 that they took the plunge, losing all the necessary days at once. The whole subject must have been a nightmare and respect is due to Celsius for his progressive views.

KELVIN

Sources agree that William Thomson (1824 – 1907), better known as Lord Kelvin (he was raised to the peerage in 1892) was an intellectual giant. He took a top first in mathematics from Cambridge and the brilliance he displayed in the examinations was such that one examiner has been reported as commenting to another "You and I are just about fit to mend his pens"(ii). At the age of twenty-two Thomson was appointed professor of natural philosophy at Glasgow.

Kelvin excelled in the field of thermodynamics. His work on the theory of heat and energy resulted in the creation of a fundamentally new way of defining temperature. His temperature scale is widely used by scientists yet little known to the non-scientific. Degrees Kelvin are effectively the same as degrees Centigrade, except that they start at a theoretical temperature which is startlingly cold – so cold in fact that it is impossible for anything, ever, anywhere, to be any colder. It is known as absolute zero and this magic temperature of 0°K is equivalent to -273°C. At this temperature not even a molecule moves, never mind a mouse.

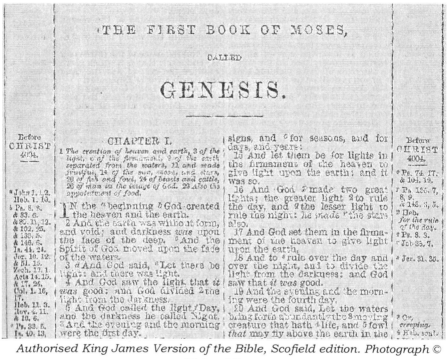

Authorised King James Version of the Bible, Scofield edition. Photograph © Richard Spence

4.6: Opening page of Genesis telling of the creation of the world, containing a note in the right hand margin 'Before Christ 4004'

Kelvin's achievement of thinking up this theoretical temperature might seem to confirm the often held view that mathematicians are abstract, head-in-the-clouds thinkers not living in the real world. But he applied his mind to all sorts of practical problems and seems to have been able to do almost everything. He was prominent for his work in submarine telegraphy, advising on the construction of the first transatlantic cable and the mechanics of laying it. He designed practical equipment to improve its function. He designed apparatus for the accurate measurement of

112

electricity. His interest in sailing led him to design an improved ship's compass that was adopted by the Royal Navy.

It is somewhat reassuring to find that even Kelvin complies with the saying that Homer sometimes nods: he did make serious errors of judgement in some aspects of science outside his field. He was convinced, for example, that X-rays would turn out to be a hoax and that heavier than air aircraft could never fly. But his real Achilles' heel concerned a topic to which he devoted an inordinate amount of time: the age of the earth. He had grown up in a world in which there was increasing discussion about this. Many bibles still included a side note in Genesis, reflecting Bishop James Ussher's calculation carried out in 1645, that the earth was created on 23rd October 4004 BC.

Kelvin's grasp of mathematics and the theory of heat combined to convince him that the age of the earth was not only much older than that, but that its age could be calculated by working out how long it had taken to cool down from a molten state to its current temperature. Kelvin's theorising resulted in his finally estimating the earth's age at about 40 million years. Geologists, and Darwin, did not agree but Kelvin regarded both geology and biology as unsound because neither was founded on the rigorous mathematical analysis that had proved unfailingly reliable in his other activities. Kelvin was crashingly wrong – probably more than thirteen billion years wrong – but to be fair he did indicate that his estimate might need revision in the event of a source of energy hitherto unknown being discovered. At that time no-one had yet heard of radioactivity. And he was certainly much nearer the mark than Ussher.

RADIOACTIVITY

Radioactivity is complicated and is made worse by the plethora of units of measurement, virtually all of which are named after scientists in the field. Only three are discussed here, and a word of explanation may be helpful to reduce confusion. The essential thing, before making any kind of measurement, is to decide what you actually want to know. If, like the earlier scientists who were unaware of its dangers, all you are interested in is how radioactive something is, in other words how energetically it is emitting radiation, then the curie is one of the appropriate units. This refers to a number of (nuclear) disintegrations per second.

The problem with disintegrations per second is that they give no indication of how dangerous the radioactivity is which, by and large, depends on how much energy is absorbed by someone or something. Absorption varies considerably according to the source of the radioactivity, how far away it is and the type of rays emitted (alpha rays are much more harmful than beta or gamma rays). The appropriate measure for absorbed radiation used to be the roentgen (although this has now been superseded). But should you need radiotherapy none of these units is much help because what both you and the radiologist want to know is 'how much harm will it do?' not just on one occasion but cumulatively. This is where the sievert comes in. Calculation of this is a bit of an art form as it aims to take into account, inter alia, body weight and how the radiation enters the body.

Let us begin with the discovery of X-rays.

ROENTGEN

Wilhelm Conrad Roentgen (Röntgen) (1845-1923) was a most unlikely candidate for making the sensational discovery of the existence of X-rays. He was the son of a cloth merchant and had no scientific background. He did not particularly shine at school, apart from being good at rigging up bits of kit. He was expelled from secondary school, albeit unfairly after being wrongly accused of drawing a caricature of one of the teachers. He went on to the local university but did not have the necessary qualifications to be properly enrolled as a student there.

Things then began to look up. Roentgen found that it was possible to study mechanical engineering at Zurich provided

114

he passed their entrance examinations. He may not have been outstandingly brilliant in an abstractly mathematical way but his enquiring mind, together with careful observation and a practical ability to design experiments, certainly made him an outstanding scientist. In 1901 he received the Nobel prize for physics.

Before Roentgen's discovery other scientists had established that when an electric current is passed through a glass vacuum tube containing gas at an extremely low pressure, cathode rays are produced and the tube lights up with a ghostly fluorescence. It was also known that cathode rays could not pass through glass, but could pass through thin metal plates inserted inside the tube. In order to study cathode rays outside the vacuum tube a physicist called Phillip Lenard had designed the 'Lenard tube', which was a vacuum tube with an aluminium foil window at one end. Lenard was able to show that cathode rays passed through the window but that, having done so, they dissipated in the air within a few centimetres.

Roentgen turned his full attention to investigating cathode rays. In November 1895 he was working with a Lenard tube and, just beyond the aluminium window, had set up a scientific plate coated with a chemical sensitive to cathode rays. When the tube was turned on the plate began to luminesce as he expected. He then wondered what would happen if the plate were placed near cathode rays that had been produced in an ordinary vacuum tube. To be able to see whether the plate would again luminesce he had to block out all the light created within the tube. He therefore fitted a jacket of black card round the tube and tested its efficacy by extinguishing the light in the room and passing an electric current through the tube. No light escaped but he noticed that the scientific plate, some distance away, was glowing. He knew that cathode rays could not survive in the air at that distance so realised that the effect must have been caused by a different sort of radiation. Not knowing what these mysterious new rays were, he called them X-rays.

He experimented for a further six weeks and found that photographic plates were sensitive to these rays, which were happily passing through both the glass tube and its black jacket. He then used photographic plates to record how well these rays were able to pass through all sorts of other things: metals, books, glass, wood. He even got his wife to hold her hand between the vacuum tube and the plate to see if the new rays would go through flesh. When the plate was developed it showed the faint outline of her hand, her ring and, wonder of wonders, details of the bone structure inside.

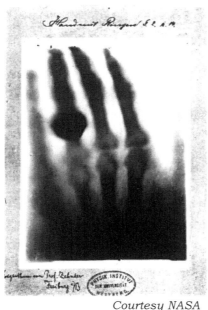

Courtesy NASA

4.7: "Hand mit ringen"

A print of one of the first X-rays by Roentgen taken on 22nd December 1895 and presented to Prof Ludwig Zehnder of the Physik Institut, University of Freiburg, on 1st January 1896.

The image is of the left hand of Roentgen's wife. Her comment on looking at it was "I have seen my death".

By the end of the year Roentgen had presented a paper to a scientific society and sent his friends New Year greetings with an off print of the paper and copies of some of the pictures he had taken. Within a week news about the sensational Roentgen Rays hit the headlines. The benefits for medical science were obvious, but certain members of the public had reservations. The prospect of being able to see a picture of one's own skeleton gave some feelings of a premonition of death.

The exaggerated modesty of late Victorian England also found the concept hard to come to terms with – a company even advertised clothing claimed to be X-ray proof. Those who were not so modest enjoyed the latest popular verses:

> The Roentgen Rays, the Roentgen Rays,
> What is this craze?
> The town's ablaze,
> With the new phase
> Of X-rays ways.
>
> I'm full of daze,
> Shock and amaze,
> For nowadays,
> I hear they'll gaze,
> Thro' cloak and gown – and even stays,
> These naughty, naughty Roentgen Rays.(iii)

By the 1950s public understanding had swung to the other extreme. X-rays were regarded as so commonplace and harmless that most shoe shops were equipped with machines used for X-raying children's feet in their new shoes to be certain that the shoes allowed enough room for growth.

Despite his fame Roentgen always remained a quiet and unassuming man, hating publicity and steadfastly avoiding any limelight. It is fitting that Roentgen rays eventually became universally known as X-rays, the term he himself always used, allowing his name to fall into comparative obscurity. But one would like to think that the professional in him would have been satisfied to know that his name has been widely used by radiologists and others working in the field, as a scientific unit for measuring the amount of exposure to the rays discovered by him.

CURIE

The curie represents something approaching half a million disintegrations per second and was named in honour of Marie

Curie (née Maria Sklodowska) (1867 – 1934). Her story is inspiring – she was clever, modest, caring, hardworking and dedicated.

Marie Curie was born in Warsaw. At that time Warsaw was in Russia: geographically Poland did not exist, having been carved up by Russia, Prussia and Austria in 1795. Two of Marie's uncles had been sent to Siberia for participating in a recent uprising. Teaching in Polish was a criminal offence, but despite all a strong sense of Polish identity remained.

Marie left school at the age of 16 having won the girls' gold medal. She was passionate about science and wanted to continue her studies, but no higher education was available for females and the family could not afford to send her to study abroad. She began teaching and became involved in a nationalist movement, reading to women workers in Polish. Because of these activities it became prudent for her to leave Warsaw and she took a post as a governess in a country village. When her younger sister left school an agreement was reached between them whereby Marie would continue working and use her income to finance her sister's medical studies in Paris. Her sister, when qualified, would do the same in return.

Thus it was that in 1891 Marie was eventually able to go to the Sorbonne to study science and mathematics. She was a brilliant student, burning the midnight oil and surviving on little more than bread and scrape. For her doctoral thesis she chose to study the recently discovered radiation from uranium – 'uranium rays'. These had been virtually ignored by the scientific establishment whose attention was absorbed by the very recent and more superficially exciting discovery of X-rays.

Normally the characteristics of a chemical compound depend on the arrangement of atoms within each molecule. Marie discovered that the amount of radiation produced by different compounds of uranium was not affected by what the particular compound was, but depended only on the amount of uranium it contained. In those early days when practically nothing was known about radiation her conclusion was a breathtaking example of lateral thinking. She realised that the radiation could not be the result of how the atoms were arranged within a molecule and must therefore come from within the uranium atom itself.

Her next step was to look at all naturally occurring ores containing uranium and she found that pitchblende (a blackish oxide of uranium) produced far more radiation than the amount of uranium in it would suggest. Her deduction was that the additional radiation must be produced by some other more active element in the ore.

In 1895 Marie married Pierre Curie. Their marriage was very much a meeting of minds and together they set to work. They succeeded in refining pitchblende to such an extent that they were left with a substance that produced 300 times as much radiation as uranium. They presented a paper outlining their work, coining the word radioactivity to refer to what had until then been thought of as uranium rays, and suggesting that the new element (if that was what it was) should be called polonium, in honour of Poland – a country still without geographical existence. By 1898 they had good grounds for saying that there was yet another strongly radioactive element present in pitchblende. They proposed calling that one radium.

To prove the existence of radium the Curies needed to extract it from the pitchblende. Pitchblende was costly, they were not well off and they knew that a huge amount would be needed to produce only a minute amount of radium. Fortunately Marie's brain was not only scientific but also practical. The mining of pitchblende, like the mining of most things, resulted in substantial slag heaps and Marie arranged for a sample of slag to be sent to her. She thought, quite rightly as it turned out, that radium might also be present in the slag.

The Curies were happy in their work and with each other but their lives were arduous. With no financial resources they were lucky to be given the use of what was little more than a shed. Their work, carried out mostly on old wooden tables in this unheated, uninsulated, leaky building and sometimes also in the yard outside, was physically demanding. The slag had to be refined and analysed – Marie worked with 20 kg at a time and was sometimes stirring a boiling mass from dawn till dusk. From several tons of slag they were ultimately able to obtain one-tenth of a gram of radium chloride.

In addition to all this they were bringing up their small daughter and both of them were teaching in order to earn an income. Their health suffered. No-one at that time had any idea of the effects of radiation on the body and such was the Curies' delight in their work that Pierre often kept a small amount of a radium salt with him in his pocket, while Marie liked to keep some by her bedside because it was luminous. The notebooks in which they kept details of their work are still so radioactive that they can only be inspected by researchers who are wearing protective clothing and who are willing to sign a form that they carry out the inspection at their own risk. But the Curies achieved international renown for their achievements and were awarded the Nobel prize for physics in 1903.

In 1906 Pierre was run over and killed by a horse-drawn wagon. Marie was devastated but continued with her scientific work and eventually succeeded in isolating pure radium. In 1911 she was awarded another Nobel prize, this time for chemistry, but the French Académie des Sciences did not consider that Marie's scientific achievements and international renown were adequate to outweigh her inferior status as a foreign female. Her nomination for election to the Académie was turned down.

Marie Curie's personal financial position was by now secure, but the expense of obtaining radium to develop further research remained a problem. The Curies were scientists, not business people, and had refused to patent their work, feeling that their methods and discoveries should be freely available to all. An American female journalist who met Marie was horrified to hear that, whilst some fifty grams of radium was available in the US for scientific research, there was barely one gram in the whole of France.

$100,000 RADIUM GIFT TO MME. CURIE

Harding Makes Presentation at White House Reception to Woman Scientist.

BRILLIANT THRONG PRESENT

President, Ambassador Jusserand, the Guest of Honor and Others Make Brief Addresses.

By CONSTANCE DREXEL.

A small, frail-looking little woman, with a face of cameolike delicacy under the black of a plain but becoming hat, walked up the aisle behind the President of the United States. It was Mme. Marie Curie, and the great mo-

Courtesy Radiological Society of North America, and U.S. Library of Congress

4.8: From the front page of the Washington Post, May 21, 1921

The journalist took this cause to heart and organised a huge fund-raising project amongst the women of America, the target being to raise enough money to be able to present Marie with one gram of radium. The campaign was successful and the radium was presented to Marie personally by the US President. She needed the radium but hated the publicity involved.

Marie died in 1934 of leukaemia, caused by exposure to radiation. The following year her daughter and son-in-law were awarded the Nobel prize for chemistry in recognition of their own work in connection with radioactivity, but in due course her daughter also died of leukaemia caused by exposure to radiation.

SIEVERT

Those undergoing radiotherapy and even just X-rays owe a great deal to Rolf Maximilian Sievert (1896 – 1966). He was a Swedish professor of radiation physics who was a pioneer in the fields of radiation dose measurement and radiation protection. When the use of diagnostic and therapeutic radiation began, it was not initially subject to any restrictions or guidelines. Dosages varied from place to place and even from doctor to doctor. And at the very beginning no-one was even aware that there was any danger at all. It was Sievert who set up an organisation to supervise the control of radiation doses, Sievert who pressed for radiation protection laws and Sievert who, in order to avoid unjustifiable risk to patients, developed a system for adjusting the simple measure of a radiation dose by a quality factor to produce an indication (now measured in sieverts) of the biological effects.

Sources of radiation are not only found in hospitals. Passengers on commercial airline flights are exposed to radioactivity, for example, and low levels of it are found in many foods. The man in the street knows that radiation needs to be avoided where possible but remains none the wiser as to whether a dose of, say, one sievert or one million sieverts is dangerous. In recent years an informal and distinctly less esoteric measure has gained popularity, given somewhat spurious authority by the use of its acronym: the BED. These letters stand for the Banana Equivalent Dose, and one BED represents the amount of radiation absorbed by your body when you eat a banana.

ELECTRICITY

GALVANOMETER and GALVANIZE

Those who studied science at school will have come across a piece of kit called a galvanometer that can detect and measure the strength of an electrical current. The name of the apparatus honours Luigi Galvani (1737 – 1798), who studied medicine at the University of Bologna and who eventually became professor of anatomy there. However, even those who have never had anything to do with science will have come across Galvani's name in the sense of galvanising someone or something into action, a phrase that originally used to refer to stimulation by use of a galvanic electrical current but which is now used in other contexts.

Galvani married the daughter of one of the professors at Bologna and she took a great interest in helping him with his experiments, many of which took place in the garden. He referred to this when writing up his scientific work and wrote a loving biography about her when she died. After her death Galvani's world began to fall apart: he missed her support and companionship and his experimental work seemed to be contradicted by another scientist (Volta – see below). French troops invaded Bologna and anyone in public office was required to swear an oath of loyalty to Napoleon, but Galvani was a devout Catholic and to him such an oath was anathema. Banned from teaching because he refused to swear the oath, he lost his job, his income and his pension. His friends eventually managed to obtain a decree exempting him from the oath and reinstating him on the basis of his scientific achievements, but he died before it could come into effect.

Galvani studied electricity in the context of frogs or, to be more precise, the legs of dead frogs. All you ever wanted to know, and more, about electricity in frogs' legs was discovered by Galvani and, as in so many scientific experiments, accident played an important role. Galvani already knew that static electricity could make muscles contract and wanted to find out more about it. This had its problems because at the time there was no source of continuous electricity – batteries had yet to be invented (see Volta again). He therefore made do with a machine that could build up enough static electricity to result in it discharging a spark into the air. One day Galvani was working on the nerve in a dead frog's leg with a metal scalpel when the nearby machine happened to discharge its spark: at that moment the frog's leg twitched.

For the next ten years Galvani carried out further detailed

research and here the layman's idea of the mad scientist is unusually apposite. He decided to investigate the effect on muscle of that other great source of electricity in the air, lightning. He rigged up a wire from the side of his house, connecting it to the nerve in a frog's leg, with another wire from the muscles down into the well to ensure that it was properly earthed. He then thoughtfully drew a picture of it all so that future generations could see exactly what his garden looked like as a result.

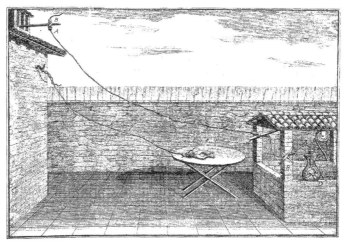

From 'De viribus electricitatis in motu musculari commentarius' 1791, courtesy Luigi Galvani Bicentennial Celebrations Bologna

4.9: Galvani's 'atmospheric discharge detector'

Half frog, with the nerves connected to the lightning conductor and the muscles connected to the water of the well

All he had to do now was watch and wait for a thunderstorm. Sure enough, when there was a flash of lightning nearby the leg was 'galvanized into action'. In other words, it twitched.

His next step was to try and get the same effect from atmospheric electricity without a thunderstorm. He used brass hooks to hang a range of frogs' spinal cords (with legs attached) from an iron railing round the garden and noticed that when a leg touched the railing it twitched. He refined the experiment using a small metallic arc of zinc at one end and copper at the other to demonstrate that the leg of a dead frog always twitches if the nerve is touched with one end of the arc when the muscle attached to that nerve is in contact with the other end of the arc.

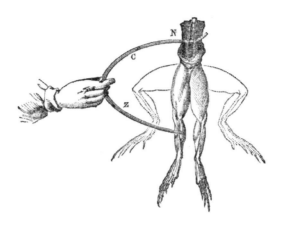

4.10: Illustration of Galvani's twitching frog leg, when touched with an arc made of zinc and copper

The conclusion that Galvani drew was that all muscles contain traces of 'animal electricity' generated by the brain, flowing into the body through the nervous system and stored in the muscle in tiny amounts. His friend Volta interpreted the results differently, thinking that the electricity was 'metallic electricity' generated by the touching of two different metals rather than coming from within the muscle. In the course of his own experiments Volta proved his point. Nevertheless, Galvani was not wrong and carried out further work which showed that dead muscle could be made to twitch using a single metal or even without any metal at all. This led to controversy at a scientific, though not a personal, level: in fact it was Volta who later coined the phrase 'galvanic current'. At the time Galvani appeared to be the loser: in contrast to Volta's fame Galvani kept a low profile and, as his results did not immediately lead to anything useful, their importance was not recognised. But many years on, his work is regarded as having laid down the foundation of a new branch of science that we now know as electrophysiology.

VOLT

For the technically minded, one volt is the amount of electrical potential needed to send a current of one ampère through a piece of wire or other conductor that has a resistance of one ohm. Alessandro Giuseppe Antonio Anastasio Volta (1745 – 1827) and his achievements are now comparatively unknown, but pretty well everyone who has used anything electrical has heard of the shortened (mercifully, very shortened) version of his name. Volt is not merely an esoteric word known only to scientists: this is worldwide recognition and could justly be considered the crowning glory of a famous and successful life.

Volta grew up in a world where electricity was a new phenomenon attracting a great deal of interest. His years of research culminated in his most important contribution to the field: the battery. Before then it had been extremely difficult to study electricity because there was no reliable source, apart from either the tiny amounts of 'animal electricity' demonstrated by Galvani or a machine that delivered a single, sudden, electrical discharge. Volta's battery became known as the Voltaic pile because it consisted of a stack of alternating discs of zinc and silver (or copper), separated by discs of leather soaked in salt water. Volta's fame became such that he was invited by Napoleon to give a personal demonstration of his invention, and he had honours heaped upon him, including a prestigious medal from the Royal Society.

Where did the idea for the voltaic pile come from? Volta's friend Galvani had been doing detailed research on 'animal electricity' and had concluded that it was the result of electricity produced from within frogs' muscles. Volta was initially convinced by that argument but later disagreed, thinking that the electricity was more likely to have been produced by the linking of two different metals, the twitch in the frog's leg merely indicating that electricity was passing

126

along it. He therefore started experimenting without frogs and found that different strengths of current could be produced using different combinations of metals, the strongest being produced by zinc and silver, although even then the current was so tiny that there was no apparatus capable of demonstrating it. The only way Volta could detect the current himself was to use his tongue to complete the circuit, in just the same way as today one tests a battery to see if it is dead by touching the top terminal with one's tongue when holding a finger against the bottom of it.

Photo © User GuidoB/ Wikimedia Commons

4.11: A voltaic pile - Alessandro Volta's electric battery

Volta wanted to take this discovery further, but it was still a long way from a tingle on the tongue to a battery. In studying 'animal electricity' he read about a type of electric ray called the torpedo fish that can deliver a powerful electric shock. The organ with which it does so consists of a column of alternating discs of different tissues and it was this that led Volta to try reproducing the design. It also explains why he called the invention an 'artificial electric organ'. The key to his success was that he had inserted a piece of wet material between each pair of zinc and copper (or silver) discs, thereby separating each pair from the adjacent pairs, but in a way that allowed the electricity produced by each pair of discs to accumulate with that produced by all the others.

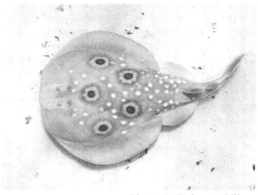

Photo © Roberto Pillon

4.12: Common torpedo fish
(light brown with large blue spots)

But what of the man himself? When he was very young his parents thought he must be backward as he did not talk until the age of four. He was born into a noble family, but they were not wealthy and he had to earn his living. He was heavily lent on to enter the priesthood or to study law, but by his late teens had determined to become a physicist. His scientific activities were not limited to electricity. While on holiday by Lake Maggiore he was at the lakeside, poking about in the water with a stick, when he noticed he was dislodging bubbles of gas from the mud at the bottom. He collected the gas, calling it 'inflammable air from marshlands' and on further analysis discovered it was mainly composed of a hitherto unknown gas: methane.

Volta's nobility turned out to be a disadvantage as under the prevailing law it prohibited him from marrying the opera singer with whom he was in love and with whom he carried on an affair for some years. He was nearly fifty before he eventually married someone else, but the marriage does seem to have been happy. He had four children and after he achieved success and fame he wrote lovingly to his wife referring to the sweetness of domestic life. In 1819 he resigned his official positions and retired to his country estate.

WATT

Ever since the achievements of James Watt (1736 – 1819) were honoured by the adoption of the watt as a measure of electrical power, his name has appeared on countless trillions of light bulbs. It has therefore become such a fundamental part of everyday life that it occurs to hardly anyone that Watt was actually a person. Even those who do know of him do not associate him with light bulbs, since his work had nothing to do with electricity, although it did have everything to do with power.

The young Watt, like several other eminent scientists, was a sickly child and hardly went to school. Instead he pottered about in his father's workshop (his father was a ship's chandler) making models. He went to London to serve an apprenticeship as a scientific instrument maker, but poor health prevented him from finishing the training and he returned home to Scotland. Popular history regards him as the inventor of the steam engine, but that is not right. It was as a result of repairing an early steam engine that Watt had his brilliant idea of improving the design, by cooling the steam using cold water injected into a separate condenser instead of into the piston cylinder. This resulted in a fourfold increase in efficiency. Watt patented his design and went into business with Matthew Boulton.

Boulton was a very astute businessman. He successfully applied for an Act of Parliament to extend Watt's patent for twenty-five years. Customers had to pay a royalty, usually calculated as a third of the annual fuel savings made by them as a result of using a Boulton and Watt engine. It therefore became important to be able to compare amounts of energy. To do so Watt introduced the notion of horsepower, based on the amount of work expected in one day from an average workhorse, operating machinery by walking round a circular track harnessed to a wooden shaft attached to a central pivot.

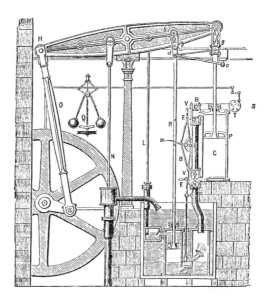

4.13: Sketch of a steam engine designed by Boulton & Watt, 1784

The steam engine was Watt's 'baby' – he was continually improving it and was anxious to prevent anyone else from entering the field. One of his employees came up with a design for a high-pressure steam engine, but Watt saw to it that the idea stopped there. In fact high-pressure engines were to be the way forward – literally. Such engines would be powerful enough, yet light enough, to be mounted on wheels and thus open the way to locomotive power and the railway revolution. Watt died an extremely wealthy man, but the world had to wait until his patents expired before high-pressure engines could be developed.

AMP

It is hard to believe that anyone could become a professor of mathematics without ever having been to school or university, but André Marie Ampère (1775 – 1836) succeeded in doing so.

He was educated at home by his father, a merchant who was largely self-educated himself and who took the task very seriously. It is said that André used pebbles and biscuit crumbs to solve complicated arithmetical sums when he was still too young to recognise written numbers. At the age of eleven he found he was unable to pursue his interest in mathematics through a particular book as it was written in Latin and also needed a grasp of calculus to understand it. He therefore set to work and within a few weeks he had sufficient knowledge of both subjects to enable him to study the text.

Courtesy California Digital Library, University of California

4.14: Portrait of André-Marie Ampère

Brains are not everything and life was hard for Ampère. He not only had to cope with tragedy, but also suffered from depression. In the 1790s France was not a safe place to be and when Ampère was still only in his late teens his father was sent to the guillotine. Ampère was devastated and for months could do nothing, although he eventually recovered through finding an interest in botany. He married, but after only five years his wife died and he never really came to terms with his loss. He made a disastrous second marriage and within the year he and his second wife were no longer on speaking terms. He had a poor relationship with his son, and his daughter married an alcoholic and moved back into Ampère's house with her husband, bringing much unhappiness.

Ampère worked on physics and chemistry as well as on mathematics and in 1820 was inspired by the report of an experiment in which electricity passing through a wire had been found to create a magnetic effect. Ampère threw himself into investigating this and within a week presented a paper setting out his own detailed findings on the relationship between electricity and magnetism. He continued to work diligently in both the practical and theoretical aspects of the field, establishing a way of measuring the amount of electricity flowing through a conductor and setting the foundation for the development of the new science of electromagnetism. His name is now a household word as a result of the decision to use his name for the standard unit of electrical current.

OHM

When thinking about how electricity works it is recommended that the non-scientific reader thinks of having a shower (strictly for clarification purposes, not cleanliness, so don't rush off ....). The best showers deliver lots of water, pounding the shoulders so hard that it is as good as a massage. If yours only produces a measly trickle you might find that the water pipe supplying it is too narrow and you need a larger pipe. Or you might want to install a power shower that forces the water through the pipes much faster. Or both.

George Simon Ohm (1787 – 1854) was familiar with the concept of water pressure, and that the resistance to it offered by a piece of piping depended on both the diameter of the pipe and the pressure of the water. With this in mind he set about studying the same things for electricity. He wanted to investigate the resistance to different electrical pressures (i.e., voltages) offered by different types and lengths of wire (i.e., conductors). He discovered that for any particular wire there is a constant ratio between the level of voltage and the amount of electrical current flowing. Returning to the analogy of a water pipe, it was natural for him to think of that constant ratio as the resistance of the wire. Ohm's studies established a cornerstone of the theory of electricity known as Ohm's Law and it was in recognition of this discovery that the standard unit for the measurement of resistance, the ohm, was named. (As his name inconveniently begins with the letter O, which risks unavoidable confusion with the digit 0, the symbol for ohm is written as a capital omega (Ω), presumably because of the similarity in sound.)

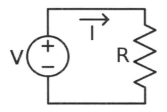

Diagram of an electrical circuit to demonstrate Ohm's Law: I=V/R

where V = voltage of battery, I = strength of current measured in amperes, R = resistance measured in ohms

Ohm's career is rather sad and to some extent he was his own worst enemy. Recognition came very late and much of his life was spent in penury. As far as education was concerned, school offered little more than learning by rote and it was his father, a locksmith, who did an impressive job in teaching him maths, science and philosophy. Undue enthusiasm for ice-skating, dancing and billiards resulted in young Ohm's university career coming to a premature end and he had to take a job teaching mathematics. Private study led to the award of a doctorate and for a time he taught maths both at university level and in schools. After thirteen years in which his career had progressed little he published his private studies about electricity, but unfortunately the paper was not well received. His mathematical explanations were criticised, no prestigious university post was offered and he left his job – it being a moot point whether he jumped or was pushed. His next publication was a paper on acoustics that fared even

133

worse when his mathematics were proved to be wrong. It was another fifteen years before the importance of his work began to be recognised and only two years before his death did he finally achieve his heart's desire by being appointed professor of physics at Munich University.

FARAD

If you are not a scientist the farad is probably another unit of which you have not heard, but you will almost certainly know of the Royal Institution's scientific annual Christmas lectures for children, now shown on television. These were started in 1826 by Michael Faraday (1791 – 1867). And in 1991, to celebrate the 200th anniversary of his birth, a new £20 note was issued, the back of which had an illustration depicting Faraday lecturing at the Royal Institution.

4.15: Series E £20 note featuring Faraday

Faraday was born in London and came from a devoutly religious background. The family was poor: he had little to eat and even less education. He never learnt any mathematics, but had an innate feel for the links between various fundamental concepts in physics and is widely regarded as the greatest experimental genius of all time.

At the age of thirteen he began work as an errand boy for a bookbinder and was then taken on for seven years as an apprentice. By good fortune this gave him access to scientific books and he took the opportunity of reading those he came across. He was given a ticket to attend a series of chemistry lectures delivered by Humphry Davy at the Royal Institution and took careful notes that he then bound into a book. By the age of twenty-one he was so determined to "enter into the service of science"(iv), as he put it, that he wrote to Sir Joseph Banks, President of the Royal Society, to ask for guidance on how he might do so. Banks did not reply. Faraday's next step was to write to Davy enclosing the bound lecture notes and asking for a job. Davy advised him to remain a bookbinder, but very shortly afterwards Davy's assistant was in trouble with the police for brawling, so Davy offered the job to Faraday. Faraday accompanied Davy on an eighteen-month scientific tour of Europe and never looked back. His scientific career developed and at the age of thirty-three he was made a Fellow of the Royal Society, despite the jealous opposition to his election by Davy, who was by then its president.

Because it had been shown that electricity created a magnetic field, Faraday was convinced that the principle should also work the other way round, that magnetism could be used to make electricity. He eventually devised an experiment that succeeded in doing so. In contrast to the prevailing view of how electricity worked, he formulated his own intuitive view of why this happened, simply in terms of lines of force. Maxwell (see below) later expressed Faraday's idea in mathematical terms to construct the theory of electromagnetism: the farad is a measure of electrical capacitance, relevant to that theory.

Faraday was involved in a large number of other projects including the way lighthouses were lit, the investigation of explosions in coalmines, and pollution of both air and water. He even wrote to The Times complaining about the terrible smell of the Thames: "The appearance and the smell of the water forced themselves at once on my attention. The whole of the river was an opaque pale brown fluid. In order to test the degree of opacity, I tore up some white cards into pieces ... and then dropped [them] into the water... before they had sunk an inch below the surface they were indistinguishable"(v). This resulted in a much publicised cartoon in Punch Magazine.

FARADAY GIVING HIS CARD TO FATHER THAMES
And we hope the Dirty Fellow will consult the learned Professor.

Courtesy The Victorian Web

4.16: Cartoon published in Punch, 1855

In retirement Faraday was awarded a modest pension and a royal grace-and-favour house at Hampton Court. He was a man of integrity with a strong sense of religion and aware of the corrupting influences of pride and fame. He turned down the offer of a knighthood, preferring to remain just 'plain Mr. Faraday'(vi).

MAGNETISM

GAUSS

The strength of a magnet is measured in gauss but since this is not normally something one thinks about in daily life 'Gauss' is not a widely known name. Yet it is said that, in the modern world, the mathematical genius of Carl Friedrich

Gauss (1777 – 1855) has only been surpassed by that of Sir Isaac Newton.

Gauss came from a poor German family and his father, who has been described as domineering and uncouth, wanted him to go out to work rather than study. Fortunately Gauss's exceptional ability at an early age was brought to the attention of a member of the aristocracy, who paid him a stipend from his mid teens and for much of his adult life in order to give him the opportunity to remain in education and pursue research.

Gauss's love was mathematics, in which he made a range of discoveries. One of his proudest achievements was the first major discovery in the study of geometry since classical times: he constructed a 17-sided polygon using only a ruler and compasses. His mathematical approach to astronomy brought him a considerable amount of popular fame. An asteroid had been spotted and its position observed over a short distance before it disappeared behind the sun. Gauss astonished everyone by successfully forecasting where it would reappear, but he retained a sense of aloofness from his colleagues by not revealing how he had calculated it. Some of Gauss's most productive time was spent working with magnets and, with the physicist Wilhelm Weber (see below), he laid the foundations for the modern study of magnetism.

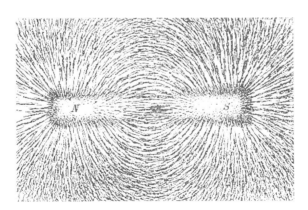

4.17: The magnetic field of a bar magnet revealed by iron filings on a piece of paper placed over the magnet

Those who knew Gauss considered him somewhat cold and secretive. He had few friends and few peers with whom he could discuss ideas. Much of his work was never published and if a colleague claimed to have discovered something, Gauss had the annoying habit of claiming (probably quite correctly) that he had already thought of it himself some time ago. He did have a very happy marriage and was devoted to his first wife, but after only four years she died in childbirth and although he was able to carry on with his work, he never really got over this personal tragedy.

WEBER

Wilhelm Eduard Weber (1804 – 1891), professor of physics at Gottingen, was versatile. He carried out pioneering work on magnetism with Gauss (see above) and wrote learned papers with his brothers, one of whom was an anatomist and the other a physiologist. He also did a great deal of work in the field of electrodynamics, in the course of which he calculated how fast an electric current flows through a wire. He found it to be very close to the speed of light but it took a later physicist, Maxwell (see below), to realise the significance of this. The weber is a unit used in electromagnetism to measure the strength of magnetic flux.

All this high-powered, energetic scientific work is rather esoteric and of more interest to the layman is an invention Weber set up in 1833. Did this invention win him fame and prestige? No. It was never published as a scientific advance worthy of note. Was it for commercial development, leading to wealth and fortune? No again, although later on others came up with similar ideas that were of immense use both commercially and militarily. Weber's invention was used merely for convenience. He set up the world's first working electric telegraph system, connecting his physics laboratory to the astronomical observatory where Gauss worked some three kilometres away. The project was not without its problems: the wire, strung over intervening houses, kept breaking and each time had to be replaced by a more robust wire. So in the

138

end it probably created more work than it saved, but the fact that it worked at all must have been immensely satisfying.

MAXWELL

At an Edinburgh school in the 1830s a shy boy who spent his time drawing diagrams and making models was thought by his schoolmates to be so thick that his nickname was 'daftie'. But a few years later, when mathematics and science were introduced into the curriculum, they realised they were dramatically mistaken. This was James Clerk Maxwell (1831 – 1879), who by the age of fourteen had already written a learned mathematical paper read to the Royal Society of Edinburgh.

Maxwell was an intellectual giant. On reading the papers in which Faraday set out his ideas arising from his experimental results in the fields of electricity and magnetism, Maxwell developed Faraday's concepts and formulated the mathematical link between the two fields: the maxwell is another unit used for the measurement of magnetic flux. He confirmed Weber's measurements of the speed of electricity and, realising that it was approximately the speed of light, drew the implication that the basic laws of electromagnetism must also apply to light. This theory led to Hertz's discovery (see below) of the existence of radio waves, although it was not until Hertz had made his discovery that Maxwell's theory became generally accepted.

In other scientific fields Maxwell also made substantial contributions. His theoretical work on Saturn's rings led him to conclude that the rings had to be made up of tiny particles, a fact now confirmed by space exploration. His work on colour vision led him to be the first to demonstrate colour photography, for which, being a true Scot, he used a piece of tartan ribbon.

At a more practical level Maxwell, as the first Cavendish Professor of Physics, was closely involved in the design of the scientific laboratory at Cambridge University, founded in memory of the physicist Henry Cavendish. Cavendish had been as eccentric as he was brilliant and published practically nothing during his lifetime, leaving his scientific work contained in twenty packages of disorganised, unread papers. Maxwell undertook the heroic task of editing these, leading to the revelation that several scientific discoveries, attributed to various people now well-known for having made them, were really rediscoveries having actually been proved years earlier by Cavendish. It was just that nobody knew about them.

4.18: Saturn eclipsing the sun, seen from behind, from the Cassini orbiter

While Maxwell was ensconced at the Cavendish a handful of women, ignoring the widely promoted view that book-learning was inappropriate for females and potentially damaging to their health, had had the temerity to cross the hallowed portals of Cambridge University in search of higher education. One or two of these were even given special permission from the authorities to sit the Tripos exams, although it was not until the late 1940s that degrees were actually conferred on those who passed. Maxwell must have been quite a modern man for his day, as he enabled – encouraged would be putting it too strongly – the women's lib movement to edge forward a fraction of an inch by allowing females to pursue their studies in his precious Cavendish Laboratory, provided always that they did so only during the long summer vacation when he was away in Scotland.

TESLA

Er ... who?   Nikola Tesla (1856 – 1943) had a prickly personality, few friends and an obsession for cleanliness and feeding pigeons.   Penniless, he emigrated from his native Serbia to the United States and soon obtained a job with Edison working on direct current (DC) electricity, but left shortly afterwards following a disagreement.   Tesla favoured the use of alternating current (AC) instead and designed electrical equipment to enable its introduction.   His designs were successfully used at the Niagara Falls for the supply of electrical power to New York, and AC came into general use across most of the world.

Photo © John W. Wagner

4.19: Bronze bust of Tesla
sculpted by R. Farrington Sharp, as presented to educational institutions

Tesla also patented designs for radio (wireless) broadcasting and was working on a huge project in connection with this when the funding ran out and it had to be abandoned.   In the meantime Marconi had won fame for having invented the radio and for the first wireless transmission insisting, when challenged, that he had not seen Tesla's work.

In 1956 the tesla was adopted as the international measure of the strength of a magnetic field.   This was no doubt useful for those in scientific circles but hardly impinged on the consciousness of "the man on the Clapham omnibus"(vii).

141

Even if all the passengers on such a vehicle pooled their general knowledge to compile a list of famous scientists, Tesla's name would almost certainly not be on it. But he is not without his fans. There is even a website, supported by those who feel passionately that his achievements should have earned him more lasting fame, that seeks to rectify the situation by selling T-shirts bearing his name as a logo. The proceeds are used to commission bronze busts of Tesla (set in black granite and weighing over a hundred kilograms), which are then presented to a variety of respected educational and other appropriate institutions.

The advent of MRI (magnetic resonance imaging) scanners, however, may well do more to bring Tesla's name to public attention. You might, for example, come across a '3 tesla whole body scanner' if you have to attend hospital for an MRI scan. Each scanner is calibrated in teslas according to the strength of the magnetic field it uses and its tesla rating is included as an essential part of the description of every scanner.

OTHER UNITS

HERTZ

Maxwell's thoughts on electromagnetism (see above) had thrown down a gauntlet to the scientific community and the German physicist Heinrich Rudolf Hertz (1857 – 1894) was the one to pick it up. Maxwell had theorised that light was a form of electromagnetic radiation and had gone on to postulate that, in addition, long wavelength electromagnetic waves with similar properties (now known as radio waves) ought to exist. Hertz' experiments discovered the existence of these radio waves and demonstrated that they behaved in the same way as light, proving that Maxwell was right. However, he had no idea of the importance of his discovery, commenting merely that it was "of no use whatsoever"(viii). In recognition of his achievement his name is now used as the international unit of frequency and appears in all the daily newspapers as an integral part of the guide to the day's radio programmes. But Hertz' abilities were not limited to the field of science: he was also an enthusiastic linguist and learnt both Arabic and Sanskrit.

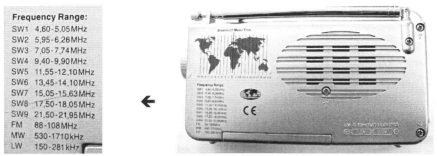

Photo © C.M.Wiles

4.20: The back of a radio, showing frequencies in megahertz

On the centenary of Hertz' death a postage stamp was issued in Germany in his honour. How times had changed. Previously he had been celebrated in Hamburg, his place of birth, where the town hall is decorated with a number of plaques bearing portraits of its most eminent citizens, including Hertz. But his was one of six such plaques removed by the Nazis because they related to Jews, although Hertz himself was a Lutheran and his father, although born Jewish, converted to Roman Catholicism before his son Heinrich was born. The plaque was replaced soon after the war.

ÅNGSTRÖM

The ångström is the only unit of length to make it into this chapter and it is short. Very, very short. If you put ten million of them in a row you still end up with a line only one millimetre long. However, it is frequently said that size is not always everything and it would be a mistake to confuse small with insignificant.

This particular length was named after the quiet and modest Anders Jonas Ångström (1814 – 1874) who was born

143

in Sweden during a solar eclipse. Perhaps he was therefore doing no more than following a destiny already written amongst the stars when he decided to dedicate years to the mapping of the solar spectrum. He listed the wavelengths of over a thousand spectral lines, using a unit of measurement that he found convenient for recording these wavelengths, which were tiny. Ångström was one of the founders of spectroscopy and with the development of this field of science a general need arose for an appropriate unit of length in which to record measurements. Eventually the one Ångström himself had used was officially recognised and named after him. It seems a pity that the ångström has not been adopted by the Système Internationale, which uses the somewhat more prosaic nanometre (equal to ten ångströms) instead.

DECIBEL

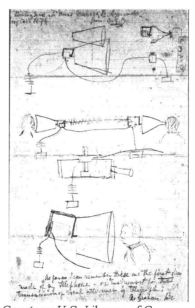

Courtesy U.S. Library of Congress

4.21: Bell's first drawings of his telephone, 1876

Bell's handwritten annotation reads: As far as I can remember these are the first drawings made of my telephone or 'instrument for the transmission of vocal utterance by telegraph'.

144

"Mr. Watson, come here; I want to see you"(ix) said by Bell to his assistant, has its place in history as the first telephone conversation.   Alexander Graham Bell (1847 – 1922), who patented the telephone, was born in Scotland but emigrated to the United States.   He was a professor of vocal physiology, developed a system for teaching the deaf how to speak and opened a school to train teachers to teach the deaf how to put his system into effect.   He also worked more generally on acoustics and it is for this reason (as well as perhaps the aptness of his name) that the bel, a measure of increase in sound volume, was named after him.   The bel itself is seldom used but the decibel, or one-tenth of a bel, is well-known.

History is not always straightforward and others also claim to have invented the telephone.   Two deserve particular mention.   The first involves almost split-second timing.   In 1876 Bell did succeed in patenting his invention, but only just. A little later on the same day that Bell lodged his application, and within a few hours – some say half an hour – of his having done so, the lawyer of a certain Elisha Gray also lodged an application in respect of a similar invention.   It is therefore quite possible that poor Elisha could actually have thought up the telephone first but that his lawyer just lingered too long over his toast and marmalade that morning.   Those few hours gave Bell his patent, opening the way to fame and fortune.

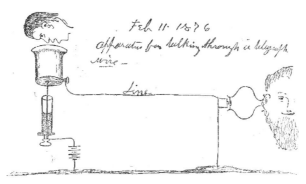

Courtesy University of Virginia

4.22: Gray's notebook entry that led to his caveat

Then there is the sad tale of Antonio Meucci. He was an Italian immigrant to the United States who spent years working on an electrical device to communicate speech along a wire, spending every cent he had on the project. He demonstrated an early version of his invention and in 1860 a report on it was published in New York's Italian language newspaper. Meucci continued to improve his design but could not afford a full patent, so in 1871 he protected his work by registering a caveat – a one-year renewable notice of an impending patent application.

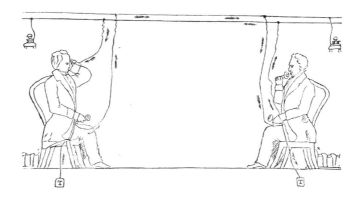

4.23: Copy of a drawing filed with Meucci's caveat demonstrating his invention

Meucci then sent his working models and technical details to the Western Union telegraph company in the hope of interesting them in a contract, but he got nowhere and when he asked for the return of his property was told it had been lost. By 1874 Meucci's financial plight was so desperate that he did not pay the $10 needed to renew his caveat and eventually he went bankrupt. Early in 1876 Bell was granted a patent, but in 2002 the US House of Representatives, noting that if Meucci's caveat had been renewed no patent could have been issued to Bell, passed a resolution that Meucci's invention of the telephone should be acknowledged. They also gave the story a somewhat sinister slant, noting that Bell had carried out experiments in the same laboratory where Meucci's models and designs had been stored, but Bell's working notes and records do suggest that he was doing no more than working independently in the same field.

Bell himself was known to dislike the telephone and apparently silenced his own by stuffing it with newspaper saying "I never use the beast"(x). So all those who have been driven dotty by its intermittent ringing, interrupting work, leisure or even theatrical productions, may comfort themselves with the knowledge that at least there was some small element of poetic justice.

DOBSON UNIT

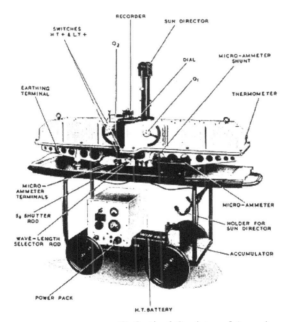

4.24: Dobson's ozone spectrophotometer, 1968 model

How do we actually know that in the 1980s something very alarming started happening to the ozone layer? We would probably still be waiting to find out had it not been for the lifetime's obsession of the British meteorologist Gordon Miller Bourne Dobson (1889 – 1976). He designed and made the necessary measuring instruments to record levels of ozone in the atmosphere (now measured in units called Dobson units) and used them to research how these ozone levels varied with latitude, the weather, the seasons and from year to year. And he started all this in the 1920s, long before anyone knew of the dangers posed by CFCs.

Dobson's interest had arisen out of earlier work on meteor trails when he realised that the temperature of the stratosphere could be much warmer than expected. He had correctly concluded that it must be because ultra-violet radiation was being absorbed by ozone molecules. During his lifetime the value of his work was recognised by scientific colleagues but it was only after his death, when a hole was suddenly found to be developing in the ozone layer, that the importance of measuring ozone levels came to public attention.

MACH NUMBER

It was not until Concorde led to the establishment of a scheduled supersonic airline service across the Atlantic that the technical jargon 'Mach 1' began to emerge from the dark recesses of the world of aeronautical engineers and reached the general public.

What happens as an aircraft approaches a speed of Mach 1, the speed of sound? Whole books are written on the subject but the essence of it is that the smooth lines of air-waves flowing past the aircraft start to break up into shock waves in the shape of a cone, with the nose of the aircraft at its apex, somewhat comparable to the bow wave of a motor boat. This turbulence shakes the aircraft about, creates serious vibration, alters its flying characteristics and makes the needle on the wind-speed gauge wobble around in a way referred to as 'Mach jump'. If atmospheric conditions are right, vapour clouds will form in the areas of low pressure round the aircraft, which disperse once Mach 1 is achieved.

Those for whom some considerable time has passed since the first flush of youth still tend to think not of Mach 1 but of 'breaking the sound barrier'. That idea was apt in the early

148

days: the buffeting experienced by an aeroplane as it approaches the speed of sound resulted in the first British plane designed to fly at such speeds falling apart on its test flight in 1946. In reality the problem was a design barrier rather than a sound barrier and within two years it had been solved in the United States – funding for continued aeronautical research not being a priority in post-war Britain.

Photo by Ensign John Gray, Courtesy U.S. Navy

4.25: FA-18 Hornet breaks the sound barrier

This measure of speed is named after the Czechoslovakian physicist Ernst Mach (1838 – 1916), who worked in optics, mechanics and wave dynamics, establishing the principles of the science of supersonics. He became increasingly fascinated in the philosophy of science and developed the concept that so-called scientific laws are no more than a way of thinking and only useful in order to help the mind make sense of observed experimental data. This led him to reject the newly developing theory that all matter is composed of atoms, since at that time atoms were too small to be seen and, to his way of thinking, such a theory was therefore unnecessary.

NEWTON

'Unhappy' is the only way to describe Newton's childhood. His father died before he was born, his stepfather would have nothing to do with him and he did not get on well with the grandparents who brought him up. He grew up bitter, bad-tempered and notorious for his rages. He could not bear to be criticised and should another academic disagree with his opinion he would wage a spiteful campaign to humiliate his opponent.

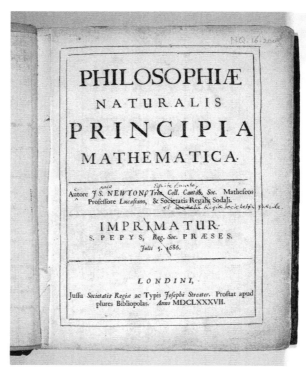

4.26: Opening page of Sir Isaac Newton's own first edition copy of his Principia with his handwritten corrections for the second edition

Newton was a late developer. Even after he had been studying at Cambridge for four years there was little sign that he was rather bright, let alone anything special. But the university then closed because of the plague and Newton had to return to the country. He began to come into his own and there was much more to him than just the notorious falling apple. Within two years he had made major, fundamental contributions to the sciences of mathematics, optics, physics

150

and astronomy. Shortly after this he was appointed to the Lucasian Chair of Mathematics and in due course his "Principia", generally regarded as the greatest scientific book ever written, was published.

After the age of forty-five Newton faded out of academic life. The University of Cambridge appointed him as their Member of Parliament and he became Warden, then Master, of the Royal Mint. His standing in the scientific world remained such that he was elected President of the Royal Society. Unfortunately he used the appointment to spend much of his time furthering his dispute with a rival academic.

The newton is an international unit of force that is used in the measurement of acceleration.

TORR

Consider three apparently random things: a small child's encounter with magic, a problem for Italian pump makers, and barometers. All are linked through the ideas and scientific work of the son of an Italian textile worker who, after Galileo's death, ended up being appointed to the post of Official Court Mathematician to the Grand Duke of Tuscany. That man was Evangelista Torricelli (1608 – 1647).

The child playing in a bath with a beaker full of water thought that when she turned the beaker upside-down under the water and slowly pulled it up out of the bath, it must be magic that kept the water inside the upside-down beaker making it very heavy. She was disappointed that every time she tried to lift the beaker, no matter how carefully, the magic stopped as soon as the rim of the beaker broke the surface of the bath water, when the water inside fell back into the bath with a disappointing gurgle. If only it would stay in the upside-down beaker long enough to be lifted high up over the bath water the resulting splash when it fell out might then have been quite impressive. Making no progress with the magic she decided instead to cover the flannel with soap on one side and blow through it from the other to make lots of bubbles, which would have the added advantage of providing misleading evidence that soap had been diligently applied to muddy knees. It was thanks to Torricelli that the child's father was able to explain that it is the weight of the air pressing on the surface of the bath water that keeps the water in the beaker while it is being pulled up. There was trouble about the mud, though.

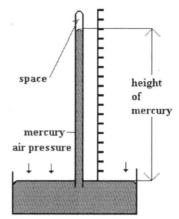

Courtesy University of Queensland

4.27: Diagram of a mercury barometer demonstrating the space (vacuum) at the top

Makers of early suction pumps for draining mines had been infuriated to find that no such pump would work for raising water more than about 32 feet. To raise it more than that meant that a series of pumps was needed in order to pump the water up in separate stages. Galileo had been consulted as to the reason but had been unable to shed any light on it. Torricelli's explanation was that the weight of the column of air stretching from the surface of the water in the mine up in to the sky must have been counterbalancing the weight of the 32 feet of water.

Developing his idea, Torricelli thought that, since mercury is so much heavier than water, the weight of the air would only be able to counterbalance a much shorter height of mercury. This would have the advantage of allowing experimentation with equipment of a much more practical size. So he tried his idea out, using a long glass tube closed at one end (instead of the child's beaker) and mercury (instead of bathwater). He found that he was right: the height of mercury supported in the tube by the outside air pressure was about 76 centimetres (30 inches). If the glass tube were any longer than that, the mercury slid down inside it to about the 76 cm level. He even thought that the space that this left at the top of the tube must be a vacuum – an empty space containing nothing, not even air. However, he did not press the point because he was reluctant to get involved in any controversy – ever since Aristotle, scientists had believed that it was impossible for a vacuum to exist. Nevertheless, Torricelli's understanding of the concept of air pressure had led him to invent an instrument that could measure such pressure: the barometer.

Since the introduction of the metric system (Torricelli himself talked of cubits) air pressure is normally measured in millimetres of mercury and a pressure of 760 mm of mercury, or one standard atmosphere, is known as 760 torr.

PASCAL

Those who think of Blaise Pascal (1623 – 1662) as simply a philosopher may be surprised to find his name as a unit of pressure. Pascal was famous for his philosophical and religious treatises and was an extremely devout Christian. He was also a gifted mathematician, despite his father who held the unusual view that his son should not be allowed to study mathematics until he was fifteen and who, to this end, had banned all books on the subject from the house.

Pascal carried out a number of experiments on atmospheric pressure and established that at the top of a mountain this is lower than it is at the bottom – at least he was the one who had the idea, although ill health prevented him from doing the legwork himself. He also addressed the awkward problem of what, if anything, was in the space at the top of Torricelli's barometric tube. Pascal eventually satisfied himself that Torricelli was right and that the space must indeed be a vacuum.

The idea took hold and it was only a few years later that a certain Otto von Guericke carried out a great deal of work involving vacuums and invented a way of pumping air out of containers. Now von Guericke was no shrinking violet. A life spent hidden away in a laboratory toiling over tiny quantities of stuff was not for him. Oh no, he went for Size. In 1657 he organised a public demonstration of the power of atmospheric pressure in what has subsequently become known as the Magdeburg experiment, after the name of the town where it was carried out.

4.28: Contemporary drawing of Guericke's Magdeburg experiment in 1656

4.29: Detail from previous drawing

This was such an historic and impressive event that in the year 2000 it was re-enacted in Devon with the aid of a grant from Copus (Committee on the Public Understanding of Science). It involved putting two large, heavy-duty hemispheres together using an airtight seal and pumping out all the air inside. This created a vacuum and the two halves of the sphere were therefore held together by nothing more than the air pressure outside it.

The aim of the experiment was to demonstrate the power of air pressure by using horses to try and pull the hemispheres apart. And just as had been the case in 1657, even the sixteen working carthorses brought in for the occasion, pulling with all their strength, did not succeed.

BEAUFORT SCALE

In view of Britain's reputation over the centuries as a sea-faring nation it is satisfying to find that the person who thought up the now internationally used scale for the measurement of wind speed was an officer in the Royal Navy. The Beaufort scale, in contrast to other units of measurement in this chapter, began as a distillation of practical experience rather than the product of hopeful scientific experiment.

Sir Francis Beaufort (1774 – 1857) came from a modest background in Ireland and at the age of thirteen joined the Navy as a midshipman. By 1805 he had risen to the rank of commander but was then seriously wounded in action, sustaining two sabre cuts before being shot at point blank range with a blunderbuss. To everyone's surprise (including his) he survived, despite the harrowing experience of having fifteen pieces of shot removed by the surgeons at a time when no-one had ever heard of anaesthetics.

Unfortunately a sixteenth piece of shot remained in Beaufort's lung and he was no longer fit for active service. In 1829 he was appointed Hydrographer to the Navy, a position with responsibility for mapping coastlines and providing information on winds, tides and currents. This was an inspired appointment. In those days more ships were lost through shipwreck than through enemy action and Beaufort's powers of organisation, diligence and obsession for detail produced the first accurate naval charts for many areas. He commissioned the second voyage of the Beagle (made famous by Darwin) under the command of Robert FitzRoy and it was on this voyage that Beaufort's scale was first used officially.

FitzRoy was a good friend of Beaufort and went on to become the first director of the body founded in 1854 known as the 'Met Office'. Insomniacs and other devotees of Radio 4's shipping forecast will feel well acquainted with him as it is this FitzRoy who, in 2002, was paid the compliment of being awarded his own sea area, previously named Finisterre.

© *User Emoscopes/ Wikimedia Commons*

4.30: Zones used by the UK shipping forecast

Beaufort was not the first to tackle measurement of wind speed. Earlier attempts consisted of a list of general

156

descriptions of wind in increasing order of strength from calm, through breeze and gale, to storm and tempest. In 1780 a more precise list was published by a meteorological society in Germany, defining wind force by reference to its observable effects on land. On that scale, at level one leaves rustled and at level four twigs and branches broke off. Beaufort devised his wind scale in 1805 for his own personal use when keeping a ship's log and he began simply by allotting the numbers 0 - 13 to general descriptions of increasing wind strength.

Although experienced seafarers in the days of sail must have been very sensitive to differing wind strengths, it is astonishing to realise just how accurately Beaufort felt able to assess it. His original table shows that he could distinguish between four levels of breeze and no less than six levels of gale. The entries in his log even used half strengths as well, so he must have been very confident in his assessments.

Courtesy Pearson Scott Foresman

4.31: A frigate

Within a few years Beaufort modified his scale and introduced a refinement that was to set it apart from all others. He included a note of the sails that a fully rigged frigate (a type of man-of-war) would carry corresponding to each number on his wind scale or, for lighter breezes, the

157

vessel's speed in knots. This produced a definition of wind strength that was sufficiently objective to form a more or less standard system of assessing wind at sea.

Beaufort's criterion 1832(xi)

Beaufort Number	Description	Beaufort's Criterion	
0	Calm	Calm	
1	Light Air	Just sufficient to give steerage way	
2	Light Breeze	With which a well-conditioned	1 – 2 knots
3	Gentle Breeze	man-of-war, under all sail and 'clean full', would go in smooth water from …	3 – 4 knots
4	Moderate Breeze		5 – 6 knots
5	Fresh Breeze		Royals
6	Strong breeze	In which the same ship could just carry close hauled …	Single reefs and top gallant sails
7	Moderate Gale		Double-reefs, jib, etc.,
8	Fresh Gale		Triple-reefs, courses etc.
9	Strong Gale		Close-reefs and courses
10	Whole Gale	With which she could only bear close-reefed maintop-sail and reefed fore-sail	
11	Storm	With which she would be reduced to storm staysails	
12	Hurricane	To which she could show no canvas	

Courtesy The Met Office

One might be forgiven for wondering why, now that sailing frigates are a rarity and accurate wind speed measurements can be made scientifically, Beaufort numbers are still used at all. There are two steps to the answer. First, Beaufort

158

numbers proved to be so useful that in 1838 their use became mandatory: the Commissioners of the Admiralty ordered their use in all ships' logs. The scale thus became well established throughout the Royal Navy. Secondly, it was very much in the Admiralty's interest to be instrumental in the early development of weather forecasting. Following severe storm losses to the British fleet during the Crimean War, the Admiralty began work on setting up a global weather information network to provide warning of approaching storms. For a long time information about wind speeds at sea could still only be obtained from the mariners who were out there and for whom there was no alternative other than to use the Beaufort scale with which they were already familiar. Although the invention of the cup anemometer (that small whirligig device seen on the top of weather stations, consisting of three cups sideways up, attached to a framework that spins horizontally in the wind) in 1846 had made accurate wind speed measurement on land possible, these readings were converted into Beaufort numbers to provide consistent data. The new science of weather forecasting that grew out of the Admiralty's weather observation network simply continued to use the Admiralty's existing system.

As the rig of naval sailing vessels changed the scale evolved. With the coming of steam it was no longer relevant to refer to the amount of sail, so the scale was adapted by Sir George Simpson to refer instead to the appearance of the sea, including the height of the waves. He subsequently extended the scale further for use on land and later added specific wind-speeds when accurate scientific measurements became available. In 1944 five further wind forces (13 – 17) were added to accommodate powerful hurricanes and cyclones.

RICHTER SCALE

The Richter scale is named after Charles Francis Richter (1900 – 1985), an American seismologist who worked at the California Institute of Technology. Like Beaufort, Richter initially devised the scale for his own use. And again like

Beaufort, he was not the first in his field to do so. Previously Mercalli had produced a table of 'felt intensity' that listed twelve different levels of earthquake and provided a description of the effects of each. Mercalli's table, with some modification, is still in use and the precision of his descriptions makes it straightforward to apply(xii). Level three, for example, refers to "vibration like passing of light trucks" and notes that hanging objects swing. At level six his table specifies that "... Persons walk unsteadily... Furniture moved or overturned... Small bells ring (church, school)...". And at level seven, as well as "Difficult to stand... Waves on ponds... Large bells ring...", the table notes the fascinating phenomenon that hanging objects (which were busy swinging at level three) now merely quiver.

4.32: Earthquake in Italy, 5th Century BC, as drawn by Lycosthenes in 1557

One gets the impression that Richter happened to be in the right place at the right time. While he was doing what he himself describes as the routine work of cataloguing the shallow earthquakes that are common in southern California, he wanted to be able to grade them according to size. In contrast to Beaufort, who devised his wind-scale to overcome

160

the lack of objective measurements, Richter had access to vast amounts of data but no simple, yet scientifically meaningful, way of ranking them. The Mercalli scale was all very well as far as it went, but it only looked at the effect of an earthquake and this depended not just on its size but also how far away it was and how far underground it was, as well as the structure of the local subsoil, not to mention the vulnerability of local architecture.

Richter eventually found that, for the earthquakes he was dealing with, there was an approximately consistent mathematical relationship between the maximum movement of the ground (as recorded on a seismograph) and the distance from the earthquake's epicentre. This enabled him to set up a theoretical 'standard earthquake' to which all others could be compared. As his standard he opted for an earthquake that, at a distance of 100 km, produced a trace amplitude (the record of ground motion as shown on a seismograph trace) of one micron (a millionth of a metre). He then defined the size of any earthquake as a ratio of its trace amplitude at that distance to the trace amplitude of his standard earthquake. In order to avoid ending up with cumbersome numbers in the millions, he used a ratio not of the amplitudes themselves but of the logarithms of the amplitudes. So as you go up the Richter scale each whole number represents an actual increase in the recorded ground movement of ten times that of the previous scale number. Thus the movement recorded at level five is 1,000 times that at level two.

In 1935 Richter published his scale, designed to apply only to those earthquakes he had been cataloguing, and called it the magnitude scale. He and his senior colleague Beno Gutenberg then carried out further work to extend the scale to surface earthquakes worldwide and, later, to deep earthquakes. This was a massive task and some, including Richter himself who never referred to 'the Richter scale', felt that the name of the scale should have paid tribute to Gutenberg as well.

We are so used to hearing simple Richter scale numbers bandied about that it is easy not to realise that earthquakes are extraordinarily complicated. They don't just make the earth shake near the epicentre, they create shock waves that travel in all directions. Several kinds of shock wave travel along the earth's surface (the ones mainly responsible for any damage) and others travel not round, but through, the earth. Then of course there are aftershocks as well. So although a number on the Richter scale makes the size of an earthquake sound very precise, there is still a great deal of room for manoeuvre over which shock waves to use for the basis of various mathematical calculations. The scale therefore provides no more than a rough estimate of an earthquake's strength.

Because the Richter scale is essentially a system of calculations based on readings from seismographs, there is no top limit to it. The earthquake that caused the devastating tsunami at the end of 2004 was estimated at 9.3; the highest number yet recorded is 9.5 for the Chilean earthquake in 1960. In practice, however, it is highly unlikely that any earthquake will reach level 10.0 But, as Richter himself said, "that is a limitation in the earth, not in the scale"(xiii).

CHAPTER FIVE

MEDICAL

Medical eponyms could fill a whole book on their own. Not only have they already done so, but books have even been written on eponyms occurring within a single specialty. This chapter considers a select but eclectic assortment, chosen either because they commonly feature in ordinary conversation or because there is something particularly fascinating about them. They are listed from Alzheimer's to Zimmer.

ALZHEIMER'S DISEASE

The German physician Alois Alzheimer (1864 – 1915) was a warm-hearted, cheerful chap with a great enthusiasm for combining scientific research with medical practice. He had a happy marriage to a woman wealthy enough to allow him financial independence and was lucky enough to have a close and lasting friendship with a scientific colleague with whom he could discuss and exchange ideas. The atmosphere in his anatomical laboratory, despite being thick with the smoke of his cherished cigars, encouraged research and he enjoyed teaching those who worked there.

Today his name means the distressing mental deterioration that can eventually lead to a complete inability to wash and dress oneself, sometimes involving loss of memory to the extent of being unable to recognise one's nearest and dearest.

It is a sword of Damocles that those beyond the first flush of youth imagine poised over them every time they cannot find the word they want or end up in a room having forgotten why they went in there.

The first description of the clinical and neuropathological features of Alzheimer's disease was presented in 1906 by Alzheimer while he was working in a research clinic in Munich. The case he described related to a woman who had died at the age of only 51 years and his presentation appears to have been aimed at drawing attention to the fact that dementia akin to senile dementia could occur in comparatively young patients. However, the head of the clinic claimed this to be the first recognised case of a new disease – perhaps such a 'discovery' would have lent weight to the clinic's prestige – and accordingly named it after his colleague.

This was not Alzheimer's only achievement. He was a psychiatrist and, in contrast to the newly-emerging psychoanalytical approach being developed by Freud, Alzheimer researched the biological basis of mental illness. He concentrated on anatomical analysis of the brains of psychiatric patients and for a long time many in the medical establishment paid little attention to his work, regarding it as mere dissection. But Alzheimer's work was far more than that. His post-mortem brain studies were in each case guided by the clinical features of that patient's mental illness. He did eventually achieve recognition before he died and is now regarded as the founder of modern neuropathology, a discipline closely linked to clinical neuroscience.

CAESARIAN (or Caesarean)

The earliest successful Caesarian on a woman who survived the operation is recorded as having been performed in about 1500. The unfortunate woman who made history in this way was one Madame/Frau/Signora Nufer, who had been in labour for several days. Her husband Jacob, a Swiss pig-gelder, performed the operation. It is not recorded whether she was still conscious at the time but one fears she must have been. In comparatively modern times explorers have reported witnessing such operations being carried out by native healers who appeared to be well experienced in the procedure. One such operation was observed in Uganda in 1879, the patient being anaesthetised with banana wine and the wound dressed with a paste made from certain roots.

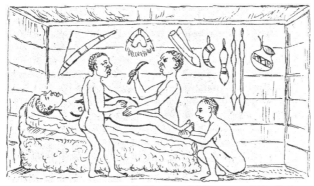

Courtesy U.S. National Library of Medicine

5.1: Successful Caesarian section performed by indigenous healers in Uganda, 1879

The origin of the obstetric term Caesarian section derives in some way from the Latin verb to cut (*caedo, caedere, caesum).* Exactly how, and from which Caesar it does so, is not clear. Dictionaries reflect the popular understanding that Julius Caesar – the one who invaded Britain – was delivered in this way. That seems highly unlikely to have been the case for three reasons. First, his mother is known to have survived his birth by many years – admittedly possible but hard to believe considering the risks, particularly the risk of infection. Secondly, he was not the first to bear the name – indeed it was already being used by the Caesar "family" almost as a surname. Thirdly, the belief that Julius Caesar was delivered by a Caesarian does not seem to date back any earlier than the 1500s.

Since dictionaries show that the word 'Caesarian' first appeared in English in about 1600, it would be easy to assume that its incorporation into the language was based on the received wisdom at that time regarding the birth of Julius. But even if that were to be the case, it is necessary to consider why the name was already in use within his family. A likely possibility is the legend related by the Roman historian Pliny, that it was the first and original Caesar (not that Pliny or anyone else seems to know exactly who he was or when he lived) who was cut out from his mother and was named accordingly. It would certainly be understandable that such a remarkable event would have been celebrated by repeated use of the name in subsequent generations. A second possibility, supported by some medical dictionaries, is that the name of the operation has come from a Roman law known as the *Lex Caesarea*. That law laid down that if a heavily pregnant woman died, her baby was to be cut out in order to save its life and, if it failed to survive, to be buried separately. The law was itself so named either because its contents related to cutting or because it was enacted at a time when one of the Caesars was emperor of Rome.

COLLES' FRACTURE and SMITH'S FRACTURE

Should you trip and fall over, stretching out your hand to break the fall, you might, if you are unlucky, end up with a Colles' fracture. That is, a fracture of the lower end of the main bone in your forearm (radius) with the fragment of broken bone pushed 'like this'. By contrast, if your hand had not been outstretched but had been flexed so that your weight had fallen on to the back of it, then you might have a Smith's fracture instead, in which the fragment of broken bone had been pushed 'like that'. For the more anatomically minded, 'this' is in the direction of the back of the wrist, whilst 'that' is in the opposite direction towards the inside of the wrist. So just take care when roller-skating unless you want to know about these fractures in uncomfortable detail.

In cases of injury it is not always easy to determine the exact nature of a fracture and before the invention of X-rays it could be next to impossible. Abraham Colles (1773 – 1843), a professor of anatomy and surgery in Dublin, and Robert William Smith (1807 – 1873), a professor of surgery also in Dublin, each published a paper describing in detail the type of fracture that now bears his name. Knowing exactly what to look for when examining a patient with a fractured wrist enabled such fractures to be more easily distinguished and therefore treated appropriately.

Courtesy U.S. Library of Congress

5.2: A man on pedalled roller skates, 1910

Colles came from a humble background. His father was in charge of a stone quarry, but died when Colles was still only six. His mother was determined that her children should nevertheless receive a good education. It is said that Colles' choice of career was influenced by his childhood discovery of an anatomy book lying in a field after a recent flood. He returned the book to its owner, but the doctor told him he could keep it. Later Colles graduated from Trinity College, Dublin with an arts degree but he had at the same time been studying surgery. He completed his medical education in Edinburgh, then walked from there to London (he must have been fit because it only took him eight days), to extend his experience of surgery before returning to Ireland.

The grapevine has it that both Colles and Smith suffered a fall at some point in their lives, with the intriguing result that Colles suffered a Smith's fracture, and vice versa.

CROHN'S DISEASE

By permission of University of Glasgow Library, Special Collections

5.3: 'An old crone': the Newbury witch

Once upon a time a woman diagnosed with Crohn's disease was told by her son that she could now expect to grow a few whiskers and develop a large wart on the side of her nose. She responded by telling him smartly not to be so cheeky, emphasising the correct spelling of the condition. Despite the unfortunate homophone, premature aging is not one of the symptoms of Crohn's disease, but it can be an extremely nasty disease. It is increasingly common, yet the cause is still unknown. It involves, amongst other things, inflammation of the gastro-intestinal tract, the symptoms of which include pain, diarrhoea and what can be only politely be described as social embarrassment. Although incurable, much can be done through treatment with steroids and other drugs to minimise its effects, but even so some sufferers end up requiring repeated abdominal operations to remove sections of the affected bowel.

Burrill Bernard Crohn (1884 – 1983) grew up in New York and was one of twelve children born to a German-Jewish immigrant family. His father was a stockbroker and managed to make enough money to provide the basic necessities. Despite the prevalent anti-Semitism that made it difficult for Jews to get into medical school at that time, Crohn qualified as a doctor. He practised at the Mount Sinai Hospital and it was there that he developed his interest in gastro-intestinal illness, carefully recording his observations.

Quite a number of cases of a disease similar to Crohn's had been described in early medical literature but it was not until 1932, when a scientific paper describing fourteen cases was published jointly by three colleagues, that the disease acquired its name. That paper referred to it as "regional ileitis". Others referred to it by using the name of the first of the three alphabetically listed authors: Crohn, Ginzburg and Oppenheimer. Crohn himself remained modest about his achievements and only ever referred to the disease by the name used in the publication.

DOWN SYNDROME

John Langdon Haydon Down (1828 – 1896) was born in a village in Cornwall and left school on reaching the age of fourteen to go to work as an assistant in his father's grocery shop. He became a pioneer in the care and education of the mentally handicapped, particularly children, and was apparently inspired to do so by an incident that happened when he was eighteen. When sheltering in a cottage from a storm he had met a feeble-minded girl (as he described her in the language of his time) and longed to be able to do something to help her.

He first trained as an apprentice to a barber-surgeon but realising he would need more knowledge of science to become a medical practitioner he took a course in pharmacy. Eventually he enrolled as a medical student, graduating with a fistful of gold medals in recognition of his academic talent. Instead of pursuing a medical career in a university hospital as his tutors and colleagues expected, he surprised everyone by accepting an appointment as Medical Superintendent at the 'Royal Earlswood Asylum for Idiots'.

The Asylum had recently been heavily criticised and Langdon Down was appointed to 'turn it round'. He threw himself into the task and transformed its reputation. He set about introducing some sort of consistency in approach by classifying the different types of cases being cared for there. In doing so he was heavily influenced by the then current vogue for ethnology, which promoted the view that the shape of the head was an indicator of the shape of, and hence the extent of development of, the brain beneath. This was a time when the differences in head shapes of different racial groups was thought to indicate differences in learning skills. Langdon Down allocated each of his cases to a specific racial type, based on facial appearance and measurements of the head. Do not jump to the conclusion that this meant Langdon Down was a racist. Far from it. Because the different conditions suffered by his (almost entirely Caucasian) patients presented superficial similarities in appearance to those of different racial origin, he concluded that this must not only indicate that were there no hard and fast differences between racial groups but also "furnish some arguments in favour of the unity of the human species"(i). In the end he gave up this method of classification, finding it not very useful. After his work at the Asylum he set up his own care home that was run by three successive generations of his family, before eventually being absorbed into the NHS.

Langdon Down was the first to notice that there was a particular group of patients who shared certain marked similarities in appearance, including an unusual crease straight across the centre of the palms of the hands, and he recorded an accurate and detailed description of their condition which he (incorrectly) believed was caused by tuberculosis. In his original paper he categorised such patients as of the Mongolian type, in reference to their typical flattened facial profile, and thereafter the condition became referred to as Mongolism.

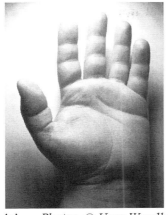 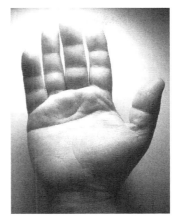

(a)   *Photos © User Wurdbender/ Wikimedia Commons*   (b)

5.4: Adult Hands
(a) showing normal creases   (b) showing a Simian crease

In the early 1960s there was universal pressure from those in the scientific establishment investigating the condition to have it renamed because the existing name was felt to be both misleading and embarrassing. This, combined with an understandable complaint from the People's Republic of Mongolia to the World Health Organisation, succeeded in getting it officially renamed as Down syndrome.

The Law of Eternal Cussedness of Things decrees that if you are related to anyone medical the chances are that you are likely to end up with a medical condition or disease that lies within your relation's particular field of specialty. Langdon Down's family is an example, as one of his grandsons was found to have Down syndrome.

EUSTACHIAN TUBE

The Eustachian tube connects the middle ear to the throat and is named after the Italian anatomist Bartolomeo Eustachio (Eustachius) (c.1524 – 1574). Most people remain blissfully unaware of its existence unless it becomes blocked after catching a cold, affecting the hearing. Eustachio was the first to publish an accurate anatomical description of what he called the tuba auditiva, but he cannot claim actually to have discovered it. A description of such a tube in goats was made two thousand years earlier, and for some considerable time had led to a belief that goats could breathe through their ears.

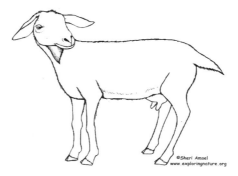

Drawing © Sheri Amsel

5.5: Domestic goat

We know that Eustachio must have had a good education because he was able to edit Greek text and to make his own translations of text written in Arabic. He studied medicine and was appointed professor of anatomy at the University of Rome. This gave him access to the bodies of those who had died in local hospitals and thus an opportunity to pursue detailed anatomical studies. Eustachio lived during the golden age of anatomy, when the true intricacies of the human body had only recently begun to emerge from religious myth. A brief diversion into the story of dissection will help in the understanding of his achievements.

One of the very earliest anatomists had been the Greek physician Galen but, owing to religious scruples, he had been forced to rely on the dissection of apes rather than humans. He lived during the second century A.D. and produced an apparently authoritative overview of anatomical findings. Unfortunately Galen was more than a little dogmatic and began his work with certain preconceived ideas. One was that 'spirits' (not unlike the 'humours' of Shakespearian times) travelled from the liver, heart and brain through the veins, arteries and nerves with an ebb and flow movement akin to breathing. Another was that the body and every structure in it had been made by the Creator and was perfect in its design. Galen's beliefs fitted in well with the newly established Christian religion, the leaders of which heralded his work as holy. In the eyes of the church, therefore, further research was close to blasphemy and physicians who criticized Galen were subject to punishment. The wholesale adoption of Galen's work by the church held back the development of the science of anatomy by hundreds of years, and the pursuit of understanding was not helped by the fact that Galen was wrong in some respects and was not above describing non-existent structures 'found' on dissection, simply because he thought they must be there somewhere.

Courtesy U.S. National Library of Medicine

5.6: Frontispiece of Bartholomaei Eustachii's Romanae Archetypae Tabulae Anatomicae, published 1783

Despite the church's hard line, interest in anatomy continued. Eventually the church agreed to permit dissection of executed criminals and this led to the rather gruesome spectacle of dissections being carried out in public. The

173

professor in charge, duly enthroned on a podium, would read Galen's text aloud while some junior who had drawn the short straw had to cope with the embarrassing problem of demonstrating the truth of Galen's (sometimes incorrect) words about the corpse. The whole procedure appears to have been quite a lengthy social event requiring refreshments. We are told that "the sessions were long and collations were served."(ii). Anatomical studies by Leonardo da Vinci paved the way for further research by the Italian Vesalius, considered to be the 'father of anatomy', whose book published in 1543 contained accurate illustrations of his dissections of the human body and whose work landed him in trouble with the Spanish Inquisition.

Eustachio was initially critical of Vesalius for doubting Galen, but as his experience of dissection increased he, too, became sceptical of some of Galen's claims. Eustachio, together with another artist, made detailed, accurate anatomical drawings of his dissections, from which forty-seven copperplate engravings were prepared with a view to illustrating Eustachio's planned major new work on anatomy. In contrast to the wood cut illustrations used in Vesalius' work, these engravings were able to show his findings in far greater detail. Unfortunately Eustachio died rather suddenly without completing his magnum opus and only eight of these engravings were published during his lifetime.

Following Eustachio's death no trace of the missing plates could be found despite intensive searches. He was undoubtedly a master of anatomy, but his place in history has been seriously undermined by the Mystery of the Thirty-Nine Missing Engravings. In the end it turned out that he had given them to his co-artist, but it was not until 1714 that they were traced and were then published by courtesy of the Pope. Whilst these illustrations were still useful even without any of Eustachio's intended text, by the time they were published much of the new detail discovered by him had already been found by others. The value of his work, that should have resulted in a giant step forward in the science of anatomy and indeed would have done so had it been published as planned 160 years earlier, was therefore greatly diminished.

FALLOPIAN TUBE

The Italian anatomist Gabriello Falloppio (1523 – 1562) was a contemporary of Eustachio and so was working at a time when, as we have just seen, the traditional views of anatomy were being challenged. The study of anatomy was just beginning to break free of the stranglehold of the church and was an exciting new field open to discovery. Fallopio, or Fallopius for those who prefer his Latin name, concentrated on dissection of the human head and reproductive organs. He described in detail the tube down which an ovum passes on its way to the uterus, that is now called the Fallopian tube.

In his early life Falloppio was not well off and had to enter the church in order to earn a living, taking up the study of medicine only when he was older. At that time there was fighting between Italy and France. Soldiers being what they are, syphilis tended to follow in the paths of armies and the disease had therefore been named in several European countries according to the nationality of the most recent invading army – conveniently ignoring the fact that there would certainly have been local cases of the disease prior to the army's arrival. In an attempt to control the spread of the current epidemic of what the Italian Falloppio would have called 'the French disease', Falloppio invented an early kind of condom made of linen. His record of clinical trials involving 1,100 men shows that these devices were most effective in protecting from infection. They were said to have been tied in place with pink ribbon in order to increase their appeal to the ladies.

HEIMLICH MANOEUVRE

Since the inception of the Heimlich manoeuvre in 1974, the name of Dr. Henry Jay Heimlich (b1920) has become well-known across the world. The manoeuvre is used to rescue someone who is choking. Should you ever be tempted to suck cough sweets at night, read the following cautionary tale and reconsider.

One night a young couple retired to bed after an exhausting day dealing with professional commitments and the demands of two young children. The wife was doing her best to ignore a tickle in her throat, but since it tended to wake her up at night she had a tube of pastilles at the ready on the bedside table. As feared, she woke up coughing and still half-asleep reached for a pastille but, just as she put it into her mouth, an intense tickle produced an uncontrollable urge to cough. In order to do so she took a sudden sharp inbreath, only to find that she had inadvertently inhaled the pastille. It lodged firmly well down in her windpipe and she could not breathe at all – either in or out – neither could she speak or even grunt. Desperately shaking her husband awake she remembered, as images of her past life went before her eyes, that he had once told her of an effective procedure that could be carried out when someone choked. Although terrified, that memory left her sure of certain rescue, and her confidence proved to be fully justified. Despite being suddenly woken from a deep sleep by his speechless wife frantically gesticulating in the general direction of her mouth, her husband proved extraordinarily quick-witted and equal to the occasion. Dashing round like a knight in shining pyjamas he stood behind her, put his arms round her with his fist at the crucial spot in her upper abdomen and expertly jerked the fist inward and upward. The pastille flew half way across the bedroom and breathing was immediately restored. He got back into bad and went straight to sleep. She, by contrast, spent the rest of the night thinking "what if"... What if he had not realised what was wrong? What if he had not known what to do? What if it had not worked? What if he had been away? In each scenario the answer was certain death. Morning tea was accompanied with effulgent thanks and she asked how often he had previously been called on to carry out the manoeuvre. "Oh I've never done it before" was the offhand and somewhat disconcerting response. She never, ever used cough pastilles again.

There is much controversy over some of Dr. Heimlich's work. His view is that the famous manoeuvre should be routinely used to help cases not only of choking but also of drowning and cystic fibrosis. For the treatment of cancer, and more recently AIDS, he advocates the benefits of the deliberate infection of patients with malaria (malariotherapy) in order to activate the body's own immune system, and has carried out trials of this treatment in China and Africa. The US authorities and much of the medical establishment do not agree with his views and the clinical trials are regarded by many as unethical. Even his claim that he alone is responsible for 'his' manoeuvre has been challenged. But, whatever the truth of it all, there can be no doubt of the life-saving efficacy of Heimlich's manoeuvre in cases of choking.

HUNTINGTON'S DISEASE

This rare inherited disease, which usually only appears when those affected have reached their forties or fifties, used to be known as Huntington's chorea, in reference to some of its symptoms. Chorea means uncontrollable, irregular, spasmodic movements of the muscles, usually in the face, arms and legs. In the case of Huntington's disease this can include the whole body and the disease may also ultimately cause dementia. Other diseases, such as that which used to be known as St. Vitus dance, can also cause chorea but are not hereditary.

The American physician George Huntington (1850 – 1916) was not the first to publish a description of 'his' disease, but his was the first description to be widely read. It brought him fame at the age of twenty-two, so it hardly represented the culmination of a lifetime of toil that one might have imagined. Yet it would be wrong to assume that here was a scientific genius whose early achievement introduced a long and glittering career of discovery. Just the opposite. Huntington published virtually nothing else and spent his entire career as a country doctor who was widely respected as kind, conscientious and caring, driving out with his horse and trap to visit sick patients. Despite problems with asthma he had a happy family life. He was handsome, modest and humorous and is remembered as much for his interests in the countryside, in fishing, hunting, painting and music, as for his medical skills.

So how did it come about that someone who led such an unexceptional life produced the seminal paper on a rare disease that is still without cure? The task could only have been attempted by someone who was in the unusual position both of having come across enough sufferers to realise that these were not just one-off cases but that they conformed to a consistent pattern, and also of having information available as to how previous generations of the relevant families had been affected. Huntington's particular circumstances happened to fit the bill exactly and he himself was very observant, with a straightforward, clear way of looking at things and an equally straightforward and clear way of expressing himself.

Huntington lived in the village of East Hampton on Long Island, New York, where his father and grandfather had been doctors before him. As is the case with any rare, inherited disease, particularly in the days when populations were comparatively static, cases of that disease tended to be concentrated in the few distinct areas where an affected family had settled some time in the past. East Hampton was one such village. As a child of eight, accompanying his father on his medical rounds, Huntington recalled: "We suddenly came upon two women, mother and daughter ... both bowing, twisting, grimacing. I stared in wonderment, almost in fear. What could it mean? My father paused to speak with them, and we passed on.... From this point on, my interest in the disease has never wholly ceased."(iii). Huntington observed such patients carefully and, because he had access to the notes of both his father and grandfather covering a period of seventy-eight years, was able to build up a picture not only of the symptoms but also the hereditary nature of the disease. He drafted his paper entitled "On Chorea", setting out the symptoms, course and hereditary aspects of this unusual form of chorea that occurred comparatively frequently in East Hampton. When he moved to Ohio, he read his paper describing what he called 'the hereditary chorea' to the local medical society and it was so well received that he sent it to a medical journal for publication.

Courtesy Ria van Hes

5.7: George Huntington with his pony and trap

Subsequent researchers have endeavoured to track down the origin of the disease in the USA and believe it can be traced to three people: a man (Jeffers) and a husband and wife (Nichols and Ellfin), who all arrived from Suffolk on the same voyage in 1630. At that time the English government paid a substantial reward for the finding and denouncing of witches and many of those who had symptoms that could be interpreted as being possessed by the devil were wrongly accused. Some of these undoubtedly suffered from, or had a parent who suffered from, Huntington's disease and in consequence lived in seclusion as social outcasts. The ever-present threat of being sentenced to one of the barbaric punishments in use at the time encouraged emigration. This solved the problem for those who found that they were not affected by their parent's condition. But for others, hopes of a fresh start in life proved to have been illusory when in due course it became apparent that they had not escaped the disease. In 1653 Ellfin was hanged as a witch and her granddaughter was similarly convicted. Society and the courts cruelly took the view that the grotesque movements were the work of the devil, mimicking the death throes of Christ.

'MONTEZUMA'S REVENGE'

Revenge – for what? Initially all was going well for Montezuma (1480 or thereabouts – 1520) and his kingdom in Mexico – extremely well in fact. By the time he was appointed ruler of the Aztecs their empire was fabulously wealthy. It had conquered neighbouring tribes and kingdoms, which now had to pay tribute. There was a sophisticated taxation system and vast stores of gold and precious jewels. The empire was abundantly supplied with a wide range of provisions and other necessaries including salt, paper and cotton. Montezuma had absolute power and was regarded almost as a god – even the two hundred chieftains guarding him had to walk barefoot in his presence with downcast eyes as they were not permitted to be so presumptuous as to look upon his face. His diet was commensurate with his status, it being reported that he would be offered a choice from over three hundred plates of food, including turkey, pheasant, partridge, pigeon, venison, wild boar, hare and rabbit. All rounded off with a drink of chocolate from a solid gold cup followed by inhalation of tobacco smoke.

Apart from its wealth, the empire was also legendary for its cruelty. The Aztecs worshipped many hundreds of gods, whose strength had to be maintained through precious offerings. In a country that was so rich in gold and jewels, the most appropriate offering was considered to be a human heart – preferably that of a brave warrior – and Montezuma's sacrifice of twelve thousand captives on one occasion looks comparatively modest beside the twenty thousand once sacrificed by a previous ruler.

When Montezuma came to power, the country was approaching an inauspicious time in its religious calendar. The priorities of those responsible for electing him were therefore dominated by the need to choose someone who could deal with internal and religious affairs, rather than someone who was a statesman with a feel for dealing with representatives of foreign states. Montezuma, who had trained for leadership of the priesthood, seemed the ideal choice, but because of his background he was strongly influenced by an old prophecy. That prophecy suggested that Quetzalcoatl, the god of learning who long ago had mysteriously disappeared into the sea, would one day reappear from out of the sunrise.

Photo © ADEVA

5.8: Mid 16thC portrayal of Aztec ritual human sacrifice

And then... It was to the great good fortune of Cortéz and his Spanish troops that they arrived from the East and that they happened to do so during 1519, the very year prophesied for the return of Quetzalcoatl. This probably explains why Montezuma, instead of attacking Cortéz while he had every chance of success, showered him with gold and other valuable gifts and then allowed him to enter Mexico. This continuing policy of appeasement ended with Montezuma's subjugation, the handing over of his empire's treasure and the use of his position as ruler to maintain Spanish domination. Eventually the Aztecs could stand it no longer. They appointed a new ruler who led them into battle, but by then it was too late. Their ultimate defeat was followed by the collapse of the empire and slavery to the Spanish.

Like Montezuma himself, modern Mexico welcomes visitors from Europe. But its water, although used by the locals without ill effects, creates havoc with the unsuspecting European gastro-intestinal tract. So much so that it does indeed seem fitting that in the mid-twentieth century these unwelcome effects were attributed to the ghost of Montezuma, seeking revenge for past deceit and terrible injustice.

MUNCHAUSEN'S SYNDROME

The symptoms of Münchausen's are so bizarre as to beggar belief. And although the syndrome is unusual, it is not as rare as might be supposed – apparently most hospital doctors have come across a case. Typically such patients turn up at an Accident and Emergency Department giving false personal details and falsely claiming they are suffering acute symptoms of some sort, often abdominal pain, or bleeding from the lungs or stomach. On examination they are usually found to have a host of abdominal scars with dramatic explanations – some of which may well be true – as to why. It is not unusual for them to have some genuine illness or a medical abnormality that they use to give credibility to their history. On detailed questioning they are evasive and aggressive. The whole purpose of their behaviour appears to be to mislead those responsible for their care and to get themselves admitted to hospital for tests and exploratory operations.

As can be imagined, unless a long-serving member of staff happens to recognise the patient from previous admissions, a Münchausen's patient will waste an enormous amount of time and resources. After the usual more routine tests have been carried out and the results found to be normal, doctors move on to the more unusual tests, the results of which again prove uninformative. In the hope of finding further information that might help reach a diagnosis, those hospitals that the patient claims to have previously attended for treatment are contacted. Only gradually will the true picture emerge and as it begins to do so the patient usually realises that he (or, more unusually, she) is about to be found out and discharges himself hurriedly. Frequently he then turns up at another hospital elsewhere a few days later, under a different name but presenting similar symptoms.

Münchausen's syndrome was first described, very vividly, by Dr. Richard Asher in 1951. He gave the syndrome its name in his first paragraph: "Like the famous Baron von Münchausen, the persons affected have always travelled widely; and their stories, like those attributed to him, are both dramatic and untruthful. Accordingly, the syndrome is respectfully dedicated to the baron, and named after him." (iv).

5.9: Baron von Münchausen riding on a cannon ball

Karl Friedrich Hieronymus, Baron von Münchausen (1720 – 1797), was a German nobleman who served in the Russian army fighting against the Turks. He was a passionate sportsman and hunter and, at the age of forty, retired to his country estate to pursue these interests. He became well-known locally as a raconteur, probably using a modest amount of poetic licence (but no more than that) for greater

183

effect when recounting his experiences. It is therefore not he himself but an acquaintance of his, a certain Rudolf Erich Raspe, who is responsible both for the lasting fame of the Baron and the attribution of wild exaggeration and untruthfulness.

Raspe had moved to London and was in financial difficulties. In order to find a quick source of income, he published anonymously a small volume called 'Baron Münchausen's Narrative of his Marvellous Travels and Campaigns in Russia', allegedly recording the Baron's exploits as related by him to his drinking companions over a bottle of wine. The book did include some of the Baron's own tales but also a number of fictitious ones. It sold well and over the following years each new edition included further fictitious stories added by a variety of writers.

The book begins by telling of the Baron's narrow escape when out hunting in Ceylon. The story goes that he had suddenly found himself in a tight spot with crocodile infested water on his right, a precipice on his left and an angry lion charging at him from behind, whilst immediately in front was a forty foot long crocodile intent on eating him, with jaws open at the ready. The Baron at this point fell down in fear, at the very moment when the lion sprang. The lion consequently misjudged his attack and jumped too far, with his head ending up stuck in the crocodile's mouth. Whilst the two creatures were struggling to disengage themselves, the Baron recovered himself and with remarkable presence of mind cut the head off the lion with his hunting knife and rammed the severed head further into the crocodile's throat, thereby suffocating him. As the book continues, the credibility of the Baron's alleged narrative decreases further, relating exploits such as riding a cannon-ball and visiting the moon.

NICOTINE

Rolf Harris's song featuring his two so-called buddies, Nick Teen and Al K. Hall, used to warn of the dangers of cigarettes and drink but, although there is indeed a person lurking within the word "nicotine", he was not Nicholas. The word

184

comes from nicotiana, the Latin name allocated to the tobacco plant by Linnaeus, commemorating Jean Nicot (c.1530 – 1600) of Nimes, France.

In deciding on this name Linnaeus had not gone for any obvious choice. Nicot was a diplomat and scholar, who compiled one of the first French dictionaries and had nothing to do with discovering the tobacco plant. The first Europeans to come across it were Christopher Columbus and the members of his expedition in 1492, who on their arrival in the new world were presented with numerous gifts including dried tobacco leaves. As they had no experience of tobacco they ended up throwing much of it away.

Nor was Nicot the first European to smoke tobacco: that position is held by Rodrigo de Jerez, one of the crewmen on the 1492 expedition who, after seeing the locals smoking, decided to try it himself. He unwisely continued to indulge the habit on his return to Spain and was flung into prison for seven years by the Spanish Inquisition, which regarded someone breathing out clouds of smoke as a clear case of possession by the devil.

5.10: Engraving of a man smoking, 1575

Nicot was no explorer and did not introduce the plant to Europe, where by 1559 it had already become established in

185

France, Spain and Portugal – only arriving in England some five years later. His connection with tobacco was simply an enthusiastic acceptance and promotion of its medicinal uses that he had heard about while serving as French ambassador to Portugal. He sent snuff, made from tobacco, to the French queen to cure her (or her son's) migraines, apparently with considerable success. Soon extravagant claims were being made as to the efficacy of tobacco in curing not only headache but also toothache, worms, chilblains, bad breath, wounds and numerous other medical complaints.

All Europe, it seems, was jumping on the bandwagon of the new wonder drug but in 1604 King James (I of England, VI of Scotland), who was vehemently against it, published his "A Counterblaste to Tobacco"(v), a pamphlet decrying smoking. Though clearly based mainly on passion rather than scientific evidence it was still centuries ahead of its time and in some ways came very near the truth. It claimed that the popularity of smoking was partly due to fashion and drew attention to the enormous waste of money involved. It warned of addiction: "many in this kingdome have had such a continuall use of taking this unsavorie smoke, as now they are not able to forbeare the same, no more than an olde drunkard can abide to be long sober". It even pointed out the health risk that the smoke "makes a kitchin ... in the inward parts of men, soiling and infecting them, with an unctuous and oily kind of soote, as hath bene found in some great Tobacco takers, that after their death were opened". Its blistering summary describes smoking as "a custome lothesome to the eye, hateful to the nose, harmful to the brain, dangerous to the lungs". Having set out his views on the topic James then adopted an unexpectedly modern approach to discouraging its use. Rather than making it illegal, he instructed the Treasury to impose a heavy duty on all tobacco imports.

The Royal College of Physicians debated the King's views but at that stage was definitely not convinced. Tobacco continued to be regarded as having remarkable medicinal properties, to such an extent that during the great plague smoking was made compulsory at Eton in the belief that it would help to avoid infection.

Had anyone approached the issue with an open mind there were clear early indications that tobacco really did cause health problems. Apart from those mentioned by King James, there was a steady trickle of other warnings. In 1670 a Dutch physician summarised his factual findings on the dissection of the bodies of heavy smokers, describing the trachea as coated with soot like a cooking pot, and the lungs as dried out. Others drew attention to similar findings. Evidence as to the dangers of tobacco in the form of snuff came later when a London physician recorded his observation that the use of snuff led to "swellings and excrescences"(vi) in the nose. But by and large all these warnings were ignored. Even when scientific papers were published in Germany in the 1930s linking smoking and lung cancer, attitudes remained unaltered. The world had to wait until 1950 for the publication of a large scale scientific study(vii) that provided overwhelming evidence of the link between smoking and lung cancer before things started to change.

PARKINSON'S DISEASE

During the 1790s the events of the French revolution were leading to considerable unease in Britain. Some muttered of revolution. Others who were more moderate talked of Parliamentary reform and relegating the king to the position of merely a figurehead. But even that view, given the political uncertainties of the time, was regarded by the authorities as close to treason. Close, but not quite close enough to do anything about it, although this was not for any lack of trying. At that time treason was still defined by a statute dating from 1351 declaring, amongst other things, that it was treason "When a Man doth compass or imagine the Death of our Lord the King..."(viii). Common sense tells us that back then the word 'imagine' did not yet mean mere fanciful thought, but was used more in the sense of intend or plan. However, sophisticated legal arguments were put forward on behalf of the government that the word should be construed with a contemporary meaning. Such arguments did not convince the courts and therefore, when the so-called 'Pop-Gun Plot' was uncovered, the authorities pounced with some delight – at last they felt they had a chance of making a charge of treason stick. This plot was alleged to have been devised by a handful of members of the London Corresponding Society, a secret society dedicated to achieving Parliamentary reform. The idea was to kill the king while he was at the theatre by blowing a poisoned dart into his neck from a blow-tube. The government, seeing an opportunity to silence a society of which it thoroughly disapproved, argued that the other members of the Society must also be implicated in the plot. The whole thing turned out to be something of a fiasco but not before several of these other members had been examined under oath as to their part in it. One such was the London physician James Parkinson (1755 – 1824).

Photo courtesy C.M.Wiles

5.11: Paralysis agitans: the posture and gait of a man with Parkinson's disease

The furore caused by the Pop-Gun Plot led Parkinson to turn away from his political activities to a medical career, aimed at improving the welfare of the general population, in particular those suffering from mental illness. He was also fascinated by fossils, wrote several esoteric volumes about them and, with a group of friends, founded the Geological Society of London.

It would have been satisfying to find that Parkinson's disease, which begins with a slight shaking in the arms and legs, was so named in reference to the effects of the anxiety he must have felt during his brush with the law over a charge of treason. But the truth is more prosaic. It was his work 'An Essay on the Shaking Palsy'(ix) that provided the first clear description of the condition and some sixty years after he died its importance was recognised by a later physician, Jean-Martin Charcot, who studied the disease in more detail and named it after Parkinson.

In its advanced form Parkinson's disease involves severe tremor, a stooping, rigid posture, a fixed expressionless face and a shuffling, unbalanced walk that may break into tiny running steps. These symptoms are the result of damage to specific brain cells causing a lack of dopamine, a chemical normally produced in a healthy body. In 1982 there was a very peculiar outbreak of the disease amongst a group of students in California. They had been taking a designer 'recreational' drug that was contaminated. The result was that within hours they had developed very severe, irreversible Parkinson's disease. Some were left permanently paralysed and unable to communicate. The tragedy led to new avenues of research, which increased doctors' understanding of the disease. Unfortunately there is still no cure, although many treatments are available that can alleviate the symptoms.

RAYNAUD'S PHENOMENON

Some people who 'feel the cold' suffer from Raynaud's phenomenon, in which the blood supply to the hands and feet becomes reduced due to constriction of the blood vessels. The result is that the fingers, toes and soles of the feet (and in extreme cases even the tip of the chin) go 'dead', that is, numb and impressively white. The return of the blood supply is associated with an intense tingling and even pain if the affected area is warmed up too quickly. As the fingers begin to return to life they go a sort of bluish colour and then, especially if the warming up process is too sudden, rather a bright red, before returning to normal. This effect was first described by the French physician, Auguste Gabriel Maurice Raynaud (1834 – 1881), whereupon it became known as Raynaud's phenomenon.

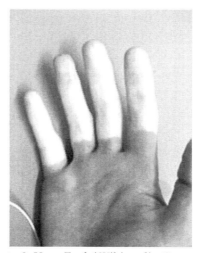

Photo © User Tcal / Wikimedia Commons

5.12: Hand of a 25 year old male showing Raynaud's phenomenon

A British gentleman, looking at the red, white and blue appearance of his hand as different parts of it were at different stages of warming, once claimed that his hand demonstrated that he was particularly patriotic because it displayed the colours of the Union Jack. Since these are also the colours of the tricoleur one wonders whether a similar thought might have crossed Raynaud's mind, but perhaps he had a different sense of humour.

Raynaud came from a well-educated family and his clinical and teaching skills as a doctor were held in high regard. He collaborated with Louis Pasteur at one stage and his publications included works on historical aspects of medical science. He was made an officer of the Légion d'Honneur but was never appointed to a senior hospital post. So his ambition of becoming a professor of medical history in Paris remained a pipe dream.

ST. ANTHONY'S FIRE

In 1951, in the small town of Pont Saint-Esprit in Provence, a great number of perfectly normal, ordinary people suddenly started going mad. Some of them also became impervious to pain and developed superhuman strength. One thought he was a tight-rope walker and decided to demonstrate his imagined skills. Another jumped out of an upstairs window because he thought could fly – and despite breaking both legs managed to run some distance down the road before he could be stopped. Another began counting and recounting the six panes of glass in his window and carried on doing it without interruption for three weeks. A child tried to strangle its mother. A man restrained in two straitjackets (a single one having proved inadequate to the task) and tied down on his bed was found soaked with blood because in his desperation to get free he had been tearing at the restraints with his teeth until all his teeth had come out of their sockets.

Some people had no hallucinations but displayed other symptoms. Many could not sleep and met in the main square at night, all night every night, walking and talking to each other. Some complained of gastric troubles whilst others suffered excruciating burning pains or felt freezing cold. Some fell into a coma, others began to develop gangrene. One man had convulsions and died. There were four suicide attempts. One of the town's doctors was himself affected and his insomnia was such that he went for eight days without sleep, using his time to care for his patients.

Ambulances, straitjackets and military help were brought in from neighbouring areas but it was some time before anyone had the slightest idea what was going on, other than that this was a dire medical emergency. The answer proved as old-fashioned as it was unexpected. All the 230 people affected were found to have bought bread from the same local bakery, bread that had been made using rye flour infected with the ergot fungus. They were suffering from ergot poisoning, or what used to be known in medieval times as St. Anthony's fire or 'holy fire'. (St. Anthony's fire was also used in the past to refer to an entirely unrelated skin complaint now known as erysipelas.)

5.13:
An ear of rye showing the growth of sclerotia (the fruiting structures of the fungus Claviceps purpurea) containing ergot alkaloids

Köhler's Medizinal-Pflanzen, 1887

Ergot fungus grows in rye kernels and, by the time the rye crop is mature, can be seen as a spike sticking out of the head of rye, described as similar in appearance to a cock's spur. Fungal spores present in the spike fall to the ground and, if the conditions are unusually wet when the next year's crop is just coming into flower, the fungus will establish itself in the new crop. Ergot poisoning was most common in those countries with a wet climate and where it was the custom to eat rye bread – notably Germany, France and Russia. Peter the Great once had to abandon a military campaign when both men and horses were suddenly struck down with ergot poisoning – on that occasion 20,000 people died from it.

There are two types of such poisoning, depending on the exact structure of the chemical produced by the fungus. One severely restricts the blood circulation, causing a drop in body temperature, a sensation of burning in the limbs (described as so painful that it felt like being burned at the stake), gangrene and death. By contrast, the mind-bending and hallucinogenic nature of the symptoms of the other type can be readily understood once it is known that the psychedelic drug LSD is derived from ergot.

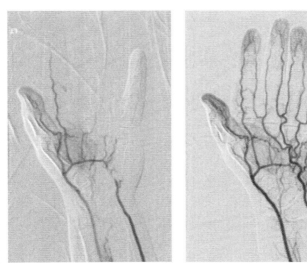

© *Korean Neurological Association's Journal of Clinical Neurology*

5.14: Angiograms showing the flow of blood to the hand in a recent case of ergotism:
before treatment   after treatment

St. Anthony's Fire was an affliction that was understandably dreaded. The contemporary description of an epidemic that occurred in Germany in 857 A.D. conveys some of its horror: "a great plague of swollen blisters consumed the people by a loathsome rot, so that their limbs were loosened and fell off before death"(x). The strange disease was regarded as either a punishment from God or created by witchcraft.

Belief in such a direct connection with the Almighty meant that prayer and intercession through the Saints was of great importance when seeking a cure. St. Anthony (A.D.251 – A.D.356), the hermit who founded Christian monasticism and spent most of his life alone in the arid Egyptian desert does not on the face of it seem the most likely source of help. His involvement arose only indirectly and it is not clear exactly when or how it did so. There is no doubt that at some time during the eleventh century the son of Gaston de Dauphiné, a wealthy French nobleman, had been struck down in an epidemic of 'holy fire'. Following Gaston's prayers his son made an apparently miraculous recovery and in 1095 Gaston, by way of thanks, built a hospital near the Church of St. Anthony at St. Didier de la Motte (now known as Sainte-Antoine l'Abbaye) in the Dauphiné region. He also founded a new monastic order known as the Hospital Brothers of St. Anthony, dedicated in particular to the care of those suffering from 'holy fire'. Over the years the order established many other such hospitals.

These events do not really explain how St. Anthony became involved in the first place and this remains a matter of conjecture. Perhaps Gaston just happened to offer up his prayers in a church dedicated to St. Anthony and so dedicated his hospital to the same saint. Or, if the illness was in those early days already known as St. Anthony's Fire, he might have travelled to Motte to pray at St. Anthony's church believing that his prayers would then be more effective. Or it might be that he went to Motte because the church there was already establishing a reputation for miraculous cures through the ownership of a holy relic, the hand of St. Anthony himself. Whatever the reason, the most likely chain of events is that the name became attached to the illness after and because of the establishment of the Hospital Brothers of St. Anthony.

SALMONELLA

Any doubts as to the quality of the salmon on one's plate implied by the name of this bacterium are quite unjustified, since salmonella poisoning is no more likely to result from eating salmon as it is from eating many other foods. Nevertheless, the implication must seem more than a little unfair to fish-mongers and those in the salmon-processing industry. Any attempt to change the name, however, (and such an attempt was once made) would have an uphill battle because the word commemorates Daniel Elmer Salmon (1850 – 1914), the specialist in veterinary medicine who is credited with having first discovered the bacterium.

Salmon set up the Bureau of Animal Industry as part of the US Department of Agriculture and was the director of it, but accreditation of the discovery to him is misleading. The bacterium was actually discovered by a researcher who was working there called Theobald Smith. Salmon clearly had great talents as an administrator (for example, he set up a system of meat inspection and required imported livestock to undergo a period of quarantine) but it does appear that he had a habit of taking the credit for work done by others, inappropriately insisting on sole or senior authorship of scientific papers. Eventually he had to resign his position after a disagreement with the head of the Department of Agriculture and he then accepted an invitation to go to Uruguay to establish a school of veterinary medicine there. Subsequently he returned to the USA and became president of the US Veterinary Medical Association. Smith went on to become a professor at Harvard and the director of the Department of Animal Pathology at the Rockefeller Institute.

TOURETTE (or Gilles de la Tourette) SYNDROME

The symptoms of Tourette syndrome are very variable and, as there is no scientific test for it, diagnosis is difficult. The symptoms comprise repetitive muscular and verbal tics, the former appearing as anything from slight twitches or sniffs to grimaces and gesticulations, the latter (when they are present) ranging from grunts and barks to involuntary, inappropriate swearing and uttering obscenities (coprolalia). The disorder used to be considered psychiatric but although it is often associated with hyperactivity, obsessive-compulsive behaviour or depression, it is now properly regarded as a neurological movement disorder.

The condition was first clearly described in 1825 by a French physician whose patient, a member of the nobility, had starting getting motor tics as a child and went on to suffer from involuntary screams, strange cries and coprolalia. This behaviour was so socially unacceptable that she had no option other than to live in seclusion until she died in old age. With hindsight it is thought that Dr. Samuel Johnson might also have had the disorder, though in a less severe form. Certainly his friends commented on his frequent tics and gesticulations and he himself refers to efforts to overcome his 'melancholia'. None of this prevented him from living a full social life. Those who came to regard him as persona non grata did so not because of any involuntary vocal sounds – rather the reverse. He was all too good at expressing his sometimes insulting opinions, as exemplified by his well-known definitions(xi) of oats ("A grain, which in England is generally given to horses, but in Scotland supports the people.") and pension ("Pay given to a state hireling for treason to his country") – the latter definition causing some embarrassment when he subsequently accepted an annual pension from the king.

Courtesy Dr. Olivier Walusinski

5.15: Front page of *Le Pays Illustré* from December 1893, with sketch of a patient's attack on Dr. Tourette

It was another Frenchman, Georges Albert Edouard Brutus Gilles de la Tourette (1857 – 1904), who by describing a group of several patients with similar symptoms first recognised that there was an identifiable disorder. Tourette studied hysteria, hypnosis, epilepsy and movement disorders but was also interested in art and literature. His later years are a sad story. 1893 was an "annus horribilis": his son died of meningitis, his mentor, friend and colleague Jean-Martin Charcot died, and he himself was shot by a disgruntled paranoid patient.

Tourette returned to medical practice, but a few years later became mentally ill due to neurosyphilis. He refused to go to hospital and had to be tricked into it by being told that there was a (fictitious) famous patient in a well-respected psychiatric hospital in Switzerland who wanted to consult him. On arrival he was forcibly detained and was cared for there whilst his condition continued its inexorable deterioration, leading to his death several years later at the age of forty-seven.

ZIMMER FRAME

Those with mobility problems often find it helpful to use a walking aid consisting of a waist high, lightweight metal frame on four legs. These devices are correctly referred to as walking frames, but are often referred to as 'Zimmer frames' and the word has now reached our dictionaries, albeit still with a capital Z.

'Zimmer' began as a trademark and the US corporation that first made such frames, Zimmer Inc., bears the name of one of its founders, Justin O. Zimmer (1888 – 1951). He qualified as a telegraph operator but immediately started work as a salesman for a company selling supports for fractured limbs. After twenty successful years at this he had the idea of improving the supports by making them out of the lighter weight metal, aluminium. His employers dismissed his suggestion as "just small potatoes"(xii), which he found so infuriating that he set up a new company to put his idea into effect, with immediate and long-lasting success. Curiously, the fact that the corporation produces replacement joints as well as walking frames and other orthopaedic devices has not hindered the word becoming annexed to walking frames alone.

So 'Zimmer' now refers to any walking frame, irrespective of the manufacturer, and is developing an even wider meaning by going beyond the walking frame to include all that the walking frame implies: old age. Thus, on reaching the significant birthday of forty, a man was heard to make a jocular reference to the wrongly perceived proximity of his own old age, in the request "bring me my Zimmer". In contrast an older one, after the need for a Zimmer had become well established, once commanded "bring on the dancing girls" – equally appropriately inappropriate. Common parlance has therefore enabled the word "Zimmer" to go off on an independent frolic of its own, in a way sadly denied to the user of one.

Drawing © *C.M. Wiles*

5.16: Dancing girls

CHAPTER SIX

BEHAVIOUR

SPOONERISM

The Reverend Dr. William Archibald Spooner (1844 – 1930) was a respected, modest and much loved personality. The son of a barrister, he won a scholarship to New College, Oxford, was ordained and eventually became Dean and later Warden of the College. His physical appearance was somewhat unusual in that he was an albino with a rather pink face and white hair, an unusually large head and very short-sighted pale blue eyes. It has been said that he looked like a rabbit and that the white rabbit in Alice in Wonderland may have been modelled on him. That is certainly possible – Charles Dodgson (Lewis Carroll) was one of Spooner's colleagues at a neighbouring college and Alice herself was based on one of the daughters of the Dean at that college.

Spooner's appearance, together with his well-known tendency to transpose the initial letters of words, conjures up all too easily a classic image of the absent-minded professor. It is true that his speech and actions were sometimes a little muddled and he could come up with the wrong word altogether, for example a reference to the distance "from Land's End to John of Gaunt"(i). On another occasion he is reputed to have asked "Was it you or your brother who was killed during the war?"(ii).

199

Drawing by John Tenniel, 1865

Drawing by Leslie Ward, 1898
Courtesy Bill & Julie Bennett

6.1: The white rabbit from Alice in Wonderland

6.2: Caricature of Dr. WA Spooner, M.A.

But these idiosyncrasies were on the whole no more than a minor verbal disability that might surface at moments of stress, uncertainty or embarrassment. His intellect was highly regarded, he was a good lecturer (ancient history, divinity and philosophy) and, as Warden, ran the College most efficiently. His conversation was fluent and witty and the number of spoonerisms he is reported to have said has been grossly exaggerated. Undergraduates to whom he lectured would certainly have amused themselves by making them up and many of the more widely quoted spoonerisms – such as "Is the bean dizzy?", "The Lord is thy shoving leopard" and "Three cheers for our queer old dean" – were almost certainly not actually said by him. "The weight of rages"(iii) is one of the few examples known to be genuine. He must have found his slips of the tongue infuriating: at his final college dinner the undergraduates asked him to make a speech and he simply

200

stood up, said "You want me to say one of those things, but I shan't"(iv), and sat down.

RACHMANISM

No-one had ever heard of Rachman before the 'Profumo affair' hit the headlines. During the early 1960s John Profumo, the Secretary of State for War, admitted to having a sexual relationship with Christine Keeler, a nineteen-year-old call girl. They were both guests at a private weekend party at Cliveden and the first time he saw her was when she was emerging from the private swimming pool absolutely starkers.

Photo © User Daderot/ Wikimedia Commons

6.3: Cliveden House, Berkshire, from the lawn

The affair alone would have caused much tut-tutting but there were three aspects to it that magnified Profumo's indiscretion beyond all measure, keeping the nation riveted and the newspapers happy for weeks. So scandalous were the goings-on that in some girls' boarding schools the newspapers appeared with large pieces cut out of them by members of staff, in order that the young ladies should be shielded from such sordid details.

201

Aspect number one was that Profumo had stated in the House of Commons that there was no impropriety about the relationship. By subsequently admitting to the affair he was therefore also admitting that he had lied to the House. He had no option but to resign, and his political career was finished, although he went on to do a great deal of very worthy charitable work for which he was ultimately awarded a CBE. The events were recorded at the time in a popular limerick, one version of which went as follows:

"Oh what have you done?" said Christine.
"You've disrupted the Party machine;
To lie in the nude
Is not very rude
But to lie in the House is obscene."(v)

Aspect number two was that Keeler, at the same time and unknown to Profumo, was conducting an affair with a member of the Russian embassy who was later found to be a spy. This raised issues of national security, although there was never any suggestion that Profumo had actually passed on any information that would have been useful to a hostile country.

Aspect number three was that Keeler turned out to be connected with a number of very undesirable characters. One of these was Steven Ward, an osteopath who was a socialite and counted a number of very well known people amongst his patients. With the press digging up everything they could find out about Keeler and her associates it emerged that Ward had indulged in a multiplicity of sexual shenanigans involving two-way mirrors, call girls and friends. He was subsequently prosecuted for living off immoral earnings and after his trial committed suicide.

So where does Peter Rachman (c, 1920 – 1962) fit into the story? He was a private landlord, minding his own business – very much minding it – about whom nothing much had been known. He was born in Poland and his parents were Jewish.

Soon after the invasion of Poland both parents disappeared and he was put to work in a chain gang before being sent to a Russian labour camp. When the war ended he came to Britain and became a flat-letting agent. He could be charming and as his income increased he began to live the high life in Hampstead. He wore silk and cashmere – almost unheard of luxuries in those days – and owned several cars, including two Rolls-Royces. He died shortly before the Profumo affair came to light, whilst his activities and the source of his wealth were not yet in the public domain. But Rachman was a friend of Stephen Ward and had apparently had affairs with both Christine Keeler and another of Stephen Ward's protégées. The level of press interest in everyone even remotely connected with the Profumo affair soon brought Rachman's activities to light.

To understand how Rachman ran his business an idea of the social and legal context pertaining at the time is needed. During the 1950s most people rented rather than owned their own homes and accommodation was in very short supply. The Rent Acts gave security of tenure, at pre-war levels of rent, to tenants who were already in occupation of a property. Once the property was vacated, however, the landlord was free to re-let it at whatever rent he could get, which was of course considerably higher. The legislation therefore provided a golden opportunity for the worst type of landlords. Rachman made a fortune by buying up tenanted slums, mainly in Paddington and Notting Hill, and then making the tenants' lives so unbearable that their only option was to leave. Gas, electricity and water supplies were cut off. Doors were removed from communal lavatories. On one occasion he even took the roof off a property in order to make the sitting tenant move out. Such activities were against the law, but he operated through a complex web of companies that effectively prevented any legal action because by the time the authorities had identified the property owner prior to issuing proceedings, ownership of it would have changed, probably more than once.

Drawing © C.M.Wiles

6.4: Tenanted properties á la Rachman

As soon as a property was empty, in order to be able to extract an exorbitant rent Rachman let it to those who would otherwise find it hard to get accommodation. This might be people involved in criminal activities, or it might be those who were vulnerable because of their colour. Neither legislation nor the social attitudes of the time did anything to discourage racial discrimination and as a result Rachman was able to exploit black tenants who found it next to impossible to get anywhere to live. He would grant tenancies, but at such high rents that several families had to share a single property in order to split the rent between them. Rachman was not the only landlord to operate in this way but he was the only one whose activities were all over the newspapers. Thus the word Rachmanism, referring to the exploitation and overcrowding of tenants in slum properties by unscrupulous landlords, was born.

MAVERICK

Today the word maverick refers to someone unconventional who goes his own way regardless of what others may do or think, to such an extent that one would hesitate to rely on him. Yet Samuel Augustus Maverick (1803 – 1870) was nothing if not reliable. On his death his descendants were commanded "to remember that the name they bear has long been a synonym for honor, integrity and truth"(vi). So why the mismatch? The key to the conundrum is cattle.

Maverick was part of the old Wild West when the United States were not as united as they are now. Born in the state of South Carolina, he qualified to practise as a lawyer and had political ambitions, but in 1832 the state was involved in such a row with the US government over the taxation of imports that it was threatening to secede from the Union. Maverick did not agree with the State's policy so he emigrated to San Antonio in Texas, at that time part of Mexico.

But trouble was brewing there as well. The Mexican government had rather belatedly woken up to the fact that the American settlers far outnumbered the Mexican residents. It tried to extend its control by imposing taxes, outlawing slavery and declaring martial law. The American settlers objected, raised an army and set up their own provisional government. The Mexicans recaptured San Antonio the following spring but were not fully in control: a small band of determined Texan defenders (including Davy Crockett and Jim Bowie of 'knife' fame) were holding out at the famous fortress 'The Alamo'. Maverick was deputed to go to Washington-on-the-Brazos as a representative of the Alamo garrison with instructions to sign the Texan Declaration of Independence. He duly did so and the Republic of Texas was declared, but the new country did not last long. Within ten years it had become part of the United States.

After the establishment of independence Maverick married and returned to San Antonio, but eventually went to live with his family by the sea and purchased several hundred cattle. When he finally returned to San Antonio some three years later to resume his legal career he left the herd behind under the supervision of some of his slaves.

Photo courtesy User Baseball Bugs/ Wikimedia

6.5: The Alamo Mission in San Antonio ('The Alamo') today

Meanwhile back at the ranch ... the slaves' attitude to cattle was not as assiduous as it might have been and the calves were allowed to roam freely without being branded. After several years Maverick returned with his sons and rounded them up, but by then unbranded cattle in the area had come to be thought of as "Maverick's" and the modern meaning of the word began from there.

HOOLIGAN

There are several suggestions for the origin of the word hooligan, none of which is one hundred per cent reliable. Once coined, the word quickly became established, taking a mere ten years or so to graduate from its first use in print – in newspaper reports of 1898 drawing attention to the unacceptably high levels of street crime in South East London – to books by authors such as Conan Doyle and H.G. Wells. The word clearly filled a lacuna in the language. The two most likely versions of the origin of the word share the common themes of Irish and Southwark.

An early suggestion by the dictionary was that the word might derive from the name of an Irish family by the name of Hooligan who lived in Southwark during the 1890s and were notorious for riotous behaviour. Later editions suggested additional alternative derivations, including the possibility that the word may derive from Hooley's gang or from a music hall song about a (fictional) rowdy Irish family. Another source(vii) puts forward a certain Patrick Hooligan (or Houlihan), who came to Southwark from Limerick some time during the 1850s – 1870s. He apparently took on a job as a bouncer and gradually collected together a gang that used to drink at a pub in Borough High Street called the Lamb and Flag. They were a rowdy lot and went about mugging people, vandalising the area and getting involved in street fights. During one of these fights Patrick killed a policeman, was convicted and died in prison while serving his life sentence.

TEDDY BOY

Immediate post war Britain was tired. The country was economically drained, there were food shortages and power cuts. Rationing was to remain in place for several years. There was a desperate shortage of housing. The standard working week was 48 hours. All male eighteen year olds had to serve two years' national service on active duty in the armed forces. There was no distinctive youth culture and adolescents dressed in the same way as their parents. Until the teddy boys.

The efforts of tailoring firms catering for their upper-class clientèle to re-introduce men's suits based on the style popular during the reign of Edward VII (born 1841, reigned 1901 – 1910) had an unexpected effect. This 'new Edwardian' look became adopted by gangs of young working class men, first in London and then across the country. As the look gained in popularity the clothing became mass produced and more exaggerated. The essentials were a dark frock-coat (preferably with a velvet collar), high-waisted drain-pipe trousers, a high-necked shirt and collar, pencil thin tie, brightly coloured socks and either brogues or large, suede crêpe-soled shoes that became known colloquially as brothel-creepers. An essential part of the overall look was the hairstyle: greased and combed back into a quiff in front, with the sides greased and combed back into a 'DA' (duck's arse) at the nape of the neck.

Photo © User Alchemica/
Wikimedia Commons

6.6: 'Brothel creepers'

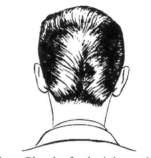

© User Charlesfrederickworth/
Wikimedia Commons

6.7: The 'DA'

Teddy boys were generally regarded as aggressive and had a bad reputation. There was a fair amount of gang warfare between them involving knife fights. In September 1953 the Daily Express, using a common nickname for Edward, referred to these 'new Edwardians' as Teddy boys, and the name stuck.

SLOANE RANGER

It is much easier to recognise Sloane Rangers than to define them. Originally the essentials for qualification as a Sloane were to be well spoken, preferably educated at a well-known private school, and to have an upper class background with enough money to live in a *des res* in West London without feeling the pinch. To this add supreme self-confidence not necessarily matched by academic ability and you begin to get the idea. A love of country sports helps, with green wellies *de rigueur*. The concept of Sloanes as an identifiable group dates from the 1970s and the phrase was probably originally coined

208

by one of the editors of Harper & Queen's before being elaborated in The Official Sloane Ranger Handbook(viii). It combined the name of the popular cowboys and Indians TV series 'The Lone Ranger' (with a hearty 'Heigh-ho Silver' for those who remember it) on to which was grafted a reference to London's Sloane Square, the central haunt of Sloanes at that time.

Photo © C.M.Wiles

6.8: (Green) Wellies with a boot remover

The Square itself was named after Sir Hans Sloane (1660 – 1753), but he was a man whose interests were certainly too intellectual to be a Sloane Ranger himself. His enquiring mind, his methodical approach and above all his diligence, took him far. By the end of his life he had become the personal physician of the monarch and president of both the Royal College of Physicians in London and the Royal Society.

Born in Ireland, as a young man he moved to London to study medicine. At that time botany was still an integral part of medical studies and he visited the newly established Chelsea Physic Garden, created by The Society of Apothecaries for the training of apprentice apothecaries in the recognition and uses of medicinal plants. Sloane then went to Montpelier to further his medical studies. When offered the post of personal physician to the new governor of Jamaica he accepted, feeling that studying medicinal plants in their natural habitat would enable him to understand more about them. The governor died just over a year later and Sloane returned to England with a huge collection of plants and other things that he had amassed whilst in the West Indies.

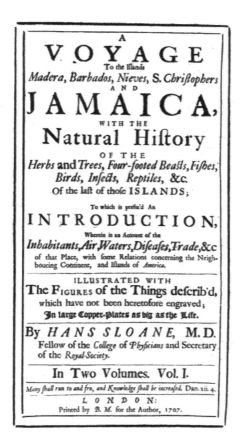

6.9:
The title page of Volume 1 of Sloane's flora and fauna of the West Indies, first published in 1707

Courtesy the Biodiversity Heritage Library and Missouri Botanical Garden, Peter H. Raven Library

He continued to collect throughout his life, buying up the collections of others when the opportunity arose, including a large number of seeds and fruits from a collector rejoicing in the appropriate name of Nehemiah Grew. As Sloane's collection expanded, so did the issue of where to keep it. An advantageous marriage eventually helped him to solve the problem by the simple expedient of staying where he was and buying the house next door. Financial security also helped

Sloane to establish a successful medical practice that included a free surgery in the mornings for those unable to pay fees. He wrote a treatise on the flora, fauna and other aspects of the West Indian islands that he had visited.

In 1720 representatives of the Apothecaries were present during the debate on a Physicians' Bill in the House of Lords, arguing that they alone were the experts on drugs and that the physicians, by contrast, knew nothing. This was an unwise assertion because Sloane was also there, representing the Royal College of Physicians. He countered, no doubt quite rightly, that he could show them hundreds of medicinal plants of which they knew nothing. More than that, Sloane was the Apothecaries' landlord, having bought the freehold of the manor of Chelsea, including the Physic Garden, some years before. Fortunately for them, Sloane's good nature was not affected by this crossing of swords. His appreciation of the fundamental importance of plants in treating illness led him, only two years later, to protect the Physic Garden by leasing it in perpetuity to the Society of Apothecaries. In return the Society was to pay an annual rent of five pounds and donate to the Royal Society dried specimens of fifty new plants every year until an overall total of 2,000 had been supplied.

SMART ALEC

A smart Alec could well be described as a clever Dick, but whereas there is no suggestion that the name Dick refers to someone in particular, there is every likelihood that the name Alec does. A certain Aleck Hoag who lived in New York in the mid 19th Century became well known for being too clever by half in the disreputable sort of way that would make him well qualified to be the smart Aleck prototype.

Aleck Hoag was a pimp and he and his partner Melinda were well organised when it came to fleecing the unwary. Initially they ran a racket, with the connivance of the local police, whereby Melinda would lure a man into a dark alleyway and while he was busy concentrating on the job in hand, so to speak, she would pick his pockets. With her arms around his neck she would then hold out behind his head whatever valuables she had found for Aleck to take them from her as he passed by. The police were useful in providing protection and, in the event of a formal complaint of theft, could arrange for the missing items to be discreetly returned to the victim's pockets – no doubt leaving him very puzzled at his apparent mistake.

However, Aleck became greedy and resented having to share his 'earnings'. He wanted to cut the New York police out of the deal, but soon found that they were harder to dupe than Melinda's clients. His new tactics required Melinda to conduct her activities beside a cemetery wall, dropping the valuables over it to where Aleck lay in wait ready to collect them. It was not long before the police found out what was going on and they were none too pleased at being left out of the scam. They insisted on a return to the former arrangements and Aleck had to think again. He realised that operating anywhere in the open air ran a high risk that he would soon be found out again, so he decided to become a 'panel thief'. In order to do this he rented two adjoining rooms, installing a curtained bed for Melinda in one room and a removable panel in the wall linking that room with the one next to it. Melinda would get her client to leave his clothes on a chair near the panel and, once in bed with him, drew the curtains round the bed. As soon as he was fully engrossed in his activities she would cough to alert Aleck waiting next door. He would come quietly into the room through the panel and, after rifling the punter's pockets, return through the panel again. He would

then go round to hammer on the door to Melinda's room in the guise of her irate husband suddenly returning home and demanding entry. Melinda would help her visitor get dressed and escape through the window in a rush before her apparent husband could break open the door, and also before her victim had had time to realise that he had been robbed.

The problem with this idea was that the visitor knew where Melinda's room was. It took only one disgruntled man, not too embarrassed to report the robbery to the police, for Aleck and

Melinda to be back where they started. But this time the police had run out of patience and decided that there was no future in continuing to co-operate with them. Melinda and Aleck were both sent to prison and there is every possibility that talk of his activities, both within and later outside the police force, led to the adoption of his name in the celebrated phrase.

DUNCE

Courtesy Research Group John Duns Scotus, Utrecht

6.10: John Duns Scotus as painted by Justus van Gent in the 15th Century

How the mighty are fallen... John Duns Scotus (?1265/70 – 1308) was an erudite scholar, theologian and philosopher. After being ordained he studied and lectured in Oxford, Paris and Cologne as well as writing numerous commentaries and treatises. He established a school of theology, much of which was based on the philosophy of Aristotle and which rejected the teaching of Thomas Aquinas. But few now have heard of him and the word that comes from his name has become used to refer to those with an IQ at the opposite end of the scale.

It is generally accepted that Scotus was born in the village of Duns in Scotland. He lived before a formal system of surnames had become established: the second and third names by which he was known identified him through his place, rather than his family, of origin. He was also referred to as Doctor Subtilis (the subtle doctor) because of his arcane philosophical and religious arguments. Much of his teaching is incomprehensible to the layman and the average mortal would be ill advised to attempt to follow the hair-splitting nuances of his theological discussions. But the importance of some of his conclusions can be readily appreciated: for example, it was his analysis that convinced the Roman Catholic Church to embrace the doctrine of the Immaculate Conception.

Drawing © C.M. Wiles

6.11: In disgrace

The teachings of John Duns Scotus gradually fell out of favour, perhaps because few of those who embraced them were blessed with an intellect commensurate with that of his own. The Dunsmen, or Dunses as they were called, appear to have proved unequal to the challenge of explaining and clarifying his complex teachings, let alone developing them any further. Thomas Aquinas came back into theological fashion and the word Duns, or Dunce, began to be applied to anyone whose reasoning was founded on old-fashioned, over-precise distinctions of dubious validity. The meaning then extended to encompass those unwilling to accept new ideas and ultimately came to be used for anyone lacking in understanding or who was just plain stupid.

During the last century John Duns Scotus enjoyed something of a revival and he was beatified in the 1990s. Academic theologians who study and accept his teachings are now (understandably) referred to as Scotists rather than either of the previously acceptable alternatives.

SILLY BILLY

Today the phrase Silly Billy sounds positively humdrum and is used light-heartedly to refer to anyone of either sex who behaves in a silly way. But the origin of the term is of the highest – indeed royal – pedigree, and the temptation of such a punchy rhyme resulted in both a nephew and a son of George III having to put up with the disparaging soubriquet.

A quick scamper through the Hanoverian family tree will set the scene. Long before Christine Keeler was heard of, Cliveden played its part in history as the home of Frederick Louis, Prince of Wales and eldest son of George II. Frederick predeceased his father and had been on such bad terms with him that his father did not even go to Frederick's funeral. On George II's death in 1760 the Crown passed directly to Frederick's eldest son, who became George III.

Frederick's offspring had a marked penchant for contracting unsuitable marriages, plus a confusing desire to name their sons William or George. George III himself only complied with the latter tendency, but the secret marriage of his brother Henry Frederick Duke of Cumberland to a woman who was a commoner persuaded George that in future he simply had to have more control over formal family relationships. The Royal Marriage Act 1772 was therefore enacted, which prohibited all male descendants of George II from marrying without the consent of the sovereign. This did not go down well with George III's siblings.

One unexpected effect of the 1772 Act was that another brother, William Henry, Duke of Gloucester, now admitted that he also had already been secretly married. This made him persona non grata and although it was eventually accepted that his marriage was valid he felt obliged to leave the country for a time. It was his son, William Frederick (1776 – 1834), said to have been somewhat intellectually challenged, who was first up for the Silly Billy nickname.

Next up was one of George III's own sons, another William (1765 – 1837), who was created Duke of Clarence and was subsequently crowned William IV. This William had a career in the Navy (entering as a midshipman and rising to the rank of rear admiral) and was highly spoken of by Nelson. As well as being called Silly Billy (though it is not clear exactly why), he was also referred to as the Sailor King. He lived for many years with Mrs. Jordan, an actress, and together they had ten children, but with the 1772 Act in force there was no question of a valid marriage.

Photo © C.M. Wiles

6.12: A groat from the reign of William IV (diameter 1.5 cm)

That deals with the Silly Billy contenders, but the catalogue of royal marriage problems continued. Another of George III's sons, the Duke of Sussex, 'married' twice, on neither occasion with the required consent, so both marriages were invalid.

George III's eldest son (later George IV) also secretly went through a form of marriage with a Mrs. Fitzherbert, again after the 1772 Act, leaving the several children resulting from it illegitimate and also leaving him available to marry one of his European cousins later on (see Brougham in Chapter Three).

Unfortunately George IV's socially acceptable bride turned out to be totally unacceptable at a personal level and in consequence the marriage produced only one child – a daughter. When she died childless at the age of 22, the royal succession was in crisis. Younger brother William (the second Silly Billy contender) was persuaded to do his duty to fill the breach by leaving his actress and marrying a young European princess. The marriage was apparently successful in that they were reasonably happy together, but unfit for purpose in that it failed to produce any offspring who survived beyond childhood.

NAMBY-PAMBY

You have to feel rather sorry for poor old Ambrose Philips (c.1674 – 1749). He seems to have been a bit of a plodder and his nickname Namby Pamby was coined essentially as a term of abuse. He did have some successes: he used to be a well-known poet and even today he merits the odd entry in the Oxford Dictionary of Quotations. But more frequently success escaped him. He set up and edited a well-regarded magazine called The Freethinker, but after 350 issues it closed down. His play 'The Distrest Mother' did well in its time, although it was mainly a translation of a work by Racine. His two subsequent plays then sank without trace and were described by Samuel Johnson as "not below mediocrity, nor above it"(ix). Philips did not struggle financially: although not wealthy his friends and patrons saw to it that he always had an income – at various times he was a tutor to royalty, a personal secretary to a prominent political figure, the paymaster of the lottery, the purse bearer to the lord chancellor, an MP in the Irish Parliament, and a judge.

Philips had the great misfortune to fall out with Alexander Pope, a controversial figure considered the leading poet of the day, who had a spectacular ability to write malicious satire. He must have made Philips' life a misery. Their mutual loathing, described as "a perpetual reciprocation of malevolence"(ix) (Samuel Johnson again), was sparked following the publication of their respective Pastoral poems in a single issue of a popular literary magazine. Philips adopted a simple, romanticised approach; Pope by contrast sought to write with elegance. Philip's efforts were eulogised, but Pope's were ignored. In order to get his own back Pope published anonymously a letter, on the face of it praising Philips' work, but beneath the surface bringing attention to the superior quality of his own. Philips could not compete with Pope's wit and was said to be so upset that he hung up a rod in a local coffee house, threatening to hit Pope with it. Pope kept out of the way for a time and Philips never had the chance to use it.

Thus the scene was set for battle in the literary world. Philips wrote a series of poems adopting a new style of such simplicity and sentimentality that today they seem more appropriate to a Victorian greetings card than to serious poetry. The beginning of one such poem sets the tone:

> "Timely blossom, Infant fair,
> Fondling of a happy pair,
> Every morn and every night
> Their solicitous delight.
> Sleeping, waking, still at ease,
> Pleasing, without skill to please;
> Little gossip, blithe and hale,
> Tattling many a broken tale,
> Singing many a tuneless song,
> Lavish of a heedless tongue; ..."(x)

Wording like this was a gift to those such as Pope and before long one of his friends published a satire, establishing the nickname for Philips that now forms part of the English language. It was headed "Namby Pamby: or, a panegyrick on the new versification address'd to A---- P---- ":

> All ye poets of the age!
> All ye witlings of the stage!
> Learn your jingles to reform!
> Crop your numbers and conform:
> Let your little verses flow
> Gently, sweetly, row by row:
> Let the verse the subject fit;
> Little subject, little wit.
> Namby Pamby is your guide;
> Albion's joy, Hibernia's pride.(xi)

Photo © Brown University USA

6.13: Title page of the Dunciad (2nd edition, 1729)

Astonishingly, critics who had supported Philips' new style of poetry also praised the parody for the same reason – its simplicity. Other parodies were published by a whole variety of writers across the country and although (mercifully) Philips had by then moved to Ireland, the situation deteriorated still further. Pope published anonymously a major parody of

219

Virgil's Aeneid, called The Dunciad, in which the goddess Dulness conducts a war against reason and light. She claims control over poetry and indicates the initials of selected poets (including Philips), referred to collectively as Dunces, as her loyal subjects writing dreary, tasteless works in support of her mission to spread dullness throughout Britain.

Philips wisely followed the advice encapsulated in the modern saying "if you can't stand the heat keep out of the kitchen" by staying in Ireland. He did not return to London until some four years after Pope's death.

CHAUVINIST

Although some have expressed doubts as to whether there really was a soldier in the French army named Nicolas Chauvin (c. 1790 - ?), several authoritative sources indicate that he did exist, that he fought courageously and was frequently wounded. His war record was such that Napoleon apparently presented him with an award and a modest pension. So far so good. But even after leaving the army Chauvin remained fiercely loyal to Napoleon. When such opinions fell somewhat out of fashion during the post-Napoleonic War years he was mocked for his out-dated attitudes. The popular theatre adopted his name and exaggerated his character, most notably when 'he' featured as a somewhat ludicrously overpatriotic young recruit in a vaudeville play(xii). His true persona subsequently became hijacked by the theatrical, extreme version.

The French word *chauvinisme* soon followed and it was not long before it found its way into English. It did so only very shortly after another word with a not dissimilar meaning – jingoism – the roots of which also derive from popular culture but this time from an English music-hall song, sung by one G.H. Macdermott. It enthusiastically embraced the British government's decision to support Turkey in the Turco-Russian war of 1877-8 by sending the Royal Navy to what was then called Constantinople. There were two verses, and after each came the chorus – the lack of rhythm in the last line making the point most forcefully and must surely have been shouted with audience participation:

> We don't want to fight, but by jingo if we do,
> We've got the ships, we've got the men, we've got the
>   money too.
> We've fought the Bear before, and while we're Britons
>   true,
> The Russians shall not have Constantinople."(xiii)

The success of the song makes one feel that had Chauvin been English rather than French he would never have been made to feel out of place.   Interestingly, while the word jingoism has remained static and the concepts it promotes have become regarded as almost archaic, chauvinism has moved with the times and the concept of chauvinism is now often referred to in the context of 'male' and 'pig'.

MARTINET

In centuries gone by armies were often something of a rabble. Jean Martinet (? – 1672) was the inspector general of Louis XIV's infantry and his approach to discipline transformed the French army into the best in Europe. Endless drilling and practice produced a body of men who could do what they were told, who could fire, recharge, reload – a time consuming business with muskets – and fire again at speed. Those commanding it were for the first time able to rely on orders being properly carried out. History is full of the names of successful commanders but even the most brilliant tactics in the world are of no use unless orders can be carried out effectively. The work of Martinet is forgotten, but it was he who was the founder of modern European military discipline that has played a crucial part in military battles ever since.

The art of waging war was fundamentally changed by Martinet in two other ways. He invented the bayonet, thereby doing away with the need for a separate troop of pike men to protect those firing muskets while they reloaded.   He also introduced the depot system for the provision of food supplies, abolishing the need for soldiers to spend time (and upset the locals by) foraging.

Despite having no place in the history books Martinet has the edge over most commanders in that his name is remembered through the English word meaning a strict disciplinarian. It was first used in this sense in England rather than in France, but that may be because in French the word already had its own meaning of a whip – a whip somewhat akin to a more merciful version of the cat o' nine tails, apparently used to bring wayward children into line. It is not clear when the French meaning of the word originated. If it predated the birth of Martinet one might speculate whether his surname played some part in the development of his passion for discipline since if the cap fits, the well-known saying advises one to put it on.

Photo © User Shattonbury/ Wikimedia Commons

6.14: 'Un martinet' (modern)

It can be imagined how popular a man such as Martinet would have been with the troops he was training. He died after he was shot from behind when leading his highly disciplined infantrymen into battle... could it really have been an accident?

DRACONIAN

In ancient times the administration of justice in Athens was a matter for the king, who had supreme power. Consideration of such issues as fairness or consistency was an inconvenience with which he had no need to concern himself. When the hereditary monarchy was abolished, the power of the king was devolved to the nobles, but although part of their job was to record the laws, the arbitrary nature of the legal system was largely unchanged. So the codification of Athenian law by Draco in 621 B.C. was a great step forward in that it limited the personal power of the rulers and gave the people of Athens the security of knowing what was within and what was against the law.

But such security alone is not enough to render a legal system acceptable. Draco had become so carried away when stipulating the appropriate punishment for each offence that the death penalty was to apply in almost all cases, driving the later orator Demades to comment that Draco's laws had been written in blood, not in ink. Fortunately this situation did not last long. Within a few years the statesman Solon had repealed virtually all Draco's laws except those relating to murder, and replaced them with something more humane.

SADIST

In 1763 a certain wealthy French magistrate arranged for his daughter to marry a young nobleman. The young man was not very well off, but to the magistrate money was not an issue since he already had plenty to spare. The particular attraction of the prospective son-in-law was that he came from a family with an enviable social status: his father had a title and his mother a position at court. No doubt the magistrate felt rather satisfied that he had found an advantageous match, but he had not done his homework. The young man in question was Donatien Alphonse Francois, Comte de Sade (1740 – 1814), now more usually known as the Marquis de Sade, and he was already showing proclivities most undesirable in either a son-in-law or a husband.

De Sade was born in Paris and sent at a young age to the family estate in Provence to be brought up by relatives. He subsequently attended a Jesuit school and then joined the army, but by the age of twenty-three had returned to civilian life. Despite his wish to marry the girl of his choice, he obediently married the magistrate's daughter as arranged and in due course they produced three children. But he showed no sign of settling down. He had his eye – more than his eye – on his wife's sister and it was also not long before he had an established mistress. He indulged himself with prostitutes, some of whom complained of ill-treatment which brought him to the attention of the police. This behaviour did nothing to endear him to his mother-in-law, who proved a woman to be reckoned with. Her fury and financial situation were such that on several occasions she was able to arrange for his arrest and temporary imprisonment. It must have been hoped that he would benefit from the experience and emerge a reformed character. No such luck.

The extent to which de Sade oscillated in and out of prison throughout his life is scarcely believable. His next arrest followed a complaint by a woman that he had stripped her naked and beaten her against her will. He alleged that she had agreed to it, and she was later persuaded to drop the charges by the offer of a suitable sum of money. He was released, but three years later he was again in prison, this time for non-payment of debts.

By 1772 the situation had become more serious. De Sade was accused of sodomy and poisoning after an evening's entertainment at which he had given several prostitutes sweets adulterated with Spanish fly, a substance that acts as an aphrodisiac in tiny doses but is dangerous in slightly larger quantities. He fled to Savoy where his mother-in-law's money and influence were again able to procure his imprisonment. In the meantime de Sade was tried in his absence at Aix-en-Provence in respect of the accusations against him and was sentenced to death. Before long he had escaped from prison in Savoy and returned to France but, after complaints of more scandalous behaviour involving a group of his servants, he fled back to Savoy, this time with his sister-in-law.

Five years later de Sade was back in Paris. Re-enter the

enraged mother-in-law. In those days there was a perfect answer available for those seriously upset by a relative, or anyone else if it came to it, provided they had enough money. De Sade's mother-in-law did. With it she bought a *lettre de cachet*: a royal warrant signed on behalf of the king, authorising the arrest and imprisonment of a person without the need for any awkward formalities such as a trial. The holder of the *lettre de cachet* merely had to fill in the name of the person to be imprisoned and meet the cost of the ensuing prison accommodation. De Sade was accordingly imprisoned and sent to Aix-en-Provence for retrial (to save the family the shame of having a relation with a criminal record) where he was found not guilty and merely warned to avoid debauchery in future. After a brief escape he was returned to Paris under guard, since the *lettre de cachet* was still extant.

Photo © User Franco christophe/Wikimedia Commons

6.15: The emerald green Lytta vesicatoria (Spanish fly, or blister beetle)

De Sade remained in prison for the next twelve years and so found himself with plenty of time for writing about his philosophy: freedom to pursue personal pleasure without regard to the law, to religion or to moral scruples. He was held first in Vincennes prison, then the Bastille and finally, after an angry outburst, in a secure mental hospital at Charenton.

These years were spent in custody solely by virtue of the *lettre de cachet*: nothing more than the say so of the king. However, with the coming of the French Revolution royal commands no longer had quite the same authority and in 1790 he was released. But the Revolution also had implications for the aristocracy and their assets: de Sade was now impoverished. He began what proved to be a permanent but probably non-sexual relationship with an actress, Mme Quesnet, and they set up home together in a modest way. As Citizen Sade he continued his writing and obtained an official post as an inspector of hospitals. For a time he stayed out of trouble, although he was mistakenly arrested and imprisoned for a year as he was thought to have been an émigré. It seems that twice during this spell in prison he narrowly escaped the guillotine, once because he had been moved to another prison and so could not be found, and on a second occasion because of an incorrect spelling of his name which resulted in the unfortunate Marquis de Salle being executed by mistake.

Photo © User Selbymay/ Wikimedia Commons

6.16: Vincennes Prison: the château today

When Napoleon came to power he considered de Sade's books so objectionable and obscene as to be unlawful. De Sade was arrested, but apparently never brought to trial – perhaps on the basis that it would have brought his books publicity. Instead he was declared insane and, after a short time in various prisons, he spent the last twelve years of his life back in the secure mental hospital at Charenton, his family meeting the cost of his board and lodging. Mme Quesnet was permitted to stay with him. On de Sade's death all his written work of these last years was destroyed on the instructions of his surviving son.

MASOCHIST

The unusual desires of Leopold Ritter von Sacher-Masoch (1836 – 1895) began when he was a child. An early sign was the unusual enjoyment he apparently derived from looking at pictures depicting cruelty, such as the martyrdom of saints. When playing hide and seek at the age of ten, he witnessed an incident involving his aunt, her furs, her lover and her effective use of a whip on her irate husband who caught them in the bedroom. His aunt, having masterfully dealt with this situation, then turned on Leopold, whose presence had by now been revealed, and whipped him. He is reported to have felt a strange satisfaction from the pain, followed by a fascination in seeing his uncle humbly return to the bedroom to beg forgiveness and accept further chastisement.

Leopold trained in the law but after graduating took up a career as a novelist. He had various sexual relationships of a sado-masochistic nature before falling in love with a woman who, so he convinced himself, was a member of the aristocracy in disguise. She went along with his pretence and they married, but in time it became clear that they were not well suited and he had to accept that his aristocratic imaginings had no basis in truth. And instead of being a woman who would dominate him, his wife was reluctant to inflict the regular whippings he craved and without which he found himself unable to pursue his writing. The marriage deteriorated further when Leopold's desire for a powerful, dominating wife led him to insist that she be unfaithful. He set up what were in his view appropriate arrangements, but this became too much for her to accept and they separated. In other ways Leopold appears to have been a kind, caring and considerate man and he subsequently developed a relationship with another woman and settled down with her. Ultimately his mental health deteriorated and he died in 1895, although it has been suggested that he in fact died ten years later after being discreetly moved to a mental asylum.

'Venus in Furs', Leopold's most well known novel, was partly autobiographical and harks back to the childhood incident involving his aunt, as well as reflecting some of his subsequent behaviour. It describes a relationship in which the main character seeks to be enslaved and whipped by his female partner. Furs feature prominently. The book must have made him something of a legend in his own lifetime since before he died the word masochism (as well as the associated word sadism) was already being used by an eminent Austrian psychiatrist in an academic study of sexual perversions(xiv).

LYNCH

The emotions invoked by the subject of lynching are encapsulated by the voice of Billie Holiday in the opening lines of the song 'Strange Fruit':

> Southern trees bear a strange fruit
> Blood on the leaves, blood at the root
> Black bodies swinging in the Southern breeze
> Strange fruit hanging from the poplar trees"(xv)

The history of lynching in the United States makes grim reading:

a) The illegality. Victims had no lawful trial. Although the perpetrators were frequently well known to the authorities, inadequacies in the legal system meant that they were seldom brought to justice. In 1932, 1937 and 1940 the House of Representatives passed anti-lynching legislation but on each occasion it failed to get through the Senate. For years such do-it-yourself administration of justice seems almost to have been regarded by the authorities as acceptable rather than murder. Those involved in carrying it out clearly felt that they did so for the benefit of the local community, and indeed were respected for it by many.

b) Its sadistic nature. Victims were often partially burnt or dismembered before being hanged, with body parts not infrequently being retained by onlookers as a keepsake.

c) The racism. About three-quarters of those who died were black. There were only four states in which no lynchings at all are recorded, but after the American Civil War most lynchings were concentrated in the Southern States and were often used as a means of intimidating the newly emancipated slaves in order to prevent them from exercising their rights.

d) The numbers involved. Records from 1882 onwards, collated mainly from postcards and newspaper articles (since administration of such so-called justice was by definition unofficial), show that well over four thousand people were killed in this way. To that number needs to be added those killings for which no documentary evidence has come to light, plus those that took place before 1882.

e) How recent it was. Lynchings by that name began in the late 1700s, but records continue up to 1968 when the Civil Rights Act finally made it possible to prosecute those involved in carrying out such crimes. And although during the twentieth century the trend was markedly downward, there was a recrudescence of lynchings during the 1920s and 1930s.

f) The party atmosphere. Photographers frequently attended and made good money selling their photographs, often as souvenirs or to use as postcards, to others who had also been there. These visual records are positively obscene, showing not only the victim but also the crowd – scores of people including women and children, excited and smiling, enjoying the event. But to put it in some sort of perspective one needs to be aware that official hangings also used to take place in public, attended by throngs of smiling spectators, until 1867 in England and 1936 in the US.

"A prospective scene in the City of Oaks, 4th March 1869"
Independent Monitor, Tuscaloosa, Alabama

6.17: Cartoon threatening that the Ku Klux Klan would lynch carpetbaggers, 1868

So who was Lynch? Most sources now opt for William Lynch (1742 – 1820). He was a plantation owner who lived in Pittsylvania County, Virginia, at a time when it was isolated and far away from the forces of law and order. To prevent illegal activity in the locality he drew up a written compact in 1780 with his neighbours for dealing with criminals without due process of law. Under the compact the signatories agreed that wrongdoers should first be warned to stop their illegal activities and then "if they will not desist from their evil practices, we will inflict such corporeal punishment on him or them, as to us shall seem adequate to the crime committed or the damage sustained"(xvi). Under Lynch's law, or Lynch law as it came to be called, the punishment was usually limited to beating or tarring and feathering; it was only later that the

230

word became specifically associated with mob rule and hanging or other forms of murder.

Taking the law into one's own hands was obviously not as unusual in Virginia then as one might have thought. Other sources come down in favour not of William but of Charles Lynch (1736 – 96), the son of Quaker immigrants from Ireland. He, too, was a prominent citizen in his locality and, with a band of like-minded neighbours took unofficial legal action. Civil disruption from a lawless crowd had threatened revolt and he, with others, took action against the leaders. In the words of the subsequent Act of Indemnity they "did by timely and effectual measures suppress such conspiracies by measures not strictly warranted by law, although justifiable from the imminence of the danger."(xvii). The timely measures included holding unofficial trials at which the accused were sentenced to whipping and conscription, but there was no question of capital punishment.

CASANOVA

Even today a life spent living between Venice, Rome, Corfu, Istanbul, Paris, London, Berlin, Riga, St. Petersburg, Warsaw, Vienna, Madrid, and Prague plus numerous other towns and cities across Europe would qualify a person as being exceptionally well-travelled. In the eighteenth century, with appalling roads and relying on ships and horse power alone, it must have been astonishing. But Giacomo Girolamo Casanova de Seingalt (1725 – 1798), who undertook all these travels, was not your average man.

The behaviour for which Casanova's name remains synonymous two hundred years after his death is simply that of a ladies' man. Even his pursuit of a career in the church did nothing to dampen his pursuit of women. But to remember Casanova simply as a libertine, even if an outrageously successful one, is to ignore the rest of his extraordinary life to which his sexual activities form little more than a colourful backdrop.

Casanova was the son of an actor, but was brought up by his grandmother who provided him with an education that enabled him to pass the necessary examinations to enter training for the priesthood. It was not long before a number of young women had succumbed to his approaches and the church authorities threw him out for scandalous behaviour. On being given a second chance Casanova secured a post in Rome in the service of the Spanish Ambassador to the Vatican and seemed well on the way to a respectable career, but scandal again intervened and he was dismissed.

By the age of twenty-one Casanova was in Venice, reduced to earning his living by playing the violin in an orchestra. His musical career lasted for even less time than his calling to the priesthood. Casanova was the ultimate Mr. Charming and he used what would now be called his 'interpersonal skills' to befriend a nobleman interested in the occult. He took charge of the nobleman's medical treatment with such success that the nobleman came to believe Casanova was blest with supernatural powers. Casanova was invited to join the nobleman's household and for some years lived almost as a son, on a comfortable allowance and travelling widely. The end result was that by the time he was thirty years old the authorities, perhaps suspicious that his extensive travels and close friendships with foreign ambassadors might indicate he was a spy, chose to take a more literal view of his charms. Casanova was arrested, found guilty of practising magic and committed to five years imprisonment in the Piombi – the uncomfortable cells, hot in summer and cold in winter, immediately under the lead roof of the Doge's Palace. Any chance of escape was notoriously slender, but after a year Casanova succeeded. Having found his way out on to the roof he re-entered the building via an attic, went down the main stairway and, again using his charm to good effect, convinced the guard at the door that he had been visiting the Palace on some official purpose and so was permitted to leave.

Casanova fled to Paris where he set up the state lottery, amassed a fortune and dined out in high society on the story of his escape. He took to travelling again and moved in the highest circles. The Pope awarded him the Order of the Golden Spur and he was received by both Russian and Polish royalty. He used his social contacts to obtain various administrative and political posts, but much of his funding was provided by a swindle in which he convinced a very wealthy, very gullible, woman that he could arrange for her rebirth as a man. Over a period of seven years he persuaded her to part with huge sums of money.

Photo © Ignazio Marconi

6.18: One of the Piombi prison cells, Doge's Palace

At the other end of the scale Casanova consorted with prostitutes, fraudsters and gamblers. Despite his charm – or perhaps sometimes because of it – he often found himself *persona non grata*. Over a period of fifteen years he was imprisoned in Paris for suspected fraud, imprisoned in Stuttgart for debt, expelled from Florence and Turin, left England because of a threatened prosecution for the non-payment of debts, fled from Poland after a scandal involving a duel, was forced to leave Vienna for contravening the laws against gambling, had to leave France in a hurry to avoid a *lettre de cachet*, was imprisoned in Barcelona, and expelled from Florence again for involvement in false bills of exchange.

Photo © User Zacatecnik/ Wikimedia Commons

6.19: Duchcov (Dux) castle in Duchcov, Bohemia

By 1774 Casanova was finally allowed to return to Venice and for eight years he worked for the state as a spy. When scandal again erupted, this time because of allegations of libel, he had to leave. Another change in career was called for and by now he seems to have been ready to settle down. He went to Bohemia where, again through a personal contact, he became the librarian at the Duchcov chateau, staying there until his death in 1798. This allowed him time to write his memoirs – and he clearly needed a great deal of time, since the written record of his eventful life extended to twelve volumes.

MACHIAVELLIAN

After being stuck for some two hundred years with a reputation for little more than devious cynicism, Niccolo Machiavelli (1469 – 1527) emerged into the light. He is now regarded as a brilliant political philosopher and the creator of modern political theory. But the description 'Machiavellian' still retains its duplicitous 'wheels within wheels' implication. The Prince, Machiavelli's most well known work, sets out his thinking on how states should be governed. That thinking was informed by his wide knowledge of politics and political systems, both historical and contemporary.

© User MapMaster/ Wikimedia Commons

6.20: The Italian States in 1494

The cynical view of human nature that forms the basis of Machiavelli's work reflected the world in which he lived. Corruption was rife, the threat of foreign invasion ever present, and there was continual jostling for power between all the individual Italian states. Insecurity hindered the development of culture and commerce. The priority in Machiavelli's political philosophy was therefore the establishment of stability and he expresses the very reasonable theory that an orderly, well-governed state is of benefit both to itself, in terms of maximising its own power, and to its people, who are enabled

235

to live in security. The prince of such a state must be perceived as setting a good example and being fair and compassionate in his dealings with his subjects. Where Machiavelli differs from modern attitudes is in the development of this theory. The role of his Prince is to present a velvet glove over an iron fist, hiding the reality of what needs to be done for the achievement of strong government. Machiavelli argues that moral scruples must, if necessary, be sacrificed and even religion might be used as a tool of power.

Machiavelli's philosophy markedly contrasts with the personality and behaviour of the man himself. He was by all accounts a generous, passionate person and something of an idealist, with a longing for an incorrupt society and a united Italy. He was born in Florence during the reign of the Medici family. By 1498 the Medicis had been deposed and the state of Florence had become a republic. Machiavelli was appointed to an important post and his involvement in foreign affairs resulted in him being sent abroad on various diplomatic missions. Foremost among these were two visits to Cesare Borgia, the ruthless and cunning ruler of a nearby state who within a short space of time had built up his own power base and was well on the way to expanding his state at the expense its neighbours. Machiavelli was impressed with the efficacy of Borgia's methods and his later political theory reflects this.

Machiavelli also undertook the re-organisation of the military defence of Florence, pressing for new laws that would allow the creation of a militia composed of native Florentines instead of relying on mercenaries. The new militia was successful in dealing with local squabbles between the Italian states, but then war between France and the pope's Holy League threatened. The republic of Florence was tiny compared with the two warring factions. Machiavelli's negotiations to try and keep Florence out of the argument were unsuccessful. Following invasion by the French, the Medici family was restored to power in 1512 and Machiavelli found himself out of a job.

Things went from bad to worse. He was suspected of being involved in a plot and was subjected to torture in order to extract a confession. He maintained his innocence and was released, but remained subject to certain restrictions on his liberty. The impoverished Machiavelli decided to retire to the country to concentrate on writing.

Desperate to earn a living and in the hope of getting another government appointment Machiavelli dedicated The Prince, his book of political theory for achieving a united Italy, to Lorenzo de Medici. This hope was only partly fulfilled. He was not able to return to the circles of power but was given the task of writing an official history of Florence. This modest appointment turned out to be something of a poisoned chalice: some years later, when Florence was once again freed from the rule of the Medici family, the new government regarded Machiavelli as tainted by this association with them and refused him further employment.

GERRYMANDERING

Those who believe that one (wo)man one vote can, in the absence of threats, be relied upon to produce a fair election result need to think again. In 1812, when the American politician Elbridge Gerry (1744 – 1814) was governor of Massachusetts, his party was expected to lose the forthcoming election. In an attempt to prevent this from happening he supported a Bill redefining the electoral districts within the state. The intention of the Bill was to redraw the boundaries of the districts unfairly, in such a way that areas with a high proportion of opposition voters would be lumped together in a few constituencies. His own party would then have an increased chance of winning the large number of remaining more marginal constituencies. The shape of one district on the resulting map looked so odd that it caught the imagination of an artist who added a head, wings and claws to the map, commenting that the district so decorated looked like a salamander. The media thus christened the creature a 'gerrymander'. Unfortunately the verb gerrymandering has subsequently proved to be very useful in describing other changes to electoral boundaries (not always limited to the U.S.), where although no equivalent mythical creature has appeared the underlying principles have remained unchanged.

6.21: Cartoon of 'The Gerry-Mander' from the Boston Centinel, 1812

Gerry was the son of a well-to-do merchant. He graduated from Harvard and joined the family business before becoming closely involved in politics. He was well known for his pro-Revolutionary views and was one of the four representatives from Massachusetts to sign the American Declaration of Independence. His subsequent political career was somewhat chequered: he held a number of high-level responsible posts but was inconsistent and had an unfortunate knack of upsetting people. Nevertheless, and despite the electoral dishonesty that incorporated his name into the language, he can hardly be considered unsuccessful because he ended up as vice-President.

BOYCOTT

Although rural life in Ireland improved somewhat after the crisis of the 1846 potato famine, the lot of tenant farmers remained very insecure. The law did not allow them to sell their tenancies. Rents were high but, if not paid, the landlord could force a tenant to surrender the tenancy without financial compensation. Consequently a poor harvest in 1879 threatened many farmers with both starvation and eviction. This led to the formation of the Irish Land League which sought to fight the farmers' corner under the slogan of 'Three F's': fair rent, fixity of tenure and free sale. Thousands of supporters attended its meetings. Some landlords and agents were forced to reduce unreasonably high rents and, where a tenant had been evicted, the League was able to dissuade anyone else from taking on a new tenancy of the farm.

One of the first landlords to fall foul of the Land League was Lord Erne. He owned a 12,000-acre agricultural estate in County Mayo and the agent who handled its administration on his behalf was Charles Cunningham Boycott (1832 – 87). Boycott was born in Norfolk, the son of a rector, and pursued a short career in the army before turning to estate management. Many of Erne's tenants could not meet their rents and the League demanded a 25% reduction. Boycott served notices of eviction and initially had to be put under police protection to save him from being attacked by angry crowds.

There then came a change in tactics. The League and its followers stopped the attacks in favour of shunning any landlord or agent who did not comply with the League's demands. Boycott was spat at and jeered. No-one would talk to him. No-one would sell him food, which had to be brought in from elsewhere by boat. His post was not delivered. No-one would work on the land he managed and at harvest time, in order to avoid the crop being ruined, fifty volunteers had to be brought in from outside the county to do the work under the protection of an escort of hundreds of police and armed soldiers. Thus it was that 'boycott' came into the language.

The costs of providing such a level of security far exceeded the value of the crop itself and the whole situation became headline news in Britain. Boycott had had enough and by December had returned to East Anglia to take up work as a land agent there.

Courtesy Maggie Land Blanck

6.22: Troops escorting volunteer labourers to Lord Erne's estate, 1880

LUDDITE

By 1811 the traditional way of life for textile workers in the North of England was changing. Skilled weavers, such as lace makers and stocking makers, had until then enjoyed a modest but reliable livelihood working on hand looms at home. They were now suddenly faced with competition from inferior but much cheaper products made using new machine-powered looms, equipment too expensive for an individual weaver to buy and too large to fit in a cottage. The textile workers were left with a choice between continuing to work as before but receiving a minute income for their efforts, or accepting comparatively unskilled and poorly paid work on the factory machines. To compound the problem the price of wheat began to rise dramatically.

Courtesy Nottinghamshire Heritage Gateway

6.23: Early 19th Century engraving showing frame-breaking in progress

It is understandable that those affected by these changes blamed their desperate situation on the new machinery. Across the North of England groups of textile workers gathered together at night to go out and smash the machines, using the pseudonym Ned Ludd (or King Ludd) for whoever was leading their particular group. The name was also used to sign letters posted up on factory doors, requiring the relevant mill owner to stop using the new machinery or risk it being destroyed. In consequence those involved in such activities became referred to as Luddites. Mill owners defended their property and the situation quickly went out of control. Armed guards shot and killed a group of attackers, the mill owner responsible was later murdered, and the attacks became increasingly violent. In 1812 Parliament passed the Frame Breaking Act making destruction of textile machinery punishable by death and after several Luddites had been hanged or transported the attacks gradually came to an end.

There was no individual Ned or King Ludd leading the Luddites – he was a mythical person. But it is probable that the name did not come out of thin air. There are reports that in a village in Leicestershire a mentally unstable apprentice called Ned Lud, Ludd or Ludlam, broke a machine in 1779 in a fit of anger, unwittingly providing a perfect *nom de guerre* for the leaders of future machine breaking activity.

HOBSON'S CHOICE

For more than sixty years Thomas Hobson (1544 – 1631) ran a regular carrier service between his premises near St. Catherine's College, Cambridge and the Bull Inn in London. His wagons, drawn by teams of six or seven carthorses, transported people, letters and goods, but he also hired out horses – the equine forerunner of RentaCar. Many of his customers were undergraduates – young, wealthy gentlemen who rode hard and fast, and horses were frequently worn out by the time they were returned.

Hobson must have been a born businessman. He quickly realised that the best horses were always the ones in demand and were thus at risk of being overworked. So, despite the danger of damaging the goodwill of his business, he introduced a system of rotation described a century or so later in The Spectator: "When a man came for a Horse, he was led into the Stable, where there was great Choice, but [Hobson] obliged him to take the Horse which stood next the Stable-Door; so that every Customer was alike well served according to his Chance, and every Horse ridden with the same Justice"(xviii). A comparatively modern application of Hobson's choice also comes from the travel business. Henry Ford is famously reputed to have said that a customer can have a car any colour he wants so long as it is black.

In April 1630 Hobson's business temporarily dwindled to nothing as Cambridge University was closed because of the plague. It was during this period of inactivity that Hobson eventually died, but he had lived for what was in those days an extraordinarily long time and by then both he and his business seem to have become something of an institution. Milton wrote two light-hearted epitaphs in his memory, claiming that if Hobson's business had just been allowed to keep jogging along then Hobson himself would have carried on as well, seemingly forever:

> .... Rest that gives all men life, gave him his death,
> And too much breathing put him out of breath,
> Nor were it contradiction to affirm
> Too long vacation hast'ned on his term.
> Meerly to drive the time away he sickn'd,
> Fainted, and died, nor would with Ale be quickn'd;
> Nay, quoth he, on his swooning bed outstretch'd,
> If I may not carry, sure Ile ne're be fetch'd,
> But vow though the cross Doctors all stood hearers,
> For one Carrier put down to make six bearers.
> Ease was his chief disease, and to judge right,
> He di'd for heavines that his Cart went light,
> His leasure told him that his time was com,
> And lack of load, made his life burdensome ... (xix)

Hobson was a wealthy man. He inherited not only his carrier business but also substantial land holdings, and he bought more land during his lifetime. Two of his daughters married well and in providing dowries commensurate with their new status he clearly parted with substantial assets, referring to these gifts in his will to explain why "my estate is much lesse than heretofore it was"(xx).

Hobson also contributed a significant amount of money to an engineering project that in 1610 dramatically improved the Cambridge water supply. This project brought clean water into the town from springs some miles away in the Gog Magog hills. Today Trumpington Road is still flanked with a high kerb beside an unusually deep gutter (drivers and pedestrians beware!), along which from time to time runs a stream of water. The casual visitor might assume that there must be a burst pipe somewhere or, if it has recently been raining hard, that there is some sort of temporary flood. Both interpretations would be mistaken.

Photo User Mammal4/ Wikimedia Commons

6.24: Hobson's conduit, Cambridge 2006

A clue as to the true explanation of the stream can be gleaned from the fact that the road itself is somewhat raised so that the water is deliberately kept within its appointed channel. This is part of what was initially called the New River but, because Hobson left money in trust for its maintenance, came to be called Hobson's Conduit. The flow of water is controlled by sluice and is still usually allowed to run between April and September.

CHAPTER SEVEN

PLANTS

Apart from finding, naming and identifying plants, botanists have sought to organise them. Most seem to have had a go at it. The earliest attempts adopted an alphabetical approach; later on certain aspects of the structure of plants were used. In this mêlée of nomenclature the eighteenth century Swedish botanist Carolus Linnaeus is the man to remember. He was the first to establish a system of classification that was both consistent and comprehensive, and it became internationally recognised. His work was continued by the Linnean Society, which is still the body responsible for identifying, documenting and classifying plants.

Linnaeus grouped plants into genera according to the characteristics of their pistils and stamens, and then identified the different species within each genus. Language barriers were avoided by the use of Latin for the names of both genera and species, so Linnaeus needed to come up with a huge number of such names. Sometimes he adopted those already used in previous attempts at classification and sometimes he made up new ones. A quick glance through any list of plants shows that absolutely thousands are named after people, frequently people of some importance to the botanical world but with no immediate connection to the plant concerned. Most – the people, the plants and the Latin names – are unknown to anyone other than serious botanists. This chapter addresses just a few plants, nearly all chosen because of their familiarity.

AUBRETIA (family Brassicaceae, genus Aubrieta)

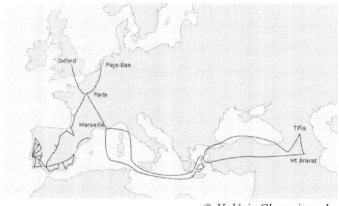

© *Valérie Chansigaud*

7.1: Route of Tournefort's Research Journeys

In 1694 the leading French botanist Tournefort published his major work on the classification of plants. It was illustrated by Claude Aubriet (1665 – 1742) after whom aubretia is named. It was this work of Tournefort that actually introduced the idea of division into genera and species, but on the somewhat uncertain basis of similarities in the flower and fruit. The book was successful on two levels. It became widely used by serious botanists of the time and later on it provided a starting point for Linnaeus.

A few years later Tournefort set off on a plant-finding expedition to the Near East. He was the first such explorer to take an artist with him in order to record his discoveries and the man he chose for the task was again Claude Aubriet. The published account of these travels was illustrated by Aubriet, whose reputation was fast becoming so well established that within a few years he was appointed official botanical illustrator to the French King, a position established a century earlier by Roi Henri IV.

246

Aubriet's work would have been well known to Linnaeus, so it is not surprising that Linnaeus named a genus after him. Aubrieta is commonly known in English as aubretia, a misspelling that perhaps developed from a mispronunciation: 'aubretia' simply sounds right to English ears in a way that 'aubrieta' does not. Although a pretty garden plant with small pink or purple flowers often seen growing on a rockery, it is a member of the cabbage family.

BEGONIA   (family *Begoniaceae*, genus *Begonia*)

7.2: Portrait of the French monk Charles Plumier

This plant was discovered and named by the French monk Charles Plumier who was one of the first, if not the first, to use the names of famous people for some of his botanical finds. He undertook three voyages to the Caribbean in search of specimens, in particular looking for the bark of the cinchona tree, which was known to have medicinal qualities and from which quinine is derived.   These journeys were very successful: many new plants were discovered and identified. Plumier was appointed to the position of Botaniste du Roi,

247

wrote several books and produced hundreds of accurate botanical drawings.

7.3: Cinchona officinalis, harvested quinine bark

Plumier's voyages were commissioned by Michel Begon (1638 – 1710), the naval administrator in charge of the galleys (rowed by convicts) at Marseilles and one time governor of the island now known as Haiti. Begon had arranged the journeys on behalf of and at the expense of the French King, and it was in appreciation of this, as well as perhaps to encourage financial support for other expeditions in the future, that Plumier chose begonia as the name for one of his discoveries.

LOBELIA (family *Companulaceae*, genus *Lobelia*)

Lobelia is another of Plumier's discoveries and he named it in honour of a Flemish physician, Matthias de l'Obel (Latinized as Lobelius) (1538 – 1616). Obel became herbalist and physician to the English King James I and was the first of many botanists to spend a great deal of time attempting to classify plants systematically rather than alphabetically. He did this on the basis of the shape of their leaves, with varying degrees of success.

248

BROMELIA (family *Bromeliacea*, genus *Bromelia*)

Bromelias grow predominantly in the Americas but the name of the family comes from Olaf Bromel (Latinized Bromelius) (1639 – 1705), a Swedish botanist known for his book on Swedish flora. As Bromel was a fellow-countryman of Linnaeus it might have been thought that Linnaeus was responsible for choosing the name, but Charles Plumier beat him to it.

The variation of plants in the bromeliad family is unusually wide in type as well as size, from very small to a plant bearing a flower spike over fifteen feet high. Some bromelias – often sold as houseplants – have thick, wide leaves that overlap at the base so tightly that they serve as the plant's private reservoir, automatically refilled whenever it rains. This enables them to be almost entirely self-sufficient and in damp, tropical climates bromelias and other bromeliads can be seen growing in the most unlikely places – often in the fork of a tree and sometimes even perching precariously on a telephone wire beside the road.

Photo © User Cody H/ Wikimedia Commons

7.4: Bromeliads growing on telephone lines in Bolivia

The most familiar bromeliad, however, grows on the ground and is the pineapple, so called because when first discovered by Columbus it was described as shaped like a pine cone. In

249

those days pineapples were valued so highly by people in the Americas that they were placed outside houses to welcome visitors, a custom that came over to Britain in the modified form of carved or sculpted pineapples on gateposts. In the 1720s the fruit itself became popular and something of a status symbol amongst the nobility, presenting head gardeners with perhaps the ultimate horticultural challenge of the eighteenth century.

The flower from which a pineapple develops grows on the top of a strong, thick stem from the centre of the plant and has a crown of short spiky leaves. If the crown is undamaged when the fruit is harvested a new pineapple plant can be grown by cutting off the crown and planting it. Have a go!

DAHLIA (family *Asteraceae*, genus *Dahlia*)

**7.5:
Dahlia coccinea,
parent of all
European 'single'
dahlias**

*From The Botanical
Magazine, 1804*

If the name Dahl merely puts you in mind of a writer of popular children's fiction then you are probably not a gardener. The dahlia, that brash – some would say rather vulgar – foreigner that brightens up even the dullest days in early autumn, is named after Andreas (Anders) Dahl (1751 – 1789).

Dahl was born in Sweden and from childhood was always interested in natural history and botany. He was one of Linnaeus's students at the University of Uppsala. Unfortunately his father's death led to a financial crisis for the family and he was unable to complete his education. Through Linnaeus's recommendation he was appointed curator of a botanical garden near Gothenburg. Two years before his death at the age of only thirty-eight, Dahl was appointed university lecturer and botanical demonstrator.

Dahlias originated in Mexico. In 1789, when Mexico still belonged to Spain, plant parts were sent from the botanical gardens there to a member of staff at the Royal Gardens of Madrid and it is thought to be that same member of staff who named the genus *Dahlia*. Three different species of plant were grown from these parts and the flowers were soon being grown across Europe. Today there are more than fifty thousand varieties, all descended from the original three plants.

SWEET WILLIAM   (family *Caryophyllacae*, genus *Dianthus*)

There does seem to be a real William behind this name, although precisely which one is a matter of debate. William the Conqueror and William Shakespeare have both been suggested, and even an early archbishop, William of York. In any event, by 1600 the name of this plant is on record[i].

However, folklore would have us believe that the name derives from William Augustus, Duke of Cumberland (1721 – 1765), one of the sons of George II. Often referred to as 'Butcher' Cumberland, he is notorious for ordering the massacre of the Scots Highlanders after defeating their army at the Battle of Culloden: an order that was interpreted by the English troops to encompass not only those fleeing the battlefield but any wounded plus onlookers as well. The Highlanders had rallied to the cause of Charles Stuart (the grandson of James II, also known as 'Bonnie Prince Charlie' or 'The Young Pretender', depending on your point of view) to support him in his attempt to depose the Hanoverians and restore the British crown to the Stuart succession.

It is said that Cumberland was asked, perhaps by an officer reluctant to participate in wholesale slaughter, to confirm in writing the order of 'no quarter'. To do this, so the story goes, he wrote on the nearest thing available which happened to be a playing card, the nine of diamonds – a card referred to ever afterwards as 'the curse of Scotland'. Unfortunately the authenticity of this tale, too, is doubtful. The phrase was probably in use some years before the battle took place and there are several alternative explanations of its origin.

Courtesy U.S. Library of Congress

7.6: 'Solomon's Glory, or the Rival Mistresses'
showing the Duke of Cumberland and his chosen girl with a group of others
jealously looking on

Be that as it may, Culloden brought an end to the hopes of Charles Stuart. By contrast, the successful removal of his challenge to the throne was cause for celebration in England. Cumberland was treated as a hero. William was the name of the day and Sweet William flowers enjoyed a patriotic popularity. The Scots on the other hand found it understandably hard to refer to anything named William as sweet and took to referring to the plant as Stinking Billy. The same name is also used for ragwort, a poisonous weed that smells horrible when squashed.

TRADESCANTIA (family *Commelinaceae*, genus *Tradescantia*)

Nothing is known about the early life of John Tradescant (about 1570 – 1638) but at the age of about thirty-nine he was appointed gardener to Robert Cecil, first Earl of Salisbury, and began work in the gardens of Hatfield House in Hertfordshire. In time Tradescant travelled widely abroad, not only to Europe but also to such places as Algiers and Archangel. Eventually Charles I appointed him Keeper of His Majesty's Gardens, Vines and Silkworms.

7.7: Tradescant's House, South Lambeth, c. 1878

In the course of his travels Tradescant collected all sorts of things that interested him. Many were plants – he was the first to grow apricots in this country – but he brought back from abroad all manner of other things as well: animals, shells, precious stones, coins and shoes to name but a few. His house became known as The Ark and members of the public could look round his collection on payment of a modest fee. It became very popular and a visit was regarded by many as essential education. Tradescant's son, also called John Tradescant, extended the collection. He followed in his father's footsteps, travelling abroad, collecting plants and curiosities and in due course becoming appointed to the same official position regarding silkworms et cetera.

The Ark was already very well established as a private museum when the younger John Tradescant met Elias Ashmole. Ashmole shared his interests, encouraged him to write a catalogue of the collection and substantially funded its printing costs. Unfortunately Ashmole's generosity was not purely altruistic. His interest extended beyond that of enthusiast, friend and patron: he wanted the collection for himself. The younger John had no surviving son and it appears he had decided that after his death his widow was to have the collection for as long as she was still alive and then it was to be given to the University of Oxford. Ashmole persuaded John, some say through trickery, to sign a deed giving the collection directly to him. Whatever the truth of it, Ashmole brought a court case against John's widow when she claimed ownership. The deed of gift was held to be valid and the collection passed to Ashmole who then presented it to the University under his own name. The enormous Tradescant collection became the basis of the Ashmolean Museum.

Ashmole's name today sounds familiar because of the mighty Museum. Tradescant's Ark is all but forgotten, although the name of John Tradescant (the elder) is attached to a genus of plants, frequently seen as small potted houseplants. But, despite all, he would perhaps have been glad that his name was not directly associated with an institution that decided in 1755, long after the dodo had become extinct, to burn as rubbish the only known complete stuffed specimen. To add insult to injury the dodo had originally been part of the Tradescant collection. A small crumb of comfort is offered by the fact that an individual curator managed to save what was left of its head and one foot from the flames.

BOUGAINVILLEA (family *Nyctaginaceae*, genus *Bougainvillea*)

The well-connected Louis Antoine de Bougainville (1729 – 1811) had several changes of career during his life but had little, if anything, to do with plants. Initially it looked as though he was going to be a mathematician, because not long after leaving university he published a treatise on integral calculus and was consequently elected a member of the Royal Society of London. But Bougainville was a man of action and this was a time of war, so he soon left academia and enlisted in the army. He set sail for Canada under the leadership of the Marquis de Montcalm and, as he could speak good English, played a key role in negotiations with the top brass of the English army. The fall of Quebec and Montreal meant there was much to negotiate and, after the total defeat of the French, their officers were returned home on parole, on the basis that they must take no part in any further military activity.

Thus Bougainville left behind both the army and the North American Indian woman with whom he had had a son. Years of boredom followed and rather than use his time to good purpose he frequented gambling dens and brothels, embarked on a series of affairs and came to the unwelcome notice of the police. Eventually he thought up a plan that would enable him to contribute once more to *la gloire de la France*. He considered that a French presence on Les Iles Malouines (the Falkland Islands) would allow France to control shipping to and from the Pacific Ocean. The French government was not sufficiently impressed to provide any finance but Bougainville was able to raise the necessary money himself. He organised and supplied the expedition, took on board a number of people wishing to settle on the islands, and set sail for the South Atlantic.

The expedition was successful. Bougainville returned to France and the following year went back to the islands to resupply the settlers with timber and food. But while he was away the Spanish government claimed ownership of the islands and the French government agreed to their claim. All Bougainville's work had been for nothing, although the Spanish did agree to pay him compensation for his efforts.

It is clear that he had by now developed a taste for travel because his next project was to become the first Frenchman to sail round the world. This time government backing provided him with two ships and he set off, calling first at Les Iles Malouines, soon to become Las Islas Malvinas, to effect their formal transfer to Spain. This was one of the earliest expeditions to include scientists, and whilst in Rio de Janeiro the expedition's botanist went ashore to collect specimens of the local plants. One of these was a climbing plant whose green leaves on the lower part of the stem gave way to a mass of small purple ones at the top. The botanist tactfully called it bougainvillea after the leader of the expedition.

Bougainville sailed on through the Pacific, past several islands where the fact that he did not land did not stop him from claiming possession of them, again for *la gloire de la France*. On to Tahiti where he stopped for nine days – long enough for the voyagers' descriptions of their stay to convey an idea of the island as a tropical paradise. It also proved long enough for many of them to catch venereal disease.

Photo © User Fred/Wikimedia Commons

7.8: Tahiti: a black sand beach

All in all, the voyage lasted for over two years. When Bougainville finally returned home he found he was a celebrity. He was appointed as an officer in the French navy, but his fame was resented by a fellow officer who implied that the appointment was due neither to high birth nor to merit but merely to the influence of the king. (This says something both about the system for naval appointments and about the popularity of the monarchy.) Bougainville challenged him to a duel for the insult and won, wounding his opponent in the arm.

The American War of Independence brought about yet another change in Bougainville's career because his ship was ordered to sail there and

became heavily involved in the fighting. A story, most probably true, is told of the ship's talking parrot. It rather wisely went missing in the early stages of the Battle of Chesapeake Bay and did not reappear for several days. When at last it did so, it was found to have lost its entire vocabulary and the only sound it would make was a rendering of the sound of cannon fire - "boom": undoubtedly a case of avian post-traumatic stress disorder.

The 1790s were a time of terrible events in France but Bougainville was fortunate. Although a staunch supporter of the monarchy he was not a member of the nobility. He kept his head down and so kept it on. Only in the last few months of the Reign of Terror was he imprisoned, but he was released shortly afterwards. A few years later he attended a reception to celebrate Napoleon's successful military campaign and the two got on well together. Once Napoleon came to power Bougainville was honoured and granted a pension, and at his end was given a state funeral.

BUDDLEIA (family *Scrophulariaceae*, genus *Buddleja*)

The buddleia, sometimes called the butterfly bush because its long, trailing flowers attract so many of them, is named after the Reverend Adam Buddle (1660 – 1715). Buddle was born and brought up in the village of Deeping St. James in South Lincolnshire and went on to read theology at Cambridge University. He was on good terms with John Ray who later became famous for his Historia Plantarum, the first comprehensive book on English plants, describing over eighteen thousand species and the first to classify plants according to their structure. This friendship developed Buddle's own interest in plants and their classification.

Eventually Buddle became rector at North Fambridge in Essex and, having inherited land and property in Lincolnshire from his uncle, had the financial security that enabled him to indulge his passion for botany. He began with mosses and grasses. His collection of seaweeds and lichens still exists, kept by The Natural History Museum in London which also has the manuscript of his unpublished complete English flora written in 1708. Because Buddle's work related entirely to British plants it seems totally inappropriate that Linnaeus should have chosen his name for a genus of plants native to tropical and subtropical regions.

CAMELLIA (family *Theaceae*, genus *Camellia*)

A word of advice. If you are fortunate enough to have acidic soil in your garden, grow camellias. In the spring before the weather is anything like warm they produce a profusion of the most wonderful exotic flowers, almost tropical in appearance. And they will even do it in that problematic shady corner.

Camellias are named after the Moravian (Czech) Jesuit brother Georg Josef Kamel (1661 – 1706) who was sent to the Philippines as a missionary. Whilst there he made an intensive study of the local flora and sent his findings back to Europe. The Jesuit library at Louvain still holds a large collection of Kamel's manuscript drawings. His text – in Latin and written under his Latinised name of Camellus – was published in England, partly in the Philosophical Transactions of the Royal Society and partly as the 1704 appendix to John Ray's Historia Plantarum. Kamel was not the first European to discover the camellia, but his published work made him an authority on all oriental plants including the camellia. Accordingly it was he whom Linnaeus immortalised when naming the genus.

Kamel was not only a botanist. His understanding of the medicinal properties of plants made him a skilled pharmacist. He discovered that one plant could be used in small quantities as a tonic and named it St. Ignatius's Bean, in memory of the founder of the Jesuits. Many years later analysis of this plant, now known as *Strychnos ignatii,* showed that it contained small quantities of strychnine.

FUCHSIA   (family *Onagraceae*, genus *Fuchsia*)

7.9:
Cannabis sativa
from Fuchs' *De*
Historia Stirpium
Commentarii
Insignes

Courtesy
Wellcome Library, London

Leonhart Fuchs (1501 – 1566) certainly never saw a fuchsia because the plant was not discovered until more than a century after his death. He was born in Bavaria and was a classical scholar, a physician and professor of medicine. His familiarity with Greek allowed him to study the original classical medical texts and consequently avoid much of the astrology and mythology that had crept into the study of medicine during the intervening years. His greatest achievement was his magnificent herbal 'De historia stirpium commentarii insignes' first published in 1542, which for a

259

considerable number of years was the recognised scientific authority on the medicinal properties of plants.

During his lifetime it was reprinted several times and was translated into several languages. In it he lists nearly five hundred plants, giving details of their medicinal properties; he also expresses great concern that few of his medical colleagues had any accurate knowledge of plants. In order to ensure that his readers could identify the plants correctly, each is illustrated with an exquisite, accurate woodcut plate in colour based on real specimens. Fuchs was responsible for the extensive research, for identifying and finding the plants, and for the text. The illustrations were the combined work of three people: an artist to do the drawings, someone to transfer the drawings to woodblocks, and a wood-engraver to cut the blocks. The book is unusual for its time in that it gives full credit to these three for their contributions, even including their group portrait.

By kind permission of University of Glasgow Library

7.10: The Illustrators of Fuchs' *De Historia Stirpium Commentarii Insignes*

POINSETTIA (family *Euphorbiaceae*, genus *Euphorbia*)

The cheerful pot plant with large red flowers that signals the approach of Christmas is not quite what it seems. It is actually a deciduous shrub growing to a height of ten feet or more in its native Mexico. And the flowers are not flowers at all, but modified leaves – the flowers themselves are white and can be seen right in the centre, looking decidedly small and insignificant. The Aztecs prized the plants, using the red leaves for making dyes and the milky sap for treating fever. Our friend Montezuma of revenge fame (see Chapter Five) was unable to cultivate them at his court owing to its high altitude, but desired them so much that he had mature plants transported up from the lowlands.

**7.11:
Joel Roberts
Poinsett, 15th
U.S. Secretary of
War**

*Courtesy U.S. Library
of Congress*

The plant initially came to the attention of the public through Joel Roberts Poinsett (1779 – 1851). He was an American statesman with a reputation for diplomacy in Latin America and was the first US ambassador to Mexico, being appointed in 1825 when Mexico had comparatively recently achieved independence from Spain. The US government had instructed him to negotiate the purchase of Texas at the knock down price of one million dollars but the Mexicans were not keen to sell and it was not long before they forced his recall. Mexico eventually lost its territory of Texas, as well as that of California, Arizona and New Mexico, in 1847.

261

Poinsett was very well educated. He studied medicine and law, spoke French, Spanish, Italian and German, and spent several years travelling across Europe and North America. He was also a keen amateur botanist and when travelling round Mexico was very taken with the beautiful plants, previously unknown to him, that had so appealed to Montezuma. He took cuttings and sent them back to his greenhouses in South Carolina. They were propagated successfully and he gave the plants to those friends who were interested in having one. Within ten years they were being referred to as poinsettias and are now the most popular pot plant in the United States.

FORSYTHIA (family *Oleaceae*, genus *Forsythia*)

The career of the very successful horticulturalist William Forsyth (1737 – 1804) ended in controversy. Born in Scotland, he had gone to London and became a gardener at Syon Park before moving on to take charge of the Chelsea Physic Garden and later the gardens of St. James and Kensington Palaces. Many of the royal trees were found to have canker and in caring for them Forsyth invented a plaster to be applied to the affected area of the tree, after the dead wood had been cut out, in order to assist its recovery.

Photo © Markus Hagenlocher

7.12: Canker on the trunk of a birch tree

At first he kept its composition secret but he reckoned without the influence of the Royal Navy, to which sound timber was of crucial importance. A Parliamentary committee conducted investigations into whether the plaster worked and was satisfied that it did. Forsyth was paid a handsome government grant to induce him to reveal its constituents: cow dung, urine, sand, lime and ash. Any 'magic ingredient' was notable by its absence. An eminent scientific colleague was incensed, practically accusing Forsyth of fraud, and bitter argument raged. Despite this Forsyth was one of the original seven founders of what is now the Royal Horticultural Society, although he died very soon after its inception. Forsythia was named in his honour by a Norwegian colleague of Linnaeus, but the plant did not come to Britain until the 1840s.

WISTERIA (or Wistaria) (family *Leguminosae*, genus *Wisteria*)

Caspar Wistar (1761 – 1818) came from a family of Quakers. He was born in Philadelphia and named after his grandfather, a well-known glass-maker. During the American War of Independence he volunteered to nurse casualties and was so affected by the experience that he decided to become a doctor. He was dedicated to his work, to such an extent that during an epidemic of yellow fever he remained in town to care for his patients even though more than half the population had left to go somewhere safer. He did catch the disease himself, but recovered. His criticism of a colleague's recommended 'depletion treatment' for yellow fever, involving frequent bleeding and purging, was so forthright that it brought to an end the former friendship between them.

Wistar's career flourished. He wrote the first American textbook on anatomy and developed new teaching aids for the subject. Some of these were carved wooden models; others, dried human body parts preserved through the injection of wax. But medicine was not his only field of interest. He was an expert on plants and fossils, he belonged to the Anti-Slavery Society and was a member, later President, of the American Philosophical Society. He held weekly social gatherings for the intellectual élite and these proved so popular that 'Wistar parties' continued to be held for many years after his death.

7.13: Bones of the prehistoric giant ground sloth from a paper published by Wistar in 1799

The genus *Wisteria* was named in honour of Wistar, the spelling with an "e" appearing to be no more than a simple mistake. Incorrect or not, *Wisteria* remains the official name, leaving it to the common name to allow the alternative spelling of 'wistaria'.

MAGNOLIA (family *Magnoliaceae,* genus *Magnolia*):
Fossilised remains show that close relatives of the magnolia are among the most ancient of trees, in existence before there were any bees or other flying insects to pollinate them. Therefore instead of producing proper nectar, they secrete a sugary substance that attracts beetles.

The magnolia is another 'Plumier' plant. He brought a specimen back with him from the West Indies in the 1690s and it seems likely that it was he who was responsible for naming the genus after Pierre Magnol (Latinized as Magnolius) (1630 – 1715), a renowned botanist, physician and Professor of Botany at the Royal Garden of Montpellier. Plumier was certainly using the name by 1703, but his was not the first magnolia to arrive in Europe. One had already been brought to England from Virginia for the Bishop of London in 1688 by the Reverend John Banister, but it somehow seems doubtful that either Banister or the Bishop would have named the plant after a botanist renowned in the South of France, even if they did know of him. The third magnolia to arrive in Europe, this time the potentially huge magnolia grandiflora, came in 1711 to Nantes from Louisiana (at that time Louisiana was French) and the name of the genus was certainly established by then.

Photo © User Pymouss44/ Wikimedia Commons

7.14: Magnolia grandiflora at the Jardin des Plantes at Nantes, planted in 1807

DOUGLAS FIR (family *Pinaceae*, genus *Pseudotsuga*)

David Douglas (1799 – 1834) was the son of a stonemason and began his career by serving seven years as an apprentice gardener, subsequently finding employment at the botanical gardens of Glasgow University. After some time, and considerable study, he was noticed by the Professor of Botany who arranged for his official appointment by the Royal Horticultural Society as botanical collector to the USA. Douglas undertook major, successful plant-finding expeditions, introducing over two hundred new species to Britain, including the Douglas fir that was named after him and also smaller plants such as the penstemon. His final journey came to a grisly end in Hawaii where he fell into a pit-trap designed to capture wild bulls and was trampled to death by one that had made the same mistake.

Unlike other fir cones, those of a Douglas fir have an obvious three-pointed bract sticking out above each scale, the central point being narrower and longer than the two on either side. A Native American myth has it that these are the tail and hind-legs of mice given shelter by the tree during forest fires.

7.15:

Cone of a Coast Douglas fir grown from a seed collected by David Douglas

© *User MPF/ Wikimedia Commons*

SEQUOIA (family *Cupressaceae*, genus *Sequoia sempervirens* and *Sequoiadendron giganteum*)

An unassuming Native American, sometimes called George Guest or Gist but better known as Sequoya(h) (c.1770 – 1843), who lived in an illiterate society and had no formal education, achieved an astonishing transformation of Cherokee culture.

Sequoya's mother was a Cherokee but little is known about his father other than that he was white, or half white. As Sequoya grew up speaking no English it is assumed that his father had abandoned him not long after his birth. Sequoya was known to be disabled and some argue that he was born so, his Cherokee name apparently meaning pig or pig's foot. But since US military records show that he enlisted and fought in the Cherokee regiment, the implication is that at least at that time he was fit for fighting. It may be that injuries received during battle were responsible for his disablement, but whatever the reason, in later life Sequoya took up the sedentary occupation of silversmith.

Sequoya became intrigued by the ability of white settlers to communicate with each other using bits of paper with marks (writing) on them that he called 'talking leaves'. The idea was completely foreign to Cherokees as their language was strictly oral – nothing had ever been written down so there was not even an alphabet – but he understood that writing was useful and could be a source of power. He determined to find a way of writing his own language and began to study the shapes of letters used in the Roman alphabet and also letters from words in any other alphabets that he could find. His initial approach was to create a separate symbol for each word but he soon discovered that this was going to be too complicated. It may be that his wife helped to focus his mind somewhat when, in a fit of frustration and rage, she burnt down the shed where he had been carrying out all his work. He then came up with a new idea: to analyse the sounds of words, reducing them to their constituent syllables. Despite the ridicule and suspicion of his tribe, he persevered. Within twelve years he had worked out that Cherokee used only eighty-five syllables and had made up a syllabary accordingly, each syllable being represented by a different symbol.

The next task was to get the rest of the tribe to use 'talking leaves'. He began with his daughter. Although memorising the number of symbols involved is at first demanding, once this has been done the system is very easy to use as all that is needed is to reproduce the sounds indicated by the symbols. Within a few days she had mastered it and this enabled him to demonstrate it to others. With his daughter out of earshot he would ask an onlooker to give him a message. Having written the sounds down he would then call his daughter to look at the writing and tell the onlooker, and anyone else present, what the message was. At first people thought he was using trickery, magic or sorcery, but the idea caught on with

267

astonishing speed and within only a year most Cherokees were able to read their own language. A Cherokee newspaper and a translation of the Bible were printed, and written records were made of the tribe's traditions, including its magic and medical cures.

Courtesy User Robfergusonjr/ Wikimedia Commons

7.16: Sequoya's syllabary

At about this time the tribe was being forced to leave its traditional homeland and was scattered across several states. Some had trekked to the new designated homeland in the west. Sequoya's great desire was to see the tribe united once more, to which end he travelled widely, using the new ability to communicate in writing to help the different groups keep in touch with each other. He died whilst visiting Mexico, contacting those members of the tribe who had settled there.

Enough of Sequoya the man. Sequoia the tree, honouring Sequoya, is also American and is famous for its size. There are two from which to choose. The species commonly called just plain sequoia, or coast redwood (*Sequoia sempervirens*), is considered to be the tallest tree in the world and can grow to over 110 metres high with a diameter at the base of 7 metres, taking some 2,000 years to do so. The species with the largest volume, regarded as the biggest tree in the world, is known as the giant sequoia, or sierra redwood (*Sequoiadendron giganteum*) and grows to some 90 metres high with a diameter of nearly 9 metres at the base. The oldest recorded such tree was found to be 3,200 years old when it was felled.

Although you might think it difficult not to be aware of the existence of something that size, the giant sequoia was little known outside its immediate locality until its 'discovery' in 1842. The following hundred years were then spent arguing about what to call it. Had the trees been the size of your average tree there might have been no problem, but it was clearly felt that such an overwhelmingly impressive species had to be named in honour of someone of commensurate stature. American botanists were working towards *Washingtonia gigantea* but after specimens of the tree had been brought to Britain a scientific description of the tree was quickly published here, naming it officially *Wellingtonia gigantea* – the Duke of Wellington had only recently died. Understandably the Americans were not happy – it was after all their tree – and an international row ensued. In the end both these names proved invalid as the genus names had already been used for other things, as had the next suggestion of *Sequoia gigantea,* but at least everyone was in agreement in describing the size. Numerous different names were then suggested but ruled out as inappropriate. Then someone busy looking at chromosomes decided that the giant sequoia was not actually a sequoia at all and awarded it a genus all of its own, calling it *Sequioadendron giganteum.* This name seems to have been accepted, despite considerable criticism. One cannot help feeling a certain respect for those Native Americans who keep out of the argument altogether and just call it 'big tree'. England, however, has resorted to somewhat underhand tactics to promote its cause. Ignoring the tree's official Latin name, it is popularly still known here as 'wellingtonia'.

LOGANBERRY (family *Rosaceae*, genus *Rubus*)

A Californian judge called James Harvey Logan (1841 – 1928) was an amateur horticulturalist who used to fiddle about with his blackberries. His plan was to cross two particular strains in order to create a bigger and better cultivar. He cannot have realised that a raspberry cane called Red Antwerp was lurking nearby. 'Twerp by name and twerp by nature: it interfered with the sex life of his plants. It cunningly came into flower at the same time as the blackberries and when Logan planted fifty seeds from his horticultural experiment, he found next year that although forty-nine of them produced his hoped-for improved fruit that became known as the Mammoth Blackberry, one turned out to be a cross between a blackberry and a raspberry. This variety became known as the Loganberry, officially called *Rubus loganobaccus*.

That, anyway, is the generally accepted version of events, although some maintain it is possible that His Honour just happened to end up with a red fruiting form of the common Californian blackberry in his garden.

BRAMLEY (family *Rosaceae*, genus *Malus*)

Photo © Marcin Floryan

7.17: Bramley apples

Was Matthew Bramley (1796–?) a botanist, a horticulturalist or perhaps just an enthusiastic gardener? No. Did he grow the first Bramley apple tree from a pip? No, that was a child called Mary Ann Brailsford. Did he make a business out of grafting cuttings from it and selling them? No, that was a nurseryman called Henry Merryweather. Bramley was simply a butcher whose only connection with apples seems to be his purchase of the house in Nottinghamshire where the Brailsfords used to live.

Mary Ann was a child who clearly liked apples, or gardening, or both, as after eating an apple one day she planted two pips from it. One pip grew into a fine seedling that by 1837 was sufficiently established to bear fruit. Bramley later bought the house and in 1856 Merryweather noticed the apples, realised that they had exceptional qualities, and asked Bramley if he might develop them commercially by taking graftings from the tree. Bramley agreed, on the sole condition that any apples sold were to be called Bramley Seedlings. Apparently no money changed hands.

Mary Ann's tree still bears fruit today.

COX'S ORANGE PIPPIN (family *Rosaceae*, genus *Malus*)

The most popular dessert apple in Britain, the Cox's Orange Pippin, was grown from a pip by Richard Cox (1777 – 1845). It is easily recognisable, not just from its distinctive colouration but also because it is the only apple whose pips rattle if you shake it. This happens because instead of being embedded in the flesh of the apple they are held loosely in a sort of cage formed by the core.

Cox was a brewer who retired from his business in Bermondsey and moved to Colnbrook in Berkshire. People in those days must have drunk every bit as much beer as they do today because on retirement he was wealthy enough to purchase two acres of land and live there with his wife, three servants and three gardeners. He was interested in fruit trees and planted two pips from a Ribston pippin that are believed to have been pollinated from a Blenheim Orange. One grew into a tree that produced the apples that we know and love today. Cox supplied a local nurseryman with some grafts from this tree and during his lifetime the apples became well-known in the area. Business then really began to take off in the

1850s when Queen Victoria's gardener brought the tree to horticultural attention at a national level.

The original tree survived until 1911, when it was blown down in a storm.

Photo © C.M. Wiles

7.18: Cox's orange pippins – before and after

GRANNY SMITH (family *Rosaceae*, genus *Malus*)

There are loads of granny smiths around – the supermarket shelves are full of them. There are also loads of fecund women who rejoice in the surname Smith, so it is hardly surprising that there are several grannies in the frame for having discovered the famous apple.

The most authentic contender seems to be Maria Ann Sherwood (about 1799 – 1870), who was born in Sussex. She married a farm labourer, Thomas Smith, and the couple with their five children later emigrated to New South Wales. In due course they were able to buy a piece of land to farm and in 1868 asked a local fruit-grower to come and look at a seedling apple that bore unusually robust green fruit, good for both eating and cooking, and excellent for storing. The seedling had sprouted from the remains of some French crab apples that had been thrown away and is believed to have been a cross between an ordinary dessert apple and the crab apple. The apples were never marketed commercially during Granny Smith's lifetime but continued to be grown locally. In 1891 'Granny Smith's seedlings' won the prize for best cooking apple at an agricultural show and their fame grew from there.

Even those reluctant to eat any fruit at all and who couldn't care less about a granny smith may still be familiar with what it looks like. A picture of one appears on the Apple Record label, a division of the company set up by the Beatles to market their records.

Photo © C.M. Wiles

7.19: Granny Smiths

GREENGAGE (family *Rosaceae*, genus *Prunus*)

Many years ago a keen gardener once gave a bag of greengages from her garden to a visiting friend. The friend, abysmally ignorant as to their flavour but anxious to do them justice, asked if she should cook them. Now, the owner of the greengage espalier was an exceptionally polite and well-mannered young woman but was unable to prevent a tiny, fleeting wince of pain from passing across her face, before smiling and responding in a confidential tone "Well you could, but we always think it's rather a waste." What an understatement! Once tasted, such a sweet fruit, redolent of summer and with a flavour to knock strawberries into a cocked hat, is never to be forgotten. Greengages sold in supermarkets bear no comparison.

In France the greengage is known as reine-claude in honour of the sixteenth century French Queen Claude who grew a large number of them in the royal gardens. She was known to encourage their spread by giving fruit to anyone who was interested in growing their own. And despite her botanical

273

interests she still found time to bear her husband seven children before she died at the age of twenty-five.

The greengage, together with many other plants, was brought to England by the botanist Sir William Gage (about 1657 – 1727). Its English name may have been born more of necessity than xenophobia. There is a suggestion that the label identifying the tree fell off during its journey from France back to Gage's home of Hengrave Hall in Suffolk, leaving its name shrouded in mystery. In due course the green plums that it produced then simply became referred to as green Gage's.

VICTORIA PLUM (family *Rosaceae*, genus *Prunus*)

These plums are named, like so many other things, after Queen Victoria. They feature in a shaggy dog story that used to be told most convincingly by a gentleman who had been brought up in the West Country. The scene is set outside Buckingham Palace in the early days of the reign of our present Queen, when the national anthem was still played at the end of every cinema showing. A time when the sentries in their sentry boxes were still positioned on the street outside the palace railings and naughty children would sometimes try and prod them in the tummy to see if they were real.

An old man from Somerset – so the tale went – had never travelled outside his home county, but wanted to visit London before he died. He accordingly packed his bags and set off to his local railway station, taking with him a large basket of victoria plums. On arrival at Paddington he boarded a bus to Buckingham Palace. Once there he strode determinedly towards the open gates leading to the extensive courtyard in front of the palace. He was accosted by a sentry:

"And where do you think you are going?" the sentry asked.

"Well, Oi do be going to take these 'ere plums to the Queen" was the response (regional accents still being very much a feature in those days).

"You can't do that." the sentry said, "You are not allowed in there".

274

"But Oi've brought them from Zomerzet for 'Er Majezty, zo Oi'm takin' 'em in." the man insisted.

Photo courtesy Petr Kratochvil

7.20: A sentry on duty at Buckingham Palace

The sentry was nonplussed but he was a kind chap. This was long before the days of Al Qaeda and he could see that the visitor meant well. Besides, the man put him a little in mind of his own father. So rather than dismissing him abruptly he opted for a more persuasive approach:

"I'm sure the Queen doesn't want your plums. She's got plenty of her own already. And anyway she might not even like plums" the sentry explained.

"Well, Oi knowz you'm wrong there" was the man's somewhat unexpected reply.

"How can you possibly know that's wrong?" queried the sentry, "You've never even met the Queen."

"No that's right. Oi 'aven't never met 'Er Majesty. But Oi knows she likes these 'ere plums cawse every time the film comes to an end in the cinema, us always zings "Zend 'er victorias".

WILLIAMS PEAR (family *Rosaceae*, genus *Pyrus*)

If you are mystified as to why tinned pears are always called Bartlett pears but you never see any Bartlett pears in the fresh fruit section of the supermarket, the answer is simple. They are actually there, but incognito.

In about 1765 a schoolmaster in Berkshire called Mr. Stair discovered (to the delight of anyone who enjoys rhymes) a pear tree that produced unusually good fruit. Some cuttings went to a horticulturalist called Richard Williams who developed and marketed the pear, using his own name for it: Williams' bon Chrétien. The pear is now universally known as just plain Williams.

Except... not quite universally. In 1799 some of Mr. Williams' trees were taken to the United States and planted on land that in the course of time came into the ownership of one Enoch Bartlett. Bartlett had no idea what the trees were but realised the quality of the fruit. Being an astute businessman he marketed the fruit commercially under his own name. It was only thirty years later, after the Bartlett name had become widely established there and some new Williams' trees were imported from Europe, that anyone realised that the two varieties were one and the same.

FILBERTS (family *Betulaceae*, genus *Corylus*)

Filberts are the nuts produced by cultivated hazel trees, whose long catkins are one of the first signs of spring, dancing in the breeze and releasing clouds of yellow pollen into the air long before any leaves unfurl. These are the male flowers: close inspection is needed to spot the tiny, bright red female flowers that look like little brushes, growing from small buds on the woody branches.

Filbert nuts are slightly longer than ordinary hazel nuts and their name, which dates from about 1390, is a reference to St. Philibert (about 616 – about 684) on whose day (August 20th or 22nd) the nuts are traditionally ripe. St. Philibert was a Benedictine abbot and bishop who founded an abbey in

Normandy but, after criticising someone of high standing at the royal court, was forced to leave. He was imprisoned for a time and then founded a monastery at his place of exile on the Island of Noirmoutier, just off the French Atlantic coast.

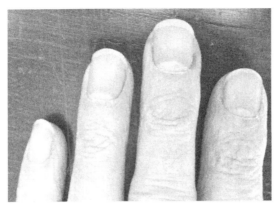

Photo © J.E. Baldwin

7.21: Filbert nails

In Victorian times, 'filbert' was a term used to describe the ideal shape for a fingernail. This appears to have been applied to nails that were naturally long and slender and the view was even expressed by some that filbert nails were a sign of aristocratic ancestry. Since a filbert nut is not very different from the distinctly short, squat hazelnut, the use of the term does seem somewhat surprising.

MACADAMIAS (family *Proteaceae*, genus *Macadamia*)

The indigenous Australians had known for years about their evergreen 'kindal kindal' trees that produced delicious nuts, but for scientific purposes the trees were discovered in 1857 by two botanists from Melbourne and Brisbane. One of these catalogued the tree and named the new genus after John Macadam (1827 – 1865). This Macadam, who was nothing to do with roads, had only recently emigrated to Australia from Scotland and had settled in Melbourne to teach at the medical school there, eventually becoming professor of chemistry.

277

Groves of trees were planted and the nut began to be grown on a commercial basis. The world's largest producer is now no longer Australia, but Hawaii.

CHAPTER EIGHT

CREATURES

Carolus Linnaeus did not confine his passion for classification to plants. His 'system naturae' extended to all living things, divided first into kingdoms. Within the animal kingdom, just as within the plant kingdom, each item was defined with a simple two-word classification denoting genus and species, as illustrated by his classification of man as Homo sapiens. The species name is not uncommonly a Latin version of the name of the person who discovered the species. There are many such names: this chapter essentially ignores all of them and only discusses a selection of creatures whose common English names reflect the name of a person.

GUPPY

A guppy is a small fish that puts one in mind of a minnow. Its native home is Trinidad where it was obviously well-known long before being discovered by Europeans. There they are simply known as 'millions', presumably in tribute to their main characteristic – an enthusiasm for, and remarkable success in, breeding. Part of the reason for this success is that the eggs are protected from predators by being hatched whilst still inside the female's body.

If life was fair these fish would be known as 'peters', since it was the German naturalist Wilhelm Peters who first described them, years before Robert John Lechmere Guppy (1836 –

1916) sent specimens to London for cataloguing. The official Latin name (Girardinus guppii) that acknowledged Guppy's apparent discovery was actually later changed, partly because of Peters' work. But by then the fish were already generally known as guppies and, whilst scientists may control and use the scientific names, their power over everyday speech is more limited. None of this should cast any aspersions on Guppy himself: by all accounts he was well known for his straightforwardness and honesty, and took the view that doing one's work well should be a sufficient reward in itself.

8.1: Portrait of a Maori man with tattoos, c.1770

Guppy's early life contained some unusual contrasts. His parents lived in Trinidad but he was born in England and brought up in a castle in Herefordshire by his grandparents. With the benefit of an inheritance he ran away to Tasmania at the age of eighteen to avoid ending up being lumbered with responsibility for the family pile. Some while later he was shipwrecked off the coast of New Zealand where he was rescued by Maoris. He lived happily with them for two years exploring the area, studying its fauna and flora, and having his back decorated with picturesque Maori tattoos. He then moved on to Trinidad where he became Inspector of Schools, pursued his naturalist's interests, married and, perhaps inspired by the example of his piscatorial namesake, had nine children.

A hint of what it must have been like to meet the man can be glimpsed from a description written by one who knew him: "... a man of remarkable individuality. Tall, gaunt, white-haired, grey-bearded, rugged in speech, combative in his opinions. A whiff of cold air seemed to go with him wherever he went. Watching him stride over the savannah, one imagined it a Yorkshire moor."(i)

PRZEWALSKI'S HORSE

Your starter for ten: what animal links France, Poland, Russia, Mongolia and Holland? The answer is Przewalski's (pronounced approximately (pr)shuh-vahl-ski's) horse – the ancient breed of wild horse that roamed across Europe and Asia thousands of years ago and believed by many to be the ancestor of all domesticated horses.

8.2: Przewalski's horse

Photo © Joe Ravi, CC-BY-SA 3.0

The story begins in France where prehistoric cave paintings include clear illustrations of this horse, depicting its beige colouration, pale muzzle and short, bristly erect mane with no

281

forelock. By the nineteenth century the last European herds of these horses in Poland and southern Russia had died out and the breed was considered to be extinct.

There was great excitement therefore when Nikolai Mikhailovich Przhewalski (1839 – 1888) found some in central Asia. Przewalski (whose name has numerous spelling options) was a geography teacher at the military school in Warsaw – at that time part of Russia. He was posted to Siberia and from there explored Turkestan, Tibet, Mongolia, and the Gobi desert. He reported back to the Tsar and wrote extensively of his expeditions, making a substantial contribution to European knowledge of the flora, fauna and geography of central Asia.

After Przewalski's discovery, a wealthy Russian landowner set up an expedition to capture some of these wild horses and bring them back for breeding purposes. This project met with very limited success. The adults were too wary and too fast to be caught and many of the captured foals did not survive for any length of time. Even those that did survive failed to thrive in captivity and, with so few distributed between zoos in a number of different countries, inbreeding became a major problem. In the meantime those horses that were still in the wild began to die out, their speed proving to be no defence against guns fired by Mongolian nomads searching for food. The last one was sighted in 1969.

With only thirteen Przewalski's horses in captivity suitable for breeding the situation was critical, but an association set up in Holland successfully established a properly organised breeding programme in an effort to prevent extinction. It has also now begun to reintroduce some animals back into the wild in Mongolia and arranged with the local government to provide them with legal protection.

JESUS CHRIST LIZARD

Imagine for a moment that you are transported – by magic carpet or aeroplane, either will do – to a foreign land. There you can bathe in a complex of natural pools and streams in waters heated by a nearby volcano, amidst a profusion of canna lilies, bromeliads and other exotic vegetation. Others are bathing, too, but there is an overall feeling of calm and peace. There you are, floating gently or even just sitting up to your neck in warm water quietly enjoying the scenery, when suddenly you hear splashing. A large lizardy thing about a foot and a half long dashes across the surface of the water just in front of you and in a fraction of a second disappears into the undergrowth beside the edge of the pool. It has gone. There is no sign of it. Looking cautiously around no-one is behaving as if anything odd has happened. You must have dreamt it – after all, the creature was apparently quite unaffected by the laws of physics.

8.3: Jesus Christ lizard, or brown basilisk

But this is no dream. You are simply in Costa Rica. When alarmed, the basilisk (known locally as the Jesus Christ lizard for reasons obvious to those familiar with the New Testament) escapes by running across water. It stays upright by trailing its long tail underwater behind it and, as long as it keeps going fast enough, its powerful back legs with large webbed feet enable it to run on top of the water for about fifteen feet before it has to resort to swimming. The splashing does draw attention to the creature but it is a spectacularly effective way of getting away form land-based predators.

Visitors to Costa Rica have no need to fear this basilisk. It is the Other Basilisk that is the problem, the one also known as a cockatrice. That one, too, has biblical connections but this time with the Old Testament. Every Christmas Isaiah reminds churchgoers that under normal circumstances a child would be in terrible danger to put a hand anywhere near its den. That kind of basilisk is a mythical creature, said to be hatched by a serpent from a cock's egg, whose breath, or even glance, is fatal.

BEWICK'S SWAN

A wild white swan flying vast distances in its migration between Western Europe and its breeding grounds on the Arctic tundra creates in one's mind's eye an image of unearthly beauty and freedom. It almost serves as an image of the soul, leaving this world and flying upwards, unfettered by the daily round, the common task. It is, in short, everything that a gravestone isn't. What better memorial could anyone ever hope for? The Linnean Society has awarded the great nature lover, Thomas Bewick (1758 – 1828), this rare epitaph.

Courtesy Art Gallery of Alberta

8.4: 'Wild Swan' engraved by Thomas Bewick c.1804

Bewick was a highly skilled wood engraver. His work is renowned for its exceptional delicacy, the product of a natural artistic talent combined with the new technique he developed

284

to allow him to engrave in much greater detail than anyone hitherto. He was born in Northumberland and spent nearly all his working life in the North East, his most famous work being his History of British Birds. At the beginning of Jane Eyre, Charlotte Brontë tells of her heroine as a young girl who, when ordered to be silent, curls up on a window seat studying this book, having selected it from the bookcase on the basis that it had pictures. Brontë also wrote a poem on Bewick's death, lamenting his passing.

Two types of swan are discussed and illustrated in Bewick's History of British Birds. He described these as the tame (or mute) swan and the wild (whistling, or hooper) swan. The two can be easily distinguished by the beginner as mute swans have orange bills and wild swans have yellow and black bills.

Despite his extensive knowledge Bewick did not have it quite right. Two similar but distinct sorts of yellow-billed wild swans can be found in Britain, but it was not until two years after Bewick died that this came to light. It took another British naturalist, William Yarrell, to realize that wild swans were not just hooper (or whooper as it is now spelt) swans but also included a second, smaller type. Yarrell was an enthusiastic member of the Linnean Society and described to them this new species. He proposed calling it Bewick's swan "thus devoting it to the memory of one whose beautiful and animated delineation of subjects in natural history entitle him to this tribute"(ii).

Recently the ornithological world has realized that the tundra swans found in the arctic are actually Bewick's swans. We are urged to call them all tundra swans, wherever they are, to reduce confusion. Despite the dictates of logic one can't help hoping, for the sake of Bewick and his remarkable work, that this idea never fully catches on. Perhaps they could all be called Bewick's swans instead.

TEMMINCK'S STINT
If you know that Temminck's stint is a bird then you must be a birder, perhaps happy to stroll round at the weekend with

a pair of binoculars and a bird book in your pocket to see what you can spot. Is it a thrush? Good. Greenfinch? Excellent. Goldfinch? Marvellous. Bit of a struggle with all those confusing waders at the estuary though. Nevertheless a wonderful relaxing day.

Photo © Andreas Trepte, www.photo-natur.de

8.5: Temminck's stint

If by contrast you can actually recognise a Temminck's stint, described by the bird book as small and drab, then you must be a twitcher. You may be one of the several hundred who raced to the coast not so long ago to see the arrival of an unfortunate American robin that had hitched a lift on a transatlantic liner, only to get a grandstand view of the poor thing being eaten by a sparrowhawk a few moments later. You will definitely possess the best pair of binoculars you can afford, with a mortgage if necessary, plus a telescope. You will be spending every evening and all weekend out with these optical aids until divorce threatens, possibly carrying on even despite being served with the petition. And, even if you are unconcerned about your image, it would never occur to you to take a bird book in your pocket because you would undoubtedly have no need of it.

But consider your plight for a moment. The thrush, greenfinch, goldfinch scenario holds no thrills and to you is merely disappointing. Driving for miles across the country when a sighting of a rare bird is mentioned on the internet must feel like a waste of time when you arrive just after the thing has flown away. And to cap it all, those wretched people at the Royal Society for the Protection of Birds tell you that two Temminck's stints are currently nesting in Scotland somewhere but insist on keeping the site a secret. What a stressful hobby to pursue – no wonder you get twitchy.

The Dutch aristocrat Coenraad Jacob Temminck (1778 – 1858) was the first director of the National Natural History Museum at Leiden and one of the first ornithologists to study an individual species of bird in detail, rather than spending all his time finding new ones. He wrote what was for many years one of the most authoritative book on birds available. But even a struggling birder could not have been tempted to take it into the field – it ran to four volumes.

JACK RUSSELL

In the days when a more robust attitude was taken about hunting with dogs the Reverend John (Parson Jack) Russell (1795 – 1883) was well-known as a keen fox-hunter. He came from an old established Devonshire family and was well-loved by his Devonshire parishioners, respected by fellow-members of the Kennel Club (he was one of the first to join), yet also welcomed by royalty on his visits to Sandringham.

Russell's lifelong passion was hunting, closely followed by an associated interest in breeding terriers. He and his friends were nearly expelled from school for getting together a small pack of hounds and regularly hunting with them. While studying at Oxford he became obsessed with finding a dog to accompany him on hunts, small enough and courageous enough to flush a fox out of its earth but also fast and with sufficient stamina to keep up with the horses. He spotted an ideal small white and tan terrier bitch and bought her from her owner, the milkman. Trump, as she was called, became the original Jack Russell and through Russell's breeding programme became the matriarch of a whole breed.

To refer to a breed, though, is rather misleading as there are different types of dog within it, creating considerable confusion. Some have smooth coats, others are wire-haired. Some have short legs, others long. Some are known as plain Russell terriers, others as Jack Russells, still others as Parson Jack Russells, and what is meant by one of these names in one country is not necessarily the same as what is meant in another. There is even a different Australian version. All this reflects the fact that for years these dogs were bred primarily as working dogs and so, in contrast to many breeds, little emphasis was placed on conforming to an exact standard. It is only in the last few years that the UK Kennel Club has recognised them at all. Even then the decision was controversial and the rules are still changing.

8.6: The Rev. John Russell: frontispiece from
Memoir of the Rev. John Russell and his Out-of-Door life
by E.W.L.Davies

The name of Trump's owner is well-known due to the dynasty Trump founded, but she herself is not entirely without memorial. Her portrait was commissioned by the then Prince of Wales (later Edward VII) and hangs in Sandringham.

Because of their size Jack Russells nowadays are often considered as more of a family pet than a hunting dog, but it is unwise to forget their breeding. There have been several cases of babies being savaged when left alone for a few moments with a group of young Jack Russells and dying from the injuries inflicted.

ST. BERNARD

You can forget the keg of brandy. This was a whim of the artist Sir Edwin Landseer who, when painting a work entitled 'Alpine mastiffs reanimating a distressed traveller', decided to adorn one of them with a small keg attached to its collar for greater artistic effect.

Alpine mastiffs are now usually called St. Bernards because of their association with the Great St. Bernard Pass, the eight thousand foot high pass across the Alps from Switzerland to Italy. The pass was used in Roman times, but its current name comes from the monastery founded there by St. Bernard of Menthon (923 – 1008). Robbers, avalanches and adverse weather made the path notoriously dangerous and the purpose of the monastery was to provide a refuge for travellers, often pilgrims making the journey to Rome. Initially the monks kept guard dogs for protection but by the eighteenth century they had realised that dogs were of help in finding and rescuing lost travellers. The monks began to breed and train alpine mastiffs and over the years these dogs have rescued more than two thousand people. Unlike the modern long-haired, positively woolly, St. Bernard these working St. Bernards were all short-haired. The monks did try crossing them with Newfoundlands to produce the long-haired variety because it was thought that this would help keep them warm, but icicles formed in their coats and snow got stuck in the long hair on their feet, making them unsuitable for rescue work. They all had to be given away.

The monastery's most famous dog, Barry, made forty rescues. He had to retire after his forty-first rescue attempt as he was repeatedly stabbed by a terrified man convinced that he was being attacked by a wolf. One is tempted to wonder if the lack of a keg had left him unaware of Barry's true identity. Barry was eventually stuffed and can be seen at the Natural History Museum in Berne. His pose used to convey a realistic image of an old, exhausted dog, close to collapse after making a harrowing rescue, but in 1923 he was remodelled and now presents a noble, heroic stance. His achievements were so outstanding that ever since he died one of the monastery's dogs has been named Barry in his honour and for a time they were all referred to as Barry hounds.

Photo courtesy Janus Museum, Bern

**8.7: Barry, exhausted
(pre 1923)**

*Photo © Natural History
Museum Bern*

**8.8: Heroic Barry
(post 1923)**

St. Bernards are known to have an innate awareness of approaching storms and unstable snow, threatening avalanches. They were trained to work in teams using their acute sense of smell to find lost or exhausted travellers, even those buried under the snow. Having found someone, one dog would stay beside him to keep him warm while the other would return to the monastery to fetch help. The dogs' extraordinary sense of direction enabled them to find their way even in blizzard conditions.

Nowadays helicopters, heat detectors and acoustic sensors for detection and warning of avalanches can do the job more effectively. In 2004, therefore, the four remaining monks reluctantly came to the conclusion that they could no longer justify the cost of, or time spent, maintaining their fifteen dogs. The meat bill alone must have been astronomical. They had intended to close the kennels and sell the dogs, but a consortium of local villages and St. Bernards' associations across the world set up a foundation to take over the financing, organisation and breeding programme of the kennels. Barry and his friends are now assured of being able to remain in their traditional home, reminding visitors of their history and thereby doing their bit for the tourist trade.

DOBERMANN PINSCHER

The employment record of Friedrich Louis Dobermann (1834 – 1894) would not suggest that he was at all exceptional. He worked in a variety of odd jobs and although there is some uncertainty, these probably included tax collector, night-watchman, skinner at the local slaughterhouse, and dog-catcher.

Courtesy Projekt Runeberg

8.9: Dobermann Pinscher, 1909

But Dobermann was driven by a passion to find the ideal guard-dog for his personal protection. Not much is known about whether it was his behaviour that made this a desirable precaution, but presumably collecting taxes did little for his popularity. He set out to breed a suitable type of terrier. He clearly had a good eye for a dog and it is believed that he crossed various breeds including greyhounds (for speed), Great Danes (for size), an early type of Rottweiler known at that time as a butcher's dog (for strength), and Manchester terriers (for tenacity), always choosing dogs that were bright and alert.

The exact details of what he did remain a matter of guesswork, as he kept no records. His breeding programme was highly successful and his dogs became renowned as working dogs, fearless hunters and highly protective. They were good ratters and were used by farmers for herding livestock. It was not long before they were being widely used by the police and even the army.

After Dobermann died his breed became known as Dobermann pinschers and within a few years the breed was recognised by the German Kennel Club under that name.

KING CHARLES SPANIEL

It is hard to think of a breed that contrasts more sharply with a Dobermann pinscher than a King Charles spaniel. The two are at opposite ends of the social scale: one has recent working class origins while the other historically hobnobbed with royalty. One is quite large with a reputation for ferocity, the other quite small and generally thought of as pretty and sweet. One a working dog, the other a lap-dog.

Further consideration can to some extent bridge the gap between them. The class system is not what it was and without doubt the companion of royalty is no longer the spaniel but the corgi. As far as function is concerned, lap-dogs (or 'comforte dogs' as they were sometimes called) were working dogs in their own way. When castles were cold and journeys in unheated carriages took forever, a dog on the lap or under the feet served as a most useful hot water bottle and, unlike any alternative, could not only be topped up with readily available cold water but could also be relied upon not to have cooled down within a couple of hours. And most self-respecting fleas, given the choice, would move to a dog rather than remain on a human host.

Photo © Darilance Cavalier King Charles Spaniels

8.10: Cavalier King Charles Spaniel

Portrait paintings from Tudor and Stuart times often include a spaniel or two, but spaniels were at their most popular during the reign of Charles II. Charles was almost always accompanied by several, even at official meetings. Samuel Pepys recorded his irritation at this when meeting the King to discuss the Navy, but Pepys, being who he was, also recorded a journey in a small boat when one of the King's dogs "dirted the boat, which made us laugh, and me think that a King and all that belong to him are but just as others are"(iii).

The King's dogs were constantly being stolen and several times he had to resort to advertising in the hope of their return. Apparently it was he who decreed that the breed should be called King Charles spaniels. It is also widely believed that Charles enacted a law, reputed to be still extant, giving these dogs the right to enter the Houses of Parliament despite any Parliamentary regulations that might exist to the contrary. Exhaustive enquiries of and by the Parliamentary authorities have unfortunately turned up nothing to support this.

Those who breed dogs often tend to get carried away with enthusiasm and, although old paintings show spaniels with a flat head and pointed nose, by the early twentieth century fashion had resulted in these characteristics being transformed into a domed head and a flat nose. It took a visiting American to start a campaign to recreate something like the original breed. This involved offering prizes at Crufts for 'look-alike' original King Charles dogs and a meeting was called for all those interested to bring copies of sixteenth, seventeenth and eighteenth century paintings in order to draw up a standard for the breed. It was decided to name it the Cavalier King Charles and in 1945 it was given official recognition by the Kennel Club.

CHAPTER NINE

INVENTIONS and DISCOVERIES

Many inventions and discoveries are commercial names or trade marks but a few of them, where use of the commercial word has become so widespread that its meaning has moved from the particular to the general, are included here. Hoover is a good example. Bakelite®, that rigid, brittle plastic that is also an electrical insulator, falls the other side of the dividing line. Although it merits its own entry in the dictionary and its use is so widespread that the word appears to be generic, it actually still refers only to a specific product. This is a pity because the story of how Leo Baekeland invented the first commercially produced plastic and made a vast fortune, and how his family's consequent financial security was unable to do anything to prevent one of his great grandsons from murdering his own mother and stabbing his grandmother, is unusual to say the least.

ORRERY
Planets in our solar system all revolve around the sun. Unfortunately they do so at different speeds and, remembering that the earth is itself a planet going round the sun, this makes it hard for the non-mathematician to visualise how the other planets move in relation to the earth. What is needed to clarify things is a visual aid. An orrery is just exactly that, a model of the solar system that fits all these relative movements together. The best place to see one working is in a science museum.

An orrery consists of a model of the sun at the centre with a number of arms protruding from it. There is a separate arm for each planet and the length of each arm shows the approximate distance of each planet from the sun. It can be wound up like a clock to show the planets moving round the sun at their appropriate speeds. The observer can then see the relationship between the planets as they move.

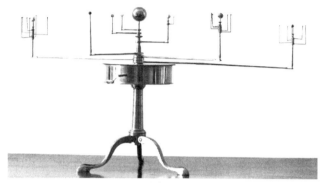

Photo © Armagh Observatory

9.1: Early mechanical orrery by Gilkerston

The word dates from 1713 and the first such model was named in honour of Charles Boyle (1674 – 1731), 4th Earl of Orrery. The Earl had a glittering military career and was also a scholar with an interest in astronomy. Towards the end of his life he was imprisoned in the Tower of London under suspicion of treason, but nothing could be proved against him and after six months he was released. Although the Earl played no part in the actual construction of the orrery, he was responsible for its creation in that it was he who commissioned it and he who arranged for the right man, probably the only man at the time with the requisite knowledge and skills, to make it: the horologist George Graham.

George Graham came from a contrasting background. He was born in Cumberland into a poor farming family and had no formal schooling. After serving seven years' apprenticeship to a clockmaker in London, he began to work for the renowned horologist Thomas Tompion. Together they made several improvements to the design mechanism of clocks and watches. Graham married Tompion's niece and Tompion bequeathed his business to Graham. Graham extended his interests into the field of astronomy making, amongst other things, a quadrant for Halley (of Comet fame) who was most impressed with its precision. Graham became known across Europe for the accuracy of his instruments and was the most celebrated clock-maker and astronomical instrument maker of his day. He was also generous, making interest free loans to friends and colleagues, often not asking for repayment. One such loan was made to enable the then unknown country carpenter John Harrison, who had an idea for the design of a marine clock so reliable that it could be used to measure longitude, to develop his idea and build the clock.

There is no suggestion that an orrery should by rights be called a 'graham' but in death the two men were honoured equally: both are buried in Westminster Abbey.

BUNSEN BURNER

Everyone who has studied chemistry at any level knows the handy little Bunsen burner that produces a clean, hot flame and is used for heating chemicals in the laboratory. But all is not what you might think. The original idea came from Michael Faraday and it was a laboratory technician at Heidelberg, Peter Desaga, who made the first one. It also seems that Desaga was responsible for developing Faraday's idea and designing the new burner, although some say that it was the professor of chemistry at Heidelberg, Robert Wilhelm Bunsen (1811 – 1899) who did this. Bunsen can certainly be regarded as responsible for the invention in the sense that he needed such a burner in order to pursue his scientific studies and so asked Desaga to make him one.

Any quibbles about the moral right to the name of the burner should not be allowed to detract from Bunsen's achievements. The most important of these was his work with

Kirchoff on spectrum analysis, in the course of which he discovered two new elements, caesium and rubidium. He also experimented for a time using arsenic compounds that were both toxic and highly flammable but, after losing the sight of one eye in an explosion and nearly dying of arsenic poisoning, he saw fit to abandon that area of research. He never married and was dedicated to his work, retiring at the age of nearly 80 to pursue an interest in geology.

PETRI DISH

What the Bunsen burner is to the study of chemistry so the Petri dish is to the study of microbiology. It is an unassuming bit of kit: an extremely shallow, cylindrical glass dish that is several centimetres in diameter with vertical sides only one centimetre high or so, plus a lid.

Photo © User Polimerek/ Wikimedia Commons

9.2: Petri dish (without a lid)

In the 1880s the German bacteriologist Robert Koch, already famous for his work on the bacterium that causes anthrax, was growing colonies of other bacteria using gelatine on a flat glass base in order to study them in detail. His assistant Julius Richard Petri (1852 – 1921), a military physician, designed the small practical dish that has been used in laboratories across the world ever since. One or two other scientists had previously designed something very similar, no doubt in response to the requirements of the new science of bacteriology, but Petri's was the one that took the name and the fame.

Later in his career Petri went on to be head of a TB sanatorium, custodian of a museum, and wrote a vast number of papers, articles and reports.   Koch received numerous honours and achieved international fame for discovering the tuberculosis bacillus, in recognition of which he was awarded a Nobel Prize in 1905.

DOPPLER EFFECT

'Neee Nor Neee Nor Neee Nor' ... A small child once thought that every police car was equipped with two sirens, each producing the same distinctive wail but at a slightly different pitch, and that they always just happened to switch from the higher pitched siren to the lower one as the car raced past him.   After all, what other explanation could there be for the change in tone?   It was clearly time for someone to explain the Doppler effect.

Doppler (1803 – 1853), whose first names appear to have been some or all of Christian, Andreas and Johann in any combination, was the son of a stonemason.   His health was never very good, so working in the family business was not really an option.   Fortunately he was brilliant at maths and he went to university in Vienna to read the subject.   His career was not straightforward.   At one stage he had given up hope of ever getting a job and sold all his possessions with the intention of emigrating to the USA, but an offer came up just in time and he went to teach in Prague instead.   Eventually he was appointed to the chair of mathematics in Prague and, later on, in Vienna.

The idea for which he is famous came from thinking about a ship moving through the waves.   He knew that a ship sailing into the oncoming waves met more waves in a given period of time than one that was stationary.   He concluded that by definition this meant that the 'wavelength' (i.e. the distance between the peak or trough of each wave) experienced by the ship as it moved towards the waves, must be shorter than that experienced by a stationary ship. He thought that the same thing must therefore be true for all other types of waves as well, including sound waves and light waves. He deduced that if a star was moving towards the earth the light waves emitted by it would be shorter, i.e., they would be closer to the ultra-violet end of the spectrum, so light from the star would look bluer. In contrast, if the star was moving away from the earth the light waves emitted would be longer, i.e., they would be closer to the red end of the spectrum and the light from the star would look redder (an effect now known as red shift). In 1843 when he came up with this idea there were no instruments available by which the minute variation in colour could possibly be detected. Nevertheless Doppler predicted that the principle would in the future provide a way of measuring the movements of stars and galaxies relative to the earth, as indeed it has.

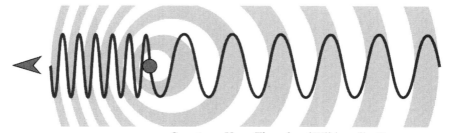

Courtesy User Tkarcher/ Wikimedia Commons

9.3: Waves emitted by a source moving from right to left

Sound travels far more slowly than light and so is much more amenable to a demonstration of the Doppler effect. In 1845 the recent development of a railway train that could reach the then terrifying speed of 40 m.p.h. enabled the Dutch scientist Buys- (or Buijs-) Ballot to carry out an experiment on a grand scale – one of the classic scientific experimental proofs of all time. It took place on the Amsterdam-Utrecht railway line. He arranged for a group of horn players to sit on an open flatbed railway wagon coupled to a steam engine.

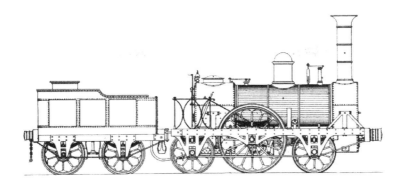

9.4: Sketch of the steam locomotive used in the Buys-Ballot experiment

The engine driver was instructed to drive full speed along the line. The horn players were instructed to blow their horns fortissimo on a long single note, breathing in relays so that the sound was uninterrupted. Buys-Ballot waited on the station platform at Maarssen and listened. In these days of small boys and police cars you don't need anyone to tell you what he heard. Within a few months Doppler refined this experiment, repeating it with two groups of trumpeters blessed with perfect pitch, one on the wagon and one at the station, who assessed by ear the interval between the two different sounds as the players went past at different speeds. We know now that at 40 m.p.h. the drop in pitch is roughly a semi-tone, increasing to a minor third at 150 m.p.h. The really clever thing is that, in the unlikely event of:

a) the train being able to race along at twice the speed of sound,

b) the trumpeters on the train not getting blown off it and having enough breath to be able to play,

c) the trumpeters on the train playing a complete tune at full blast before the train passes the station and

d) the other trumpeters who were waiting at the station having exceptionally sharp ears,

301

then the trumpeters at the station would hear the tune at the correct pitch and in the correct time but played backwards. Apparently.

PASTEURISATION

Louis Pasteur (1822 – 95) was the son of a tanner, yet became Professor of chemistry at the Sorbonne and director of the Institute founded in his honour.

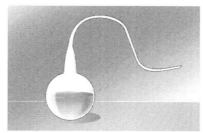

© *User YassineMrabet/ Wikimedia Commons*

9.5: Swan neck flask of similar shape to that used by Louis Pasteur

At an early stage in his career Pasteur investigated the process of fermentation, a process crucial to the wine and beer industries. He discovered that, when fermentation took place, micro-organisms only visible with the use of a microscope were always present. This finding led him to think about where these organisms had come from. Had they simply developed from within the liquid itself or, since it was known that exposure to air was needed for fermentation to take place, had they come out of the air? So he began to study the effect of different kinds of air, from city air to clear high Alpine air, on a flask of boiled (and hence sterilized) broth. He found that the cleaner the air the fewer micro-organisms grew in the broth. And when the only access to air was through a glass tube leading from the top of the flask, bent in such a way as to prevent dust particles or other contaminants in the air from falling on to the broth (a 'swan neck' flask), virtually no micro-organisms appeared, even when such a flask was placed in polluted city air. This discovery disproved the hitherto widely held theory that decaying matter spontaneously generated living organisms. In its most extreme form this old theory had suggested that maggots were actually created out of the rotting meat on which they were found.

The process of pasteurisation was a direct development of Pasteur's work on fermentation. It involves heating a liquid to a temperature in the region of 65°C – 75°C for long enough to kill off any micro-organisms already in it, then keeping it in conditions that prevent subsequent contamination. This increases substantially the time for which the liquid can be kept without spoiling, as well as protecting the consumer from infection – notably TB in the case of milk.

Photo © Krish Dulal

9.6: Silk moth cocoons in a jar

It was a natural extension of Pasteur's research for him to consider whether unseen micro-organisms in the air might not only contaminate broth, but also be the cause of disease. Crisis in the French silkworm industry led the government to call in Pasteur for advice. Pasteur identified the disease that was making the silkworms die in droves and advised that, to prevent its spread, healthy silkworms should be kept well away from the diseased ones. As a result the industry was rescued from complete collapse. Today such a basic step to stop the spread of infection is so blindingly obvious it is hard to believe that in the 1800s the idea was novel and regarded with scepticism.

From silkworms Pasteur moved on to study animal diseases. Using Robert Koch's recent discovery of the micro-organism responsible for causing anthrax, Pasteur isolated it and is credited with being the first to develop an effective vaccine against anthrax, although there is some controversy as to whether he might have used a method already discovered by someone else. He also developed a vaccine against rabies, a disease that was always fatal. Development of the rabies vaccine was still undergoing early trials on dogs when Pasteur gave it to a nine-year old boy who had been severely bitten by a rabid dog, knowing that otherwise the child was certain to contract rabies and die. The boy survived and Pasteur was the hero of the day.

SILHOUETTE

Photo © C.M. Wiles

9.7: Silhouette of the author

Before the era of photography, outline portraits used to be a cheap and popular way of recording images. They were made life size with the subject sitting between a lighted candle and a glass screen, on the other side of which was a sheet of paper on which the outline of the subject's shadow could be traced. This outline was then blacked in later, or cut out and mounted. By the late 1700s a piece of machinery had been invented for reproducing the original outline in different sizes.

The word silhouette is derived from the name of the extraordinarily unpopular French Minister of Finance, Étienne de Silhouette (1709 – 1767), but there is uncertainty as to exactly why. Silhouette had made a name for himself through his study of the English financial system and subsequently held several official appointments in France. This was a time of great extravagance amongst the French aristocracy. Silhouette was rare in that he had a reputation for economy. The king was running short of the money needed to support his part in waging the Seven Years War: Madame de Pompadour persuaded him that Silhouette would be the right man to take charge of the treasury.

The appointment was a disaster. Not only did Silhouette's abilities fail to live up to expectations, but his policies horrified the aristocracy – his own relatives included. He raised money not only by taxing their incomes but also by taxing their land. There was a storm of protest. He was ridiculed and became the butt of jokes. Within less than nine months Silhouette was forced to resign.

He retired to the country and became devoutly religious, running his own household with strict economy and passing his time by making the outline portraits that are now called silhouettes. It seems that the most likely reason for the use of his name in this way was to poke fun at the economies he introduced whilst in charge of the treasury, bearing in mind that outline portraiture was a cheap alternative to a proper painted portrait. Alternatively, it could have arisen as a reference to the hobby he took up after he was forced out of office in disgrace.

DAGUERREOTYPE

The silhouette was all very well as far as it went, but it recorded no more than an outline. A daguerreotype, by contrast, was the first type of photographic record that produced a complete image. It was not a true photograph, as we understand the word, since it was no more than a mirror image recorded directly on to a photographic plate by a chemical process. There was no equivalent of a negative and so no way that the image could be reproduced.

Nowadays a scientist tends to be thought of as someone grappling with a subject so technical and extensive that he or she is living in an ivory tower and has little time to devote to other interests. Two hundred years ago science was more straightforward and so Louis Jacques Mandé Daguerre (1789 – 1851) was able to be both an artist and a physicist. In his early career he was a scene painter for the Paris Opera. For many years he also set up a series of enormously successful Dioramas – exhibitions of large paintings on translucent material with pictures not only on the front but also on the back, so that special effects could be produced depending upon whether the painting was illuminated from in front or behind.

In the hope of being able to produce improved scenes for the Diorama, Daguerre experimented with various chemical processes. Working with a colleague, Nicéphore Niepce, he discovered that silver iodide was sensitive to light, but it took some ten years' further work before Daguerre perfected his technique. The process for making what became known as a daguerreotype was not exactly straightforward. A plate coated with silver had to be treated with iodine vapour to produce a surface coating of silver iodide. The plate was then exposed to light in a camera for some ten minutes to create an image of what was 'seen' by the camera, that could then be developed by treating the exposed plate with fumes of mercury vapour (no health and safety inspectors then). The developed image had to be fixed with a solution of salt. The picture would tarnish and eventually disappear altogether if exposed to the air, but was also so fragile that polishing would simply rub the whole thing off. The finished daguerreotype therefore had to be inserted into a sealed frame to preserve it.

9.8: 'The Artist's Studio', possibly the first daguerreotype made by Daguerre, 1837

The process had been devised in order to obtain images of scenery and within that limitation it worked wonderfully well. Such was its success that when its invention was made public in 1839 the French government bought the details of the methodology from Daguerre in order to make it available for the benefit of the whole French nation. However, the exposure time of ten minutes made it unsuitable for recording images of people. Daguerre's friend, Samuel Morse, took the method with him to the USA, where further refinement of the technique reduced the necessary exposure time to only one or two minutes, thereby tapping into a new and popular market for portraits. Daguerreotypes became all the rage, but within only a few years they fell out of favour because of the development of modern photography.

MORSE CODE

We have just met Samuel Finley Breese Morse (1791 – 1872), but his interest in daguerreotypes lasted for only a short time and was sandwiched between his two other main careers.

Like Daguerre, Morse was both an artist and a scientist. He read science at Yale University but was far more interested in art and spent much of his time there painting portraits instead of studying. Eventually he persuaded his parents to send him to the Royal Academy of Art in London for four years. He was found to be very talented but on his return to the USA there was little public interest in the historical pictures he enjoyed painting. Reluctantly he had to go back to portrait painting to earn a living and by his mid-forties he gave up painting altogether. By then he had found a new, this time scientific, interest.

It is said that Morse's enthusiasm for electromagnetism began in 1832 on board ship travelling home from France. Fellow passengers were discussing electromagnetic experiments and the speed of electricity. Morse was already aware from his studies as a young man that the passage of electricity through a piece of paper left a record of its passing by a burn mark. Morse linked these concepts together and came up with the idea of what became known as the electro-telegraph, a piece of machinery that used electricity not only to send a message virtually instantaneously along a wire from one place to another, but also to produce a paper record of that message. European scientists had already devised a system of long distance electromagnetic communication by sound alone but the brilliance of Morse's idea, and the thing that made it of enormous practical and commercial value, was what might now be called the hard copy: the paper record of the message.

Morse and his two business partners spent some years developing his idea and one of the first major problems they encountered was the fact that the longer the wire, the greater its electrical resistance and so the more feeble the electric current passing through it. This setback was overcome using the European discovery of the relay. By positioning batteries at local relay stations at appropriate intervals along the wire, the electrical signal could be boosted and communication over very long distances became possible.

This communication was still in a very limited form. Morse had begun by using a telegraphic dictionary with a number code but this was extremely cumbersome. Morse (or, some claim, his partner Alfred Vail – a suggestion always refuted by Morse) then invented a letter code using short and long electrical pulses, the familiar dots and dashes.

· · · — — — · · ·

SOS in Morse code – the international distress signal for 'Save our souls'

It is hard now to imagine a world without instant communications but before the electrotelegraph there had been no way of synchronising time across a distance. Even in a country as small as England there were variations between East and West. Accurate clocks were available and there was

Photo courtesy Rod Ward

9.9: Corn Exchange Clock, Bristol

agreement on the times of sunrise and sunset on any particular day. But the Eastern side of a country experiences sunrise sooner than the Western side, so when the sun was used as the basis for setting the time, clocks in the East indicated a particular time several minutes before clocks in the West did so. The difference between, for example, Bristol time and London time is still graphically displayed by the old clock installed in the 1840s on top of the Bristol Corn Exchange.

The new London - Bristol railway had recently opened and although Bristol carried on using its own time, the railway timetable used London time, even for the departures from Bristol. So this clock has two minute hands: one showing London ('railway') time and the other showing Bristol (or what used to be, for locals, 'real') time as eleven minutes later. It was not until 1880 that an Act of Parliament decreed that all clocks across the country were to use Greenwich Mean Time.

GUILLOTINE

In the cold world of grammar the word guillotine is described as an 'ordinary noun', but the word only has to be mentioned and imagination plunges one immediately into the horrors of the French Revolution: the unfortunate victims standing in the jolting tumbril, the jeering crowd, the diagonal blade poised between the top of the two tall posts before hurtling down at its release, the basket receiving the severed head as it falls, blood spurting everywhere as grim old crones knit nearby. Some of the emotional impact derives also from the sheer volume of indiscriminate slaughter. France was not a good place to be during the 1790s and some 15,000 heads were severed within a mere seven years.

Earlier machines for beheading people had existed – in England the Halifax Gibbet dating from the thirteenth century was one of the earliest, responsible for decapitating some eighty felons. Some centuries later a similarly designed machine, the 'Scottish Maiden', was used in Edinburgh. However, there was no generalised design for, or use of, such machines. There is also barely a mention of the guillotine being used after the French revolution, but it would be wrong to assume that that was anything like the end of it. It continued in use for public executions in France until 1939 (public executions in England ceased in 1868) and was not completely withdrawn from use until the late 1970s. Other countries also used it: during the Second World War the Nazis ordered many thousands of people to be beheaded and built a number of guillotines for the purpose.

Photo © Paul Glazzard

9.10: Replica of The Halifax Gibbet at Gibbet Street, Halifax

It was the physician and politician Dr. Joseph Ignace Guillotin (1738-1814) who put forward the idea that all prisoners condemned to death should be beheaded. A law was made to this effect in 1792. We are given to understand that beheading is a skilled and tiring task, and certainly the official executioner of the time warned the revolutionary government that in order to implement the new law some kind of machine would be needed. Dr. Antoine Louis was asked to design one that was then made and tried out on corpses. In these early days it was called a Louisette after the name of the designer. After some improvements to the design, enough machines were made to distribute them throughout France and they then became known as guillotines.

It is important to remember that Guillotin's proposal had nothing to do with the imposition of a death sentence, which was already commonplace throughout Europe. It only addressed the issue of how the sentence was to be carried out.

This usually took place in public and hitherto had involved the infliction of appalling pain, no doubt partly *pour encourager les autres*. The common man (or woman) had been expected to suffer the most. Those with money, power or influence had had a good chance of something less painful. Guillotin's proposal and the amendments to the French penal code putting it into effect were both made with the best of intentions and in the interests of equality and humanity, allowing those from the lower echelons of society who were unfortunate enough to be sentenced to death to share with the aristocracy the privilege of a comparatively painless end.

Before the guillotine the death penalty might involve any one of a number of unpleasant procedures. Beheading was probably the least gruesome, even though it usually took three or four chops with an axe to sever the head from the body. Beheading tended to be reserved for those of high social status but someone really important might be lucky enough for a sword to be used instead of an axe, when a determined slice had a good chance of carrying out the task at one go. Heretics and witches were burned at the stake – a slow process in which the victim, already tied into position, had to wait for the heat to build up once the wood beneath had been lit, although it was not unknown for the executioner to agree to hasten the victim's end in return for a suitably substantial bribe.

Breaking on the wheel was another possibility. The condemned was either tied to a wheel and beaten to death, or tied to the outside edge of the wheel of a cart that was then driven slowly down the road. Slow strangulation by hanging was widespread: if you were fortunate a nearby friend or relation in the crowd might be within reach and pull down on your feet to hurry up the process. A person found guilty of more serious offences could be hanged, drawn and quartered. This involved being taken down from the scaffold after only a short period of hanging and then disembowelled and cut into four separate pieces while still alive – eventual death being a merciful release. In some areas of France the hanging and drawing was dispensed with, the quartering being achieved more slowly by tying the four limbs to four horses which were then driven in different directions until the task was accomplished.

The carrying out of a death sentence has always had a macabre fascination, as is evidenced both by the enormous crowds attracted to watch public executions and by the popularity of the Chamber of Horrors in Madame Tussaud's, where wax images made from plaster casts of the heads of the guillotined aristocracy are still displayed. Public executions, of course, no longer happen in Europe and when the media brings film footage of such events from abroad, we are disgusted, forgetting our very recent past.

Many people must have wondered whether a person who is beheaded is aware of what has happened, even if that awareness lasts only for a moment. Reports from the time of the French revolution suggest that on occasion a victim's face showed signs of movement and a number of studies have actually been carried out. On the occasion of one execution by guillotine during the 1800s some doctors, apparently with the consent of the condemned, did their utmost to get some sort of response from him immediately his head had been severed, but without success. Other studies suggest that consciousness may remain, perhaps up to five seconds at the most.

Dictionaries include two other meanings of guillotine – not linked to Dr. Guillotin himself but to the machine that incorporates his name. The accuracy with which the guillotine neatly removed heads made the word an obvious choice for the device equipped with a large blade designed to cut easily through several layers of paper with precision. And the ruthless image of the guillotine for achieving speedy decapitation is reflected in the guillotine procedure adopted when the government wants to force legislation through Parliament: debate on each part of a Bill is abruptly halted as soon as its allotted time period has elapsed. Given that Dr. Guillotin was a politician, he would surely have been amused at such use of his name.

BRAILLE

At the beginning of the nineteenth century there was little future for a blind person. Unless the family was willing and able to provide support, most ended up as beggars.

Photo © User Kou07kou/ Wikimedia Commons

9.11: Birthplace of Louis Braille

Louis Braille (1809 – 1852) was the son of a leather worker. At the age of three he was playing in his father's workshop and accidentally pierced his eye with an awl, blinding it. The injury soon led to a severe reaction in the other eye, as a result of which he lost his sight altogether. This disaster was mitigated to some extent when, at the age of eleven, Louis gained a scholarship to the Institution Royale des Jeunes Aveugles in Paris, one of the first schools established for blind children. The boys were taught practical skills to enable them to earn a living and Louis became an accomplished organist and cellist. They were also taught to read, using the usual letters of the alphabet but embossed so that they could be felt with the fingertips.

Not long after Louis went to his new school it was visited by an artillery officer named Charles Barbier. Barbier had recently developed a system of 'night-writing' using raised dots, to allow silent communication along the battle lines when it was too dark to read and any light risked attracting enemy fire. In this system each alphabetical letter was represented by a grid or cell comprising up to twelve dots, but it had not been very successful, both because the size of the cells was unwieldy and because it was too complicated for many to succeed in mastering it.

Barbier demonstrated his system to the school. Braille realised its potential and developed it further, reducing the size and composition of the symbols to a grid of only six dots: two horizontally and three vertically. This had the key advantage of making the cells small enough to allow the whole of each 'letter' to be felt at once by a single fingertip. Letters composed of raised dots meant that they could be written much more easily than the cumbersome embossed letters, simply by pressing anything with a sharpish point against the back of the paper.

At the time no-one in authority seemed very interested in Braille's idea. Barbier was not happy about his system being modified, least of all by a blind boy. The teachers did everything to discourage an alternative to the established method of teaching reading using the embossed alphabetical letters. The boys, apparently, did use Braille's system amongst themselves and no doubt had enormous enjoyment from secret communication in 'code'.

Braille persisted and in 1827 the first book in Braille was published. Braille went on to become a teacher at his school, but his new system for reading and writing was never taught there during his lifetime. It was only some years after his death that it came into widespread, and finally universal, use. Today there are Braille typewriters and Braille printers for use with computers.

Braille died at a comparatively young age after battling for many years with tuberculosis. One hundred years later his achievement was officially recognised by the government and his body was moved to the Pantheon in Paris.

SAXOPHONE

Antoine Joseph Sax (known as Adolph) (1814 – 1894) was born in Belgium, the son of an instrument designer. He studied the flute and clarinet and began making his own instruments before he left school. He continued to experiment with innovative designs and by his late twenties had moved to Paris and exhibited some of his instruments there with great success. His set of keyed bugles was recognised as being so superior to those made by others that they became known as saxhorns, a name that upset the German inventors of the original instruments and led to considerable ill-feeling. This was exacerbated when he turned his attention to improving the standards of French military bands by, amongst other things, introducing the use of saxhorns.

Photo courtesy User Ommeh at en.wikipedia

9.12: B-flat curved soprano, E-flat alto and B-flat tenor saxophones

It was not long before Sax had invented and patented the saxophone. The well-known composer Berlioz was impressed and his support helped to win recognition for the instrument and also to secure Sax a job teaching at the Paris Conservatoire.

Despite the enormous success of his instruments Sax had many problems. He had a prickly personality with an unfortunate knack of upsetting people. He became involved in extensive litigation when competing instrument makers attacked his patent rights and consequently he twice became bankrupt. In truth, some of Sax's designs were extremely similar to those of his rivals, but his skills and attention to detail meant that his instruments were so vastly superior that they were in practice, if not in the strict legal sense, 'something else altogether'.

Ultimately Sax died in poverty, supported by a very modest pension from the French government.

SOUSAPHONE

If asked to imagine a band playing at some outside event the mind may well conjure up heartening music near a marquee, with cups of tea, sandwiches and chatter at some local event on an English summer day which threatens rain and turns rather chilly when the sun goes in. Remembrance Day is the other likely scenario, when military bands playing sombre music march with precision along Whitehall past silent, respectful crowds: cornets and trombones, horns, tubas and drums. The moment a sousaphone intrudes on the scene, the whole mental image is transformed. Suddenly one visualises the USA, with hot sunshine, nattily dressed girls waving bunches of coloured ribbons and plenty of razzmatazz.

John Philip Sousa (1854 – 1932) was one of ten children born into a musical family. His father was a trombonist in the US Marine Band and Sousa played the violin as well as a variety of other instruments. At thirteen he tried to run away to join a circus band, so his father enlisted him in the Marines. After serving his apprenticeship he left to pursue several musical interests: playing, conducting and writing various types of music, particularly military marches. When he was in his mid-twenties he returned to lead the US Marine Band for some years, then left and formed his own band that he continued to conduct until shortly before he died.

9.13: Sousaphones in a Santa Claus parade, USA

The sousaphone is a type of tuba, specially designed at Sousa's request in order to project its sound up and over the top of the band. At first its bell – the end where the sound comes out – pointed straight upwards. The instruments were consequently referred to disparagingly as raincatchers, but in the 1920s the design of the bell was altered to face the front.

FERRIS WHEEL

Chicago hosted the celebration of the 400th anniversary of Christopher Columbus' discovery of America in what became known as the Chicago World's Fair of 1893. The organisers wanted to feature a marvel of modern engineering that could rival, or even outdo, the sensationally successful Eiffel Tower then recently built in Paris. In an effort to spur civil engineers into coming up with a good idea, the Director of Works went to speak to a group of them who regularly met informally at their Saturday Afternoon Club. The first suggestion to emerge was an even bigger version of the Eiffel Tower, but the Director of Works wanted something innovative. One of the group, George Washington Gale Ferris (1859 – 1896), suggested a giant revolving wheel with spokes like a bicycle wheel that could take passengers high up into the air. Legend has it that he designed the whole thing that same evening on the back of the proverbial envelope, or in this case dinner napkin, right down to the numbers of people the wheel would carry and the cost of the tickets. But it is probable that Ferris had already thought about it a great deal, having originally got the idea from a water mill near his childhood home that was operated by a mill wheel powered by water passing underneath it.

Courtesy The New York Times Photo archives

9.14: The original Ferris wheel, built for the Chicago World's Fair 1893

The proposed wheel was certainly innovative, but initially a bit too innovative for the organisers who regarded Ferris as completely dotty. It was not until he had found private financial backers to cover the cost, plus confirmation from other engineers as to the feasibility of the idea, that his proposal was finally accepted. By then it was the beginning of winter and the fair was due to open in less than six months' time. Work had to begin immediately, in the bitter cold. On site steam was piped in to keep frost and snow at bay and to prevent the concrete from freezing before it could set properly. But despite all, the wheel was finished only six weeks behind schedule. It was 264 feet high and carried 36 cars, each of which accommodated up to 60 passengers. It proved a huge success, attracting about one and a half million visitors during the five months or so during which it was in operation. For comparison the British Airways London Eye, built to celebrate the new millennium, attracts some three and half million people annually in its 32 capsules, each accommodating a mere 25 passengers but carrying them some 200 feet higher.

In contrast to the London Eye, which continues to be a great success, the original Ferris wheel had to be dismantled at the end of the World Fair. Although it was erected elsewhere it never again achieved its former glory. Other companies copied it and Ferris became heavily involved in extensive and costly litigation to protect his rights to the design. He became obsessed with building bigger and better wheels in which no-one was interested. In 1906 his wheel was demolished and sold as scrap. Even so, it had outlasted its inventor whose wife had left him and who died, bankrupt, alone and in despair, at the age of 37.

HOOVER®

What do Hoovers and Jacuzzis have in common? The answer is that they both began in the USA as registered tradenames and that the invention of each was sparked by a medical problem. Had they remained merely tradenames they would not qualify for inclusion in this book but both words subsequently, and to the irritation of the manufacturers, became used as generic terms. In Britain use of the word 'hoover' is now so widespread that to refer to a vacuum cleaner sounds positively archaic. When the Dyson, a vacuum cleaner that looked like nothing ever seen before, initially appeared on the market, even that tended to be referred to as 'one of those funny new hoovers'. And the word 'hoover' has taken on a life of its own. It is now used as a verb and this transformation has freed it from the world of carpets: one hoovers the floor and, by analogy, a greedy member of the family might be accused of hoovering up the rest of the chocolates in the box.

9.15: Electric vacuum cleaner by Electric Suction Sweeper Company, circa 1908

It was James Murray Spangler who first had the idea. He was an inventor who had an evening job cleaning carpets in a department store. He found that the dust exacerbated his asthma, so he devised an electrically operated suction cleaner using little more than a broom handle, a pillowcase, a tin box and a fan. It worked well and he realised there could be a market for this invention, but that he needed financial backing to develop it. He persuaded a friend, Susan Hoover, to try it out. She was impressed and enthused about it to her husband, William Henry Hoover (1849 – 1932). At that time Hoover was running a saddlers and leather business but he bought the patent from Spangler, invested in Spangler's 'Electric Suction Sweeper Company' (eventually becoming its president) and in 1908 they began making the first vacuum cleaners. In 1922 the company was renamed the Hoover Company.

321

Hoover had a flair for marketing. He advertised the new vacuum cleaners with the offer of a ten days' free trial, but instead of dealing directly with each customer he arranged for the cleaners to be sent to a local retailer who could liaise with all the customers in that area. The retailer kept commission on any sales that were made and was given the opportunity to join a network of established dealers for Hoover cleaners. Hoover also trained sales representatives to demonstrate the cleaners, both at dealers' show rooms and door-to-door. Improvements were made to the design and the business thrived.

During the difficult years of the American Depression in the 1920s Hoover discreetly did much to help those in financial difficulties. He was always closely involved in the community and during the Second World War arranged for the children of employees at the Hoover plant on the outskirts of London to be evacuated to the USA and taken in by families there. He was a religious man and was widely held in great respect.

JACUZZI®

A whirlpool bath that pumps a mixture of air and water through numerous holes in its sides at a pressure that can vary from the gently relaxing to a determined pummelling approaching that delivered by a sports physiotherapist, must be the ultimate luxury. And the Jacuzzi family history is the ultimate rags to riches story.

In 1903 the seven Jacuzzi brothers plus various other relations emigrated from Italy to the USA. They began earning a living by picking oranges but soon one of them was designing and making aeroplane propellers. Before long the brothers began manufacturing aeroplanes, their business prospered and they diversified into agricultural pumping machinery.

In due course the youngest brother, Candido Jacuzzi (1903 – 1986), had a son who developed rheumatoid arthritis whilst still only a baby. The baby went for regular hydrotherapy sessions, but to alleviate his pain between visits Candido adapted the design of the agricultural pumps produced by the

Jacuzzi business. He created a portable pump that produced powerful jets of water that had a massaging effect, but which could be used by putting it into an ordinary bath. Others began to hear about it and a niche market grew amongst those who wanted one for therapeutic purposes. Later on the idea became popular as a luxury item among well-known personalities.

Twenty years after Candido first invented his portable pump a younger member of the family, Roy Jacuzzi, designed the first jacuzzi as we know it: a bath in which the piping to deliver jets of water and air is incorporated into the bath itself. Technically the word Jacuzzi only applies to baths manufactured by the Jacuzzi company. Similar baths produced by rival manufacturers should be referred to as whirlpool baths but use of the word Jacuzzi by the general public is so widespread that it has entered the dictionary, albeit with a reminder of its trademark status.

BIRO®

How did a revolutionary new type of pen designed by a Jewish man born in Budapest and manufactured by him in Argentina contribute to Britain's efforts to win the Second World War? The answer links a series of extraordinarily random events.

First, the pen had to be designed. There had been several efforts at making a pen with a small ball at the end instead of the usual nib, but the first person to make one that actually worked was Laszlo Jozsef Biro (1899 – 1985). His early career was somewhat chequered: he started medical training but then practised as a hypnotist for a time before designing the first automatic gear-box for cars. Biro then moved into journalism, but was irritated to find that constant refilling of fountain pens took time and was messy. He tried using the same quick-drying ink used by the printing press that did not smudge, but it was too thick and clogged the nib. With the help of his brother Georg he then tried changing the nib for a small ball bearing that rotated when the pen was used,

323

collecting ink from a reservoir behind the ball and transferring it on to the paper. He patented the design and began refining it.

Why did Biro leave Hungary for Argentina? By the late 1930s Nazism was spreading and the introduction of anti-Jewish laws in 1938 meant that many Jews who were able to do so left Europe. While on holiday during the mid 1930s Laszlo had happened to meet someone who was very interested in his new ball-point pen. The man turned out to be the president of Argentina, who gave Laszlo his signed card and suggested that Laszlo move to Argentina and manufacture the new pen there. Laszlo did not immediately do so but, as the situation in Europe became more dangerous, he used this contact to obtain a visa and emigrate. He set up production of ball-point pens in Argentina and in due course took on Argentinian citizenship.

Photo courtesy Adrian Pingstone

9.16: A Hurricane Mk I (R4118) that fought in the Battle of Britain

So how did the RAF become involved? A British government official in Argentina during the early 1940s happened to know that RAF navigators, flying in aeroplanes with unpressurised cabins, had problems using fountain pens because these leaked at high altitudes. He noticed that Biro's pens worked well and without leaking under these conditions. He accordingly bought British licensing rights and the pen was produced in Britain for the RAF. Shortly after the war, of course, pens of this design were made and used worldwide, and now have become so ubiquitous that 'biro', although still a trade name, has become widely used to refer to a ball-point pen of any make, without even a hint of a capital letter.

HEATH ROBINSON CONTRAPTION

Posterity has been somewhat unkind to William Heath Robinson (1872 – 1944), who was a serious artist. He began his career by illustrating classic books such as Charles and Mary Lamb's 'Tales from Shakespeare', Charles Kingsley's 'The Water Babies' and Cervantes' 'Don Quixote'. However, his name is now forever associated with cartoons of complicated and rickety mechanical contraptions, often operated by a bald man in overalls and usually involving pulleys and bits of string to achieve a simple outcome in the most convoluted way imaginable.

Even though Heath Robinson has not achieved artistic fame commensurate with that of, for example, Gainsborough or Turner, his cartoons are regarded with a great deal of affection and reach a wider public than the work of many artists, particularly through his illustrations for the Professor Branestawm books. His fame extends even to those who may never have seen one of his cartoons, through the use of his name to describe any absurdly complicated and ingenious piece of machinery.

Although the adjective Heath Robinson has now become so much a part of the English language that it merits its own entry in the dictionary, one could be forgiven for thinking that it is not really amenable to translation into other languages. The term has even failed to cross the Atlantic. But other countries have their own words for such machinery and it is not unusual for these to derive from a very similar local background. So the American term is a 'Rube Goldberg machine', after the twentieth century US cartoonist Reuben Goldberg. The Danes refer to a 'Storm P maskiner', a reference to the Danish cartoonist Robert Storm Petersen. The Turkish equivalent is a 'Zihni Sinir Proceleri', using the name of the imaginary eccentric scientist Porof Zihni Sinir, rather than the name of the cartoonist who created him. The Spanish equivalent is an 'invento del tebeo', from the name of the magazine TBO that regularly published the drawings of a Catalan cartoonist.

Those working on top-secret code breaking at Bletchley during the Second World War christened one of their machines after Heath Robinson because of the complexity of its appearance, though the level of secrecy was such that Heath Robinson himself would never have known. It was an electro-mechanical high-speed tape reader that used two separate continuous loops of teleprinter tape. One loop comprised a section of the coded text to be decrypted. The other, the key tape, was one character longer and was prepared from the details, already obtained by code breakers at Bletchley, of the code wheel patterns of the German coding machine. By running the two tapes side by side 'Heath Robinson' was able to subtract the two streams of characters one from the other, thereby testing the coded text for each possible initial starting point of the relevant code wheel. The pattern of the resulting flow of characters showed whether or not there was a possibility that further work using that particular wheel setting might succeed in deciphering the coded message.

CHAPTER TEN

MILITARY

It seems that practically every gun in existence is named after its designer. Many of these, including men with such well known surnames as Purdey, Colt, and Smith and Wesson, founded companies incorporating their own names. They do not therefore feature here because the names are commercial – usually meaning a make, rather than a type, of gun. For the same reason Beretta has to be excluded as well, despite the fascinating fact that the company, which was established hundreds of years ago, has amongst its archives a receipt dated 1526 for 296 ducats for the supply of arquebus barrels by the gunsmith Bartolomeo Beretta to the Arsenal of Venice.

The arquebus, the blunderbuss, or both, almost certainly explain the origin of the popular name for the musket used by the British army until the eighteenth century: Brown Bess. Although some take the view that the name derives from Queen Elizabeth I, the nickname did not appear until nearly two hundred years after Elizabeth died, so the disparity of dates makes the connection highly unlikely. But before saying goodbye to Bess we may perhaps pause for a moment to indulge in part of a poetical tribute to her:

> In the days of lace-ruffles, perukes and brocade
> Brown Bess was a partner whom none could despise -
> An outspoken, flinty-lipped, brazen-faced jade,

With a habit of looking men straight in the eyes –
At Blenheim and Ramillies, fops would confess
They were pierced to the heart by the charms of Brown
    Bess.(i)

STEN GUN

The sten gun is a submachine gun that was developed during the Second World War when there was a dire shortage of weapons. Its main feature was its simplicity, which meant that large numbers could be made quickly and cheaply.

Photo © Grzegorz Pietrzak

10.1: Sten Mk II submachine gun

Its connection to any name is admittedly *de minimis* but its two main designers did contribute one letter each: the S representing Major Reginald Vernon Shepherd and the T representing Harold John Turpin. The EN is taken from the end of Bren gun, where it reflected the fact that Bren guns (like Sten guns) were made by the Royal Small Arms Factory at Enfield. If the two designers felt that the 'Shepherd and Turpin' sounded too much like the name of a pub, they could still have opted for a portmanteau word such as 'The Sheppin' or some such. Respect is due for their modesty in restricting themselves to only a single letter each, but since the name itself is so short that the two letters between them account for fifty per cent of it, the word has won its place here. Just.

LEE ENFIELD

For years the British Army's standard rifle was the Lee Enfield, which dates from 1895. To understand how it got its full name one needs to be aware that an essential quality of a rifle, as opposed to a musket, is that inside the barrel there are spiral grooves known as rifling. These grooves put a spin on the bullet that results in much more accurate shooting.

Photo courtesy Swedish Army Museum

10.2: Short Magazine Lee Enfield Mk I (1903)

The action inside a Lee Enfield was designed by the gunsmith James Paris Lee (1831 – 1904), who was born in Scotland and grew up in Canada. He patented his design and, using a rifling system designed by one William Ellis Metford, produced what were known as Lee Metford rifles. When a new type of explosive came into use that could shoot bullets out of a gun faster than the gunpowder explosive that had previously been used, this was found to damage the rifling. A different rifling system, designed at the Royal Small Arms Factory at Enfield, was adopted to solve the problem. The resulting rifle, the Lee Enfield, was highly practical: millions were manufactured over many years before it finally became obsolete.

TOMMY GUN

Forget Thomas. The Tommy gun is a type of sub-machine gun, designed by an officer in the US army, John Taliaferro Thompson (1860 – 1940). He set up in partnership with another weapons designer and together they established the

Auto Ordnance Company in order to produce the gun commercially. It quickly became known as the Tommy gun, but by the time the design was finalised in 1920 the First World War had finished and most of the designers' potential market had vanished. The gun was used widely by the police, but achieved notoriety through its popularity with a number of high profile criminals during the era of prohibition. It featured in the St. Valentine's Day Massacre by Al Capone's gang in 1929 and its reputation for misuse by such men, together with the tap-tap-tap sound made when it was fired, won it the nickname 'Chicago Typewriter'. Poor sales performance eventually forced Thompson to resign the leadership of his company and it was not until shortly after he died that huge orders for the supply of Tommy guns for both European and American troops in the Second World War brought the company major success.

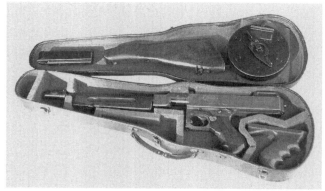

Photo © C. Corleis

10.3: Thompson sub-machine gun, stored in a violin case

BIG BERTHA

The first type of gun to be given the sobriquet Big Bertha was made at the Skoda works and used with great success by the Germans in 1914 to batter Belgian fortresses. The name arose from the mistaken assumption that the gun had been made by Krupps, the large German armaments manufacturing company, control of which at the time had passed down through the family to Frau Bertha Krupp von Bohlen (1886 – 1957).

The gun is described as a 42 cm. (16.5 inch) howitzer with a range of 15 km (9 miles). To the uninitiated, 16 or so inches does not sound at all impressive, but the reader needs to be aware that the size refers not to the gun itself but to the diameter of the shell that it fired. The shell weighed over 800 kg. and the gun was enormous, certainly too large to be moved without first being disassembled and taken piece by piece to its new site for reassembly. Even sixty years after the 1914-18 war a man who in his early teens had lived near to such a gun remembered vividly the terror induced by the appalling noise it made when fired.

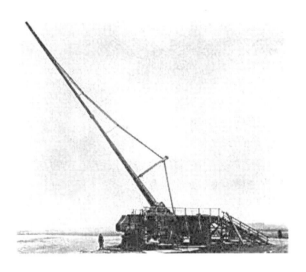

10.4: The Paris Gun 1914-1918

In 1918 Paris was shelled over a period of 140 days by 'The Paris gun', a completely different thing that this time was actually made by Krupps. It was nicknamed Big Bertha as well, presumably as a reference to the original, but it was much, much smaller with shells weighing a mere 120 kg. More a weapon of psychological warfare than one of major destructive power, its main feature was its absolutely astonishing range of 130 km. (80 miles), the shells apparently rising to an estimated height of some 40 km. (24 miles) at the top of their trajectory. Although at that distance its accuracy was understandably a bit shaky, Paris presented such a large target that the gunners could be confident of hitting it at least some of the time. The long-range shelling did create considerable alarm at first but never the wholesale demoralisation that had been hoped for by the aggressors.

LUGER

The Austrian Georg Luger (1849 – 1923) was a good marksman and during his military service he was sent to the Military Firearms School where he gained experience in automatic loading systems. After completing his military service he worked for a short time as an accountant before becoming a sales representative for a big weapons and munitions corporation in Berlin. In 1894 the company sent him to demonstrate a particular pistol, both in Germany and abroad. The pistol had its shortcomings and the criticisms that Luger received led him to make his own improvements to the design. His new pistol, the Luger, turned out to be a great success for his employers.

Luger's job came to an end in 1919, presumably on his retirement. The war had resulted in the loss of most of his invested savings and he used the rest to bring an action against his former employers over patent royalties. He remained impoverished even though, shortly before he died, the court did eventually decide the case in his favour.

KALASHNIKOV

The most famous and widespread of all submachine-guns must be the Kalashnikov. It is probably also the simplest and most basic: it is cheap to manufacture, easy to maintain and has tolerance limits so high that it can be relied on to keep firing in virtually any circumstances.

Mikhail Timofeevich Kalashnikov (1919- ?) was one of six surviving children out of eighteen born to a poor peasant family in Siberia. He worked at a train depot and was then

332

drafted into the army in 1938, where he was given some education in engineering. After three years' service he was badly wounded and during his time in a military hospital began to design guns. His efforts and talent were noticed by his superiors who sent him to the Moscow Aviation Institute to continue his design work. In 1947 he entered a national competition to design a submachine gun for the Red Army and won it with his Avtomat Kalashnikova model 1947 (AK-47). More recently he has permitted the use of his name in the marketing of various products including vodka and umbrellas.

SHRAPNEL

Nowadays shrapnel usually refers to jagged pieces of the outer casing of an artillery shell after it has been fired, but originally it meant something quite different. Shrapnel's shell, which common usage soon shortened simply to shrapnel, referred to a completely new type of ammunition designed by Henry Shrapnel (1761 – 1842).

Shrapnel was born in Bradford-on-Avon in Wiltshire, the youngest son in a family of nine children. His older brothers died without leaving any heirs and thus he eventually ended up inheriting the family home. At that time, in order to make a reasonable and socially acceptable living, younger sons traditionally went into either the army or the church. Henry Shrapnel had taken the military option and was commissioned in the Royal Artillery. His passion for invention, and in particular his determination in designing the new type of ammunition which became known by his name, absorbed a large proportion of his personal funds and a huge amount of unpaid time.

In those days wars were still being fought by infantry and cavalry on battlefields in open countryside. Success tended to go to whichever side killed the most enemy troops. Tactics were of lesser importance; the essential was firepower. Destruction produced by cannon was restricted to a comparatively small area. And the rate of casualties produced by rifle and musket fire was limited because of the time it took to reload: a trained infantryman could expect to achieve a firing rate of between two and three shots a minute.

What was really needed was something that could kill the opposition faster. Shrapnel's idea was to fill a shell not with gunpowder alone, but with small pieces of lead shot together with just enough gunpowder to make the shell explode and launch the shot it was carrying. His shell also contained a time fuse to light the gunpowder. The aim was to fire a shell to a position in the air above the enemy troops, when it would explode and the bullets mow down large numbers of the soldiers beneath. For all this to work successfully it was clearly essential that the shell exploded in the right place. The shell therefore included something that made a puff of smoke when the explosion took place, so that those firing it could see exactly where it had exploded and make any adjustments necessary before firing the next one.

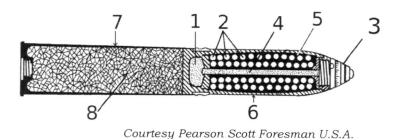

Courtesy Pearson Scott Foresman U.S.A.

10.5: Diagram of a shrapnel round (as used in World War I)

1. Small gunpowder bursting charge - fires bullets forward out of shell case.
2. Shrapnel bullets (balls).
3. Time Fuse.
4. Central tube to carry detonator flash from fuse to bursting charge.
5. Resin to hold bullets steady and give off smoke when shell bursts.
6. Thin steel shell wall.
7. Metal cartridge case.
8. Shell propellant, typically cordite or nitrocellulose.

The top brass took some convincing about the new shell but eventually it was officially adopted and used with great success. Several in the highest echelons of the army were most impressed by it and Wellington advised that its invention and use had such a dramatic effect on the war effort that it should be kept secret. He went on to suggest that since such secrecy would deprive Shrapnel of fame and honour, he should be rewarded with some form of financial compensation. Despite this, the time and money poured by Shrapnel into designing his new shell was never officially recognised other than through the payment of a modest annuity that he would have been better off without, since it resulted in his being passed over for promotion. William IV did apparently at one stage agree to confer a baronetcy on him in recognition of his services to the nation, but William died before this was done.

From Shrapnel's point of view his home country has rewarded him with little more than a new word, not even accorded the respect of a capital letter and used now to refer to something very different from his original invention. Nothing to shout, or even sing, about. But things are different on the other side of the Atlantic. Shrapnel's shell features in the USA's National Anthem, albeit not by name, and albeit in reference to an occasion when used by the British without success:

Oh say, can you see by the dawn's early light,
What so proudly we hailed at the twilight's last gleaming?
Whose broad stripes and bright stars, through the
   perilous fight,
Over the ramparts we watched were so gallantly
   streaming?
And the Rockets Red Glare, the bombs bursting in air,
Gave proof through the night that our Flag was still
   there.
Oh say does that Star Spangled Banner yet wave,
Over the land of the free, and the home of the brave?(ii)

Francis Scott Key wrote these words in 1814, after he witnessed the Battle of Baltimore. The British had been holding an important prisoner on board one of its naval vessels and Key, a lawyer, had boarded it in order to negotiate the prisoner's release. In the course of these negotiations it was thought that Key might have heard the plans for attacking Baltimore, so he was kept on board until after the battle was over. His poem describes the sight of bursting Shrapnel's shells (being shot into the air by rockets somewhat akin to a souped up version of those fired on Guy Fawkes night) and records his delight in seeing that the garrison flag remained flying, indicating that Baltimore had not surrendered. Some concept of the size of the flag can be gleaned from the fact that it could be seen at all at that distance – it measured 30 feet by 42 feet.

10.6: The Battle of Baltimore garrison flag on display at the Star Spangled Banner Centennial, Baltimore, 1914

MOLOTOV COCKTAIL

The first petrol bombs, made from bottles partly filled with petrol and set on fire as they were thrown, were used in the Spanish Civil War, and such bombs are still largely thought of as merely crude weapons, usually used in riots. By contrast the original Molotov cocktail was a distinctly upmarket version, thoroughly researched by the authorities in Finland. It was officially supplied to its army in 1939, at the beginning of what became known as the Winter War, as the primary anti-tank weapon, but it took a little time for the weapon – pitifully humble yet surprisingly effective against the might of a tank – to acquire its sobriquet.

Photo © User Ohto Kokko/ Wikimedia Commons

10.7: Molotov cocktail as produced by the Finnish alcohol monopoly ALKO 1939–1940, with a storm match for a fuse

Stalin and Hitler had signed the Molotov-Ribbentrop Pact, a non-aggression treaty that amongst other things carved up Poland between them and allocated Finland, with a total population of merely three and a half million, to Russia. There remained the minor issue of persuading Finland to agree. Russia did not consider this a problem and began simply by demanding that certain strategic ports be handed over. The request was refused. Russia invaded at the end of November 1939 with an initial invasion force of close on half a million men and some two thousand tanks, in order to take the ports it wanted. It was assumed that Finland would not try to

337

defend itself against such overwhelming odds and Russia expected to subjugate the country within about a fortnight. So confident was Russia of quick success that its troops took with them a military band to play at the expected Helsinki victory parade, rather than proper winter clothing and supplies. They were in for a shock.

Finland had had little warning of Russia's intentions and stood alone with no support from any other country. It was unprepared for war and in particular had only a minimal number of anti-tank weapons. Planning, developing or even just shopping around for weapons was by this stage totally unrealistic. An immediate and extensive supply of something with which to destroy enemy tanks was required. All that the authorities had the time and resources to do was to perfect and mass produce the petrol bomb, thereby ensuring that the thousands it was able to supply to its army worked as well and as safely as possible.

Fortunately research had found that the bottles with the best shape and size for petrol bombs were the vodka bottles produced by the state-owned company that had a monopoly on the production of spirits. These bottles also had the advantage of screw tops – such tops had been found to be safer than other methods of closure. Production of the bottles was therefore easily arranged and the same company was also employed to fill them. As to the most appropriate contents, potassium chlorate was found to work better than petrol, and adding a small quantity of tar not only helped the burning contents stick to its target but also confused those driving the tank by creating thick black smoke that prevented the crew from seeing where they were going.

The most crucial improvement over the simple petrol bomb was the use of a safer fuse, although 'fuse' is perhaps putting it a little strongly. Originally, lighting a petrol bomb called for nerves of steel: a lighted match was simply dropped into the bottle. The restricted air supply within the bottle served as a fuse, allowing the match to burn but preventing immediate explosion. The short delay gave the bomber enough time to throw bottle which, when it broke on its target, exploded as a good air supply was suddenly restored. This method had then been refined by stuffing part of an oily rag down into the neck of the bottle to close it, and then lighting the bit of rag that remained outside. The comparatively sophisticated system adopted in Finland was to close the bottle completely with its screw top and strap two special matches rather like sparklers ('storm matches') to the sides. These were lit just before it was thrown, thereby preventing explosion until the bottle had broken. The results were impressive. It is thought that during the Winter War Molotov cocktails destroyed about two thousand enemy tanks.

10.8: An unexploded 'Molotov Bread Basket' incendiary bomb

The Russian advance was supported by its air force, using bombs resembling huge versions of Shrapnel's shells that exploded before landing, releasing a large number of small incendiary bombs. The Russian radio claimed that they were not dropping bombs at all but food for the starving people of Finland. In fact the bombs did less damage than expected because of the thick snow and, in sarcastic reference to the

Russian propaganda, the Finns referred to these bombs as Molotov's breadbaskets – Vyacheslav Mikhailovich Molotov (1890 - 1986) being the Russian Minister for Foreign Affairs at the time.

Extending that train of thought, the Finns (or possibly just foreign journalists) began to call the petrol bombs that looked like vodka bottles 'Molotov's cocktails'. By March 1940, four months after the Russian invasion, the Finns had completely run out of all ammunition. But Stalin was not aware of this and spring was on its way. He was concerned that his army would find it even harder to gain ground as the snow and ice began to thaw. He also had military activity elsewhere to attend to so he withdrew, signing a treaty under which Finland ceded certain land and ports to Russia but retained its independence.

On the face of it, it seems curious that such a small weapon should have had much chance of success against a tank, and it was indeed far more successful than the Finns had dared to hope. Russian tanks had not been designed with such a mode of attack in mind and they had features that made them inherently vulnerable. The Molotov cocktail alone did not do much direct damage but one thrown to break in the right place on the back of the tank near its fuel supply had an excellent chance of setting fire to the tank's own fuel. Once that happened, the tank would fill with scorching, toxic fumes, either killing the crew or allowing them to be picked off with rifle fire as they tried to get out. Russian tanks were also not very manoeuvrable and so only suitable for fighting at medium to long range. In the thick forests of Finland the defending forces could suddenly emerge at close quarters and, ski-ing close to a tank, throw their weapons at the crucial spot for setting fire to its fuel supply, then disappear back into the forest before the tank could turn or take any defensive action.

NISSEN HUT

A Nissen hut is a very basic prefabricated shelter somewhat resembling a giant caterpillar without legs, the long body made with sheets of corrugated steel arching over into a semicircular curve, with a brick or breeze block wall at each end. These huts are associated with the armed forces and wartime activities, but in some parts of the country – where the march of development is not yet fully established – they can occasionally still be seen, used usually for some agricultural rather than military purpose.

10.9: Nissen hut near Old Romney, Kent

Although the huts can be something of an eyesore, their continued existence is proof of their usefulness and a tribute to their extraordinarily effective design. The man responsible, Peter Norman Nissen (1871 – 1930), was a Canadian engineer whose father made gold mining equipment. Nissen moved to Britain as a young man with a view to marketing that equipment but, with the onset of the First World War, he joined up with the Royal Engineers. In 1916 he was asked to design a robust, portable shelter that could be erected by four men in four hours. He met the specifications most successfully. Sheets of corrugated steel can be transported by lorry comparatively easily since they can be stacked one on top of the other to save space. And, in areas where earthquakes present a problem, the huts have the added bonus of being extremely resistant to damage because they lack the corners that are a source of weakness in a conventional building.

341

SAM BROWNE

The safety conscious cyclist wearing a flimsy, fluorescent yellow belt that consists of a waistband with a single strap passing diagonally from the left across the right shoulder may not realise that he is sporting a Sam Browne belt, one of the insignia of an army officer. Except, of course, that the military version is usually in leather or khaki webbing and not under any circumstances fluorescent.

The belt was named after General Sir Samuel James Browne, VC (1824 – 1901), who was born in India and enlisted in a regiment of the Bengal Native Infantry. He was given the job of raising a cavalry force, which became known as the 2nd Punjab Irregular Cavalry and which was soon in action on the frontier. His cavalry subsequently became part of the regular British Army and, after a number of changes of name, became known as Sam Browne's Cavalry 12th Frontier Force.

Photo courtesy User Beloochee/ Wikimedia Commons

10.10: Badge of Sam Browne's Cavalry (12th Frontier Force)

In 1858, during the Indian Mutiny, Browne charged and captured an enemy 9lb. gun (the civilian reader needs to remember that the weight relates not the gun but to the shot fired by it) to prevent it from being reloaded and fired on the advancing British infantry. During the ensuing fight with the gunners his left arm was cut off at the shoulder. He was awarded the recently created Victoria Cross for his gallantry and was subsequently decorated again for his action in the Second Afghan War, when he led a large body of troops to force a way through the Khyber Pass after capturing the key fortress protecting it.

It was the loss of Browne's left arm that made it essential for him to wear a belt so that he could carry and use his sword and pistol. A few officers used to wear belts with two vertical shoulder straps, one on each side, and so it may be that the introduction of a single, diagonal strap design was in response to Browne's particular requirements. There are claims that someone else had already invented it but, regardless of who was the first to think up the design, after Browne lost his arm he was seldom seen in uniform without one. Such a belt is now inextricably linked with his name.

MAE WEST

During the Second World War servicemen living with the constant threat of being torpedoed or shot down were issued with a sleeveless life-jacket to reduce the likelihood of drowning, the front of which was inflatable in order to keep the wearer face up and afloat. Small wonder that such a jacket became known as a Mae West, in tribute to the generous bosom of one of the first sex symbols of the silver screen – and all this before the possibilities offered by plastic surgery.

There was a great deal more to Mae West than just a voluptuous figure. She was born Mary Jane West (1893 – 1980), the daughter of a prize-fighter who ran a livery stable and of a mother who modelled corsets. Mae was on the stage from the age of five. By the time she was fourteen she already had a figure that was exceptionally well-endowed and was being billed as 'The Baby Vamp'. This did not prevent her from moving on to write, direct and star in her own plays.

Her first play to reach Broadway was simply called 'Sex' and both she and other actors in it were arrested for 'corrupting the morals of the young', although by today's standards it would hardly raise an eyebrow. She was even jailed for ten days, which brought a great deal of publicity that almost certainly benefited her career. Her next play was banned from Broadway because it concerned homosexuality, but that did not prevent it from doing well elsewhere. Within two years she had staged another hugely successful play. Censorship was very much in evidence at this time and Mae West became adept at the double-entendre, using language that in writing looked totally innocent and satisfied the censors, yet when spoken during performance with attitude and a particular tone of voice was quite the reverse.

In 1933 Hollywood beckoned. Mae West's first appearance on screen was a small part, but that was enough to turn the film into a hit. In the following year, at the age of almost forty, she starred in 'She Done Him Wrong', based on one of her earlier plays and was nominated for an Academy Award. Other successes followed.

Mae was renowned for her witty, suggestive comments: "I always say, keep a diary and some day it'll keep you"(iii), and most famous of all "Is that a gun in your pocket, or are you just glad to see me?"(iv). The government amended the censorship laws in an effort to increase its control but still found it difficult to curb her activities, her notoriety being based on innuendo rather than anything that could be pinned down in legal terms. Nevertheless, by 1943 endless official harassment led her to leave Hollywood and return to the theatre. It was not until 1975 that she appeared in another film, 'Myra Breckinridge'. It was not successful.

The image of Mae West is of an independent woman well able to look after herself. However, it is probable that she married whilst still in her teens, although she never lived with her husband. He resurfaced in the 1930s during the height of her fame and although she never admitted to the marriage she was forced to get a divorce and pay a substantial settlement in order to be rid of him.

BAILEY BRIDGE

It is not unreasonable to assume that when Sir Donald Coleman Bailey (1901 – 1985) was a small boy he must have played with Meccano®, the modelling kit involving bits of metal and nuts and bolts, because the bridges he designed and which bear his name look remarkably like complicated Meccano constructions. He was born in Rotherham and, with or without the benefit of Meccano, gained a degree in civil engineering at Sheffield. After various jobs he joined the Civil Service and by 1941 had been appointed Chief Designer at the Experimental Bridging Establishment in Christchurch. He was knighted shortly after the war for his outstanding contribution to the war effort.

The army's portable bridging equipment during the 1930s comprised a variety of bridges, designed to cope with a variety of situations. In wartime such specialist equipment was inevitably going to create massive production, training and logistical difficulties, so with the outbreak of war in 1939 the pressure was on to find something more practical. The Bailey bridge provided the ultimate solution. It was composed of a small number of standard sized parts, all of which could be loaded on an ordinary army truck. Its construction did not call for a crane and with the use of a counterbalance it could be 'launched' from one side of a river, provided the river was not too wide. No individual part needed more than six men to move it. There was enough tolerance in the design to allow the parts to be manufactured by different companies. The bridge was strong enough to carry the weight of a tank. And no matter what had to be bridged, with a little adaptation the Bailey bridge proved up to the challenge.

It began life towards the end of 1940 as a sketch on the back of an envelope that Bailey fished out of his pocket during a train journey, while returning from trials of a new military bridge that had turned out to be unsuitable for mass production. Design development, testing and production of Bailey's bridge was made a priority and in not much more than a year the army was issued with the first Bailey Bridge 'kits'. To simulate the experience of having to construct the bridges in battle conditions the Royal Engineers were trained at night in rivers in Cumbria.

Photo © Belinda Bailey

10.11: Landing pier at Southwold with a Bailey bridge beyond

The bridge was initially designed to carry tanks across a comparatively modest gap, but as the need for bridging increased it was found that construction of the standard parts could be adapted to meet other situations. Thus, wide rivers could be crossed by supporting the bridge on flat-bottomed boats or pontoons. The bridge could be strengthened by adding either extra trusses across the bottom or an extra layer of side panels. A longer bridge to cross wider spans could be made by supporting it on trestles. It could be widened to take traffic in both directions. It could be adapted for rail traffic or constructed into a suspension bridge for crossing the deep gorges of the Far East. And it could even be put together in such as way as to build a bridge that opened to allow canal traffic to pass under it.

All in all several thousand such bridges were built before the end of the war, in Italy, France and further afield, providing a crucial contribution to the Allies' success. Although these bridges were only intended for temporary use some are still functioning years after they were constructed, for example a footbridge in Suffolk over the river Blyth that connects the villages of Southwold and Walberswick.

CHAPTER ELEVEN

MISCELLANEOUS

THE FULL MONTY

Until recently this rather appealing phrase was not widely used outside the North of England, but all that changed in 1997 when it was used as the name of an award winning film in which a group of unemployed men from Sheffield turn their talents to producing, acting in and presenting an all male striptease show. The film is even responsible for exporting the phrase across the Atlantic where its meaning of complete nudity remains in keeping with the context in which it was used in the film. In Britain the phrase is not so constrained and can refer to all sorts of situations.

The film has stimulated great interest in the origin of the phrase, which still remains somewhat obscure. A recent revision to the Oxford English Dictionary(i) indicates that, although there is as yet no clear evidence, the phrase most probably derives from the name of Sir Montague Burton (1885 – 1952). Other possibilities are also mentioned, notably the widely used nickname of Field Marshal Montgomery who, even when campaigning in the deserts of North Africa, was well known for insisting on the sort of breakfast that could well be described as 'the full monty'.

From the sound of his name one could easily assume that Sir Montague Burton was born with a silver spoon in his mouth, but if ever there was a rags to riches story this is it.

348

He was originally named Meshe Osinsky and was born into a Jewish family in Lithuania during the Russian occupation at a time when the Jewish community lived in grinding poverty. The living conditions, together with the threat of pogroms, led him at the age of fifteen to emigrate to Britain where he started working as a pedlar selling accessories for the men's clothing trade.

Photo courtesy User Chemical Engineer/ Wikimedia Commons

11.1: Burton's factory in Burmantofts, Leeds, now used as a warehouse

Within three years Osinksy had established his first shop in Chesterfield selling men's suits, and it was not long before he had also opened shops in Mansfield and Sheffield. He was ambitious and also keen to fit into the customs of his new country, so he became a British citizen and changed his name to Morris Burton, later to Maurice Burton and finally to the more aristocratic sounding Montague Burton. His aim was to sell good suits at affordable prices and he advertised his principle that a man's suit should not cost more than one week's wages. His shops sold a basic option of a two-piece suit, but for a modest extra cost a customer could have 'the full monty' which included a waistcoat plus an extra pair of trousers. Success followed success. His business supplied a quarter of all British uniforms during the Second World War and one third of all demob suits after it. Eventually the

Burtons chain comprised some 600 shops. He was the biggest employer in Leeds and his employees were well looked after with a (pre-NHS) health and pension scheme, works canteens and free chiropody and dental care. Burton received a knighthood for his services to commerce and charity.

It is possible that Sir Montague Burton is also responsible for the following completely independent colloquial phrase:

GONE FOR A BURTON

This euphemism originated in the RAF and dates from the Second World War. It refers to someone who is dead or presumed dead and hence also to something that is missing, lost or broken beyond repair. It clearly relates to somebody's name and there are several possibilities to choose from.

Photo © Taro Taylor

11.2: Flying Fortress aeroplane 'gone for a burton'

Some believe that the phrase actually began its existence as a reference to the death of any pilot, implying that he needed to get a suit (from Burtons of course) either in order to be decently dressed for his funeral or simply because his career in the RAF had come to an end. Brewer's(ii) suggestion is that it began as a reference to a training school for RAF wireless operators that used to be held on the premises of one of Burton's clothing stores. Failure to complete the course successfully was said to have been referred to as 'having gone for a Burton' and the phrase subsequently became used to apply to pilots and crew who were shot down. Another explanation put forward for its origin is that a person's absence can be explained away on the basis that he had just nipped out for a pint of Burton's beer so would be unlikely to return.

TITCHY

Behind this apparently harmless and trivial word is a whole can of worms, at the bottom of which is a high society court case that had Victorian England riveted to the newspapers for months. The case concerned was an inheritance claim.

Grandfather Sir Henry Tichborne had the title and the family estate. In those days such estates were held on trusts requiring them to be passed down through succeeding generations to a male heir. Daughters usually didn't count. Sir Henry's third son James never expected to inherit, since his older brothers were both married and producing children. James was therefore comparatively free to follow his own wishes and he married Henriette who was French and stunningly beautiful, but a woman with strong views. She was violently anti-English, so the couple lived in Paris. In due course they had two sons, Roger Charles Doughty Tichborne (1829 – 1854) and Alfred. She insisted that both the boys speak French, go to French schools and be brought up as if they were French. When Roger was sixteen her husband used a family funeral as an excuse to take him over to England and, having got him there, sent him to the Catholic school Stonyhurst.

After school Roger joined the British army then decided to travel the world, starting in South America. Before long a combination of untimely deaths and a disappointing series of daughters meant that James inherited both the title and the family estate, with the result that Roger was now heir to it all.

Roger set sail back from South America, but the ship was lost at sea with no apparent survivors. Roger was officially declared dead, his will was proved and on James' death ten years later Roger's younger brother Alfred inherited. So far so good.

Henriette, however, could never accept that her elder son was dead. When her husband died she began to advertise across the world for her missing son. It was not long before 'Sir Roger Tichborne', a butcher in Australia then using the name Tom Castro, responded. Henriette was delighted, an exchange of correspondence took place, his debts were settled for him, travel money was despatched and within a couple of years the man claiming to be Sir Roger turned up. In the meantime Alfred had died, survived by a baby son. There was thus no-one alive in England other than Henriette who had known Roger as a child.

There were anomalies. 'Sir Roger' did not understand any French, nor did he have the French accent still noticeable when Roger had last been seen twelve years previously. Roger had been of unremarkable build but the claimant weighed twenty plus stone. Despite this, Henriette was adamant that her long lost son had at last been restored to her. Some others were also convinced although few (if any) within the family agreed.

The claimant began legal proceedings to have himself declared the rightful heir, but by the time the case came to court his main supporting witness, Henriette, had died. The case lasted for some three months with a wealth of witnesses being called in an attempt to establish his identity. Every day the newspapers were full of it and details of the case and of the Tichborne claimant became so well-known that across the land those of comparably impressive girth became popularly referred to as Tichborne. Eventually it was held that the claimant was a fraud, a butcher's son from Wapping whose true name was Arthur Orton. Public fascination with the case did not stop, however, as the inevitable criminal case for perjury followed. Orton was found guilty and sentenced to fourteen years' hard labour. By the time he was released his claim had been forgotten and he died in poverty.

11.3: 'The Beggar's Petition' - a cartoon from 1872 of the Tichborne Claimant, surrounded by notices reading
"I am starving" (round his neck)
"Made entirely out of my own head" (in front of model of Tichborne Hall)
"A poor man's tallent (sic): should be rewarded"
"Some has brains and no money, some has money and no brains, them as has money and no brains is made for them as has brains and no money"
"My own handwriting"

That all leaves Tichborne as merely a nickname for someone extremely fat, a name that fell into disuse as the case faded from the headlines. So how can 'titchy' possibly have come to mean someone or something very small? The answer lies in a rather podgy five year old boy, the sixteenth child of a pub landlord. The boy had been nicknamed Tichborne because of his girth, but his true name was Harry Relph (1867 – 1928) and he grew up to become a music hall comedian and dancer. Or rather, he failed to grow up: as a man he stood a mere four foot six inches in his socks. At the beginning of his career Harry wanted to adopt a stage name and remembered his childhood name of Tichborne. No longer corpulent, his most obvious feature was now his lack of height, so he plumped for 'Little Tichborne' which he later shortened to Little Tich, thereby launching the use of the word 'titchy' as a general description for someone or something unusually small. One of Little Tich's most popular routines was a dance performed wearing special boots two feet four inches long, during which he balanced on tip-toe, which must have boosted his height by an impressive fifty per cent or so.

JUMBO

For some people the perfect relaxation is to settle down on a Saturday afternoon with The Times, a cup of tea, a ginger biscuit and a pen, in order to ignore the headlines and turn instead straight to the Jumbo crossword. Jumbo (c1861 – 1885) is the exception referred to in the introduction: he was an African elephant, not a person.

In about 1861 a baby elephant was caught in the wild and sold to a zoo in Paris where he stayed for some three years. He was then transferred to London Zoo (apparently in exchange for a rhinoceros) and it was there that he was named Jumbo. Dictionaries explain that the word 'jumbo' used to be merely the second half of 'mumbo-jumbo' but leave no doubt that jumbo on its own now has the status of a new independent word, derived from the name of London Zoo's most popular attraction, the largest elephant in captivity at the time and famous for giving children rides in a howdah.

Despite all the attention and affection in which he was held, his new way of life did not suit poor Jumbo who was no doubt missing the freedom of the African plains. As he got older he became bad-tempered and had periodic fits of rage, wrecking his stall in the elephant house and breaking both his tusks. The zoo felt he was becoming a liability and so in 1882 Jumbo was sold for a considerable sum of money to the American circus Barnum and Bailey's. There was a public outcry: how dare the zoo not only sell its best loved icon but sell him to someone who would take him away, never to be seen in Britain again? On his departure one newspaper, heedless of any adverse effect on Trans-Atlantic relations and clearly ignorant of an elephant's dietary requirements, raged that Jumbo "instead of his bygone friendly trots with British girls and boys, and perpetual luncheons on buns and oranges, must amuse a Yankee mob, and put up with peanuts and waffles."(iii).

Courtesy NYPL

11.4: Jumbo's arrival in America, 1883

Sending a reluctant elephant on a long journey, especially before the days of the internal combustion engine, presented certain practical problems. Jumbo did not want to walk to the docks. Nor did he want to go into the crate prepared for his journey, but eventually he was persuaded to do so by his keeper. A team of carthorses spent the rest of the day, and part of the next, pulling the crate the four miles or so to the docks where it was transferred to a barge and taken down

355

river to Millwall before being loaded on board ship the following day for the start of the transatlantic voyage. As a special treat to keep him happy his food supplies included a sackful of his favourite onions.

Jumbo's appearance in the circus did everything his purchasers had hoped and box office receipts soared. But some three years later, after the end of a performance, Jumbo was crossing the railway to return to the circus wagons when an express train came speeding along the line and hit him. The train was derailed and Jumbo was killed.

Despite the death of their star performer the circus owners were still determined to make the most of their investment. They immediately called in a taxidermist and Jumbo's hide was stuffed so effectively that he ended up a foot taller than he had been while alive. His skeleton was also preserved and is now in the Natural History Museum in New York. Jumbo (stuffed) was put on display in the circus for several years before ending up at Tufts University where he remained until the building that housed him was destroyed by fire in 1975. A small container of ashes was retrieved, which may (or may not) contain a speck of his remains and is still kept by Tufts as a lucky mascot.

GUY

Although he has occasionally been referred to as the only man ever to enter Parliament with honourable intentions, Guy Fawkes (1570 – 1606) does nevertheless have a serious image problem. Perhaps he would be consoled to know that he has also reached a level of recognition denied to almost every other historical character. Throughout the length and breadth of Britain there can hardly be anyone who has not at least heard of his name in connection with the fifth of November. And every year since the Gunpowder Plot of 1605, whilst the country celebrates with fireworks, the Yeomen of the Guard still search the cellars beneath the Houses of Parliament before its state opening in case they find evidence of another plot to blow up not just the Monarch, but also the Lords and Members of Parliament.

GUN-POWDER Plot:

O R,

A Brief Account of that bloudy and fubtle Defign laid againft the King, his Lords and Commons in Parliament, and of a Happy Deliverance by Divine Power.

To the Tune of Sitll not too high.   Licenfed according to Order.

11.5: Heading of an anti-Catholic pamphlet from the 17th or early 18th Century

For many years the fifth of November was a public holiday. Effigies of Guy, dressed in whatever cast off clothes could be found for the purpose, appeared every November and in time the word 'guy' became used more generally to refer to anyone looking somewhat like a scarecrow. Later on its meaning widened to apply to any man, although still with some implication that he was not really respectable. Recently, reflecting its widespread use in the United States, its meaning has relaxed still further but even so it retains just a flicker of something that makes it inappropriate to use for a well-groomed man in a good suit with clean shoes.

There is no doubt that Fawkes falls on the wrong side of the dividing line between fame and infamy, but until the discovery of the Plot it appears that there was no-one to say a word against him. He came from a very respectable background: his father was a lawyer in the Protestant ecclesiastical courts. As a young man he converted to Catholicism and was described as a pious, learned, mild person who disliked disputes but was also brave and resolute. He enlisted in the Spanish army, adopting the Spanish form of his name, Guido, and distinguished himself in their capture of Calais in 1596.

What is interpreted as high treason from the point of view of the Protestant English Crown can of course also be interpreted as courageous dedication to a higher religious cause. Fawkes was not even the instigator of the Gunpowder Plot, but he was a key player because of his expertise with explosives. It was he who stayed down in Parliament's cellars that November night in charge of the thirty-six kegs of gunpowder, a slow fuse and the means for lighting it. So it was he who was discovered when the cellars were searched and he who was tortured on the rack by order of the King until forced to reveal the names of the other conspirators. He did not meet his end on a bonfire, however. He was hanged, drawn and quartered like the rest of the conspirators.

CATHERINE WHEEL

Given what eventually happened to Guy Fawkes, it is apposite that his death should be celebrated, or at least remembered, with the Catherine wheel – a firework named after another infamous method of torture and execution. In early times there were various ways in which wheels were used for killing criminals (or those merely deemed to be such). Sometimes an ordinary cartwheel would be used, placed horizontally on the ground with the victim tied on top of it with his or her limbs stretched out across the spokes. Each limb could then be easily broken with a hard hit wherever it crossed a gap between the spokes, and broken in so many places that the limbs could then all be woven through the spokes, presumably to discourage onlookers from trying anything that might land them in a similar situation.

The wheel with which St. Catherine (early 4th Century AD) was threatened had a different design. It rotated vertically and had spikes protruding all the way round the outside of its outer rim – hence the similarity to the firework. The

358

condemned person would be tied over the spikes in line with the rim of the wheel. When the wheel was rolled along its weight then drove the spikes further into the victim's body on each rotation. Mercifully for St. Catherine, legend has it that her saintly powers caused the wheel to break as soon as it touched her, so she had to be beheaded instead.

Courtesy User Dixie/ Wikimedia Commons

11.7: Early 20thC depiction of the breaking wheel as used during the Middle Ages

It was (probably) the Emperor Maximinus who saw St. Catherine as such a threat that he wanted to be rid of her. Her legend describes her at the age of eighteen as being beautiful, noble, highly educated and a recent convert to Christianity. The emperor was busy persecuting Christians, so St. Catherine visited him with the intention of persuading him not to do so. The emperor could not cope with theology himself so he sent his wisest men to argue with her. She persuaded these men of the truth of her faith, but somewhat predictably this did not go down well with the emperor who had them killed and her flung into prison. In fact the emperor appears to have had a penchant for finishing off anyone at all who disagreed with him because the next batch of converts to go the same way were his wife, the head of the prison guard and two hundred soldiers. Maximinus was ultimately left with no real alternative other than to accept the spread of Christianity or condemn St. Catherine to death. The legend ends with St. Catherine's body being gathered up by angels after her beheading and transported across the desert to Mount Sinai where the famous church and monastery bearing her name now stand.

Photo courtesy User BigRiz/ Wikimedia Commons

11.6: Two ignited Catherine wheels, spinning

For centuries St. Catherine was amongst the most revered of saints. She was adopted as the patron of virgins and scholars – both Oxford and Cambridge boast a college named after her – and also of wheelwrights. Times change and recently doubts have been expressed about not only the details of her legend but also whether she actually existed at all. In 1969 her feast day was even removed from the official list by the Catholic Church, although it has been recently reinstated.

In all probability she did exist, but it is hard to substantiate any of the details of her story.

11.8: Ring of St. Catherine, as given to pilgrims visiting Mount Sinai

BOURDALOUE

The National Trust discreetly describes a beautifully decorated china bourdaloue on display at one of its properties as "a narrow vessel used by ladies when travelling or in church". A note adds that it was so named after a clergyman famous for his long sermons: no further explanation was considered necessary.

11.9: China bourdaloue with lid

Louis Bourdaloue (1632 – 1704) was a Jesuit priest who is often referred to as 'the king of preachers and the preacher of kings'. He was a gentle, saintly man who was at ease talking to all levels of society, adopting a style of presentation appropriate to each audience. He propounded religious doctrines at length, with detailed care and irresistible logic. So popular were his discourses that crowds would gather hours in advance in order to gain seats, adding considerably to the time spent out of reach of the necessary facilities – 'portaloos' being only a recent invention. The bourdaloue, a container somewhat resembling a gravy boat in both shape and size, must have been a most welcome bit of kit for many of the female members of the congregation.

It is not recorded how matters were dealt with when the sermon came to an end, but one imagines that a used vessel would perhaps just have been left behind under the seat and a maid despatched to retrieve it afterwards.

DERRICK

One of the earliest public executioners whose name survives was Goodman Derrick (c.16th-17thC). He apparently favoured the use of a single post with an arm extending from it for a hanging and in the seventeenth century the word 'derrick' became used to refer either to a hangman or to such a gallows. In practice the word is now only used to refer to a type of crane, often one set up on a temporary basis for the purpose of loading and unloading ships but, if you stop to think about it, the similarity of such a piece of equipment to Derrick's preferred design of gallows is clear. A condemned criminal could be raised into the air and suspended from it just as easily as a consignment of goods or equipment. In years gone by the long arm of a crane was even known as a gibbet, but this has now been shortened to gib or more usually jib.

Derrick was also responsible for despatching the condemned on the permanent gallows at Tyburn (now Marble Arch) known as Tyburn tree or 'the three legged mare'. This comprised a horizontal wooden triangle supported by a tall post at each corner and it was large enough to accommodate nine victims simultaneously.

TYBURN'S TRIPLE TREE.

The coffins.   *Javelin men.*

11.10: Tyburn Tree, or the 'Three Legged Mare', c. 1680

Courtesy National Archives, Kew

11.11:
Plaque set into the pavement on the traffic island at Marble Arch

Photo courtesy User Rioverde/Wikimedia Commons

In addition, his job description required him to be handy with an axe as he carried out the more humane sentence usually passed in the case of nobility, beheading. Most beheadings took place in public outside the Tower of London on Tower Hill or elsewhere, but people with royal connections merited a private ceremony, either within the precincts of the Tower itself or on Tower Green. 'Private' in this context is a relative term as there were numerous spectators present, sometimes as many as two hundred, and the condemned was normally permitted to make a speech before the sentence was carried out. Despite the popular belief that executions on Tower Green were a frequent occurrence, such a privilege was only ever extended to seven people, most of them women. In 1601 our man Derrick had the distinction of despatching the last of the select seven, the Earl of Essex, taking a mere three blows of the axe to detach his head completely, although mercifully the Earl is said to have died after the first one.

JACK KETCH

The name of (John) Jack Ketch (16..? – 1686) was such that in the late seventeenth century those condemned to death dreaded his being the appointed executioner. He appears to have really enjoyed inflicting unnecessary suffering on his victims, either through incompetence or possibly simply to put on a good show for the attending public. In those days London had several hangmen but, like Derrick, Ketch was also an official headsman. So despite his reputation – or perhaps because of it – Ketch would appear to have risen to the top of his profession.

Following the restoration of Charles II as monarch in 1660 there was a great deal of worry about revolutionary plots – understandably, given what had happened to Charles' father. In 1678 much was made of what turned out to have been a completely fictitious 'Popish Plot' to murder the king and bring back Roman Catholicism. The outcome of the ensuing trials kept Ketch busy. First, he was responsible for despatching many Roman Catholics found guilty of involvement. Then, when Titus Oates who had invented the whole thing was found guilty of perjury and was sentenced to be publicly whipped twice through the streets of London, that sentence, too, was carried out by Ketch. The events of the Popish Plot were commemorated at the time by the production of packs of playing cards depicting the characters involved.

A few years later came the unsuccessful 'Rye House Plot' – and more new packs of playing cards – when the politician Lord William Russell was found guilty of involvement in plotting the death of the king. He was initially sentenced to be hanged, drawn and quartered, but this was commuted to beheading. However, since Ketch was the man for the job, beheading turned out to be not such an act of mercy after all. Ketch took several blows with the axe and was reduced to using it as a saw in order to complete the task. The custom was that the condemned man paid his executioner to carry out the sentence and Russell is reported to have looked at Ketch after the first unsuccessful blow and said "You dog, did I give you ten guineas to use me so inhumanly?"(iv). Whatever the exact details of Russell's beheading, it is clear that Ketch had gone too far, even for those bloodthirsty days. He was widely criticised, which drove him to publish a pamphlet(v) denying rumours that he had been drunk or deliberately incompetent and in which he blamed Russell for not keeping still during the procedure.

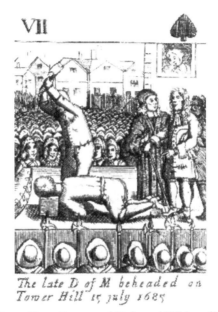

The late D of M beheaded on Tower Hill 15 july 1685

Photo courtesy User Raymond Palmer/ Wikimedia Commons

11.12: Contemporary playing card depicting Jack Ketch beheading the Duke of Monmouth on Tower Hill

Next came the rebellion in 1685 led by the illegitimate son of Charles II, the Duke of Monmouth. It was notorious for the number of people afterwards condemned by Judge Jeffries at the Bloody Assizes to be hanged, drawn and quartered – yet another gift for the makers of playing cards. Monmouth was sentenced to be beheaded and is alleged to have asked Ketch not to hack him in the way that he had hacked Lord Russell. It made no difference. Ketch was perhaps unnerved by the status and demeanour of the condemned man: this time he is said to have taken at least five blows with the axe before having to finish the job off with a knife.

The reputation of Jack Ketch was such that his name quickly became adopted as the name for any executioner, including the hangman in the new Punch and Judy puppet shows that were becoming popular at the end of seventeenth century. The puppet Mr. Punch is a rogue and early versions of the show ended up with him being hanged by the puppet hangman Jack Ketch as a punishment for his wicked deeds. Later versions have Punch tricking the hangman into putting his own head in the noose, whereupon Punch pulls the rope and it is the hangman who meets his end. It is not impossible that the change in the story was the result of the activities of a hangman who in 1718 was himself hanged after being found guilty of murder.

BOBBY

It seems that whenever the annual crime figures are released there is a public outcry for 'more bobbies on the beat'. The phrase would surely bring delight to the ghost of the former Prime Minister Sir Robert Peel (1788 – 1850) from whom this somewhat affectionate nickname for policemen was derived, though whether Prime Ministers in his day were as intent as the modern variety on leaving a 'legacy' is doubtful. If they were, Peel's would certainly have been two-edged as not only did he create the first modern Police force but he was also the bright spark who invented income tax.

The history of policing in Britain is comparatively recent. There was really none at all until Charles II introduced official night watchmen, popularly referred to as Charleys in recognition of the part the king had played in establishing the system. They quickly developed a reputation for being lazy and totally ineffective. The first real step forward was taken in 1750 by the novelist Henry Fielding who was a magistrate at

Bow Street. He set up a group of constables called Bow Street Runners – initially only six of them – whose job was to track down criminals. They were so successful that a Bow Street Horse Patrol was also established for a time. It was not until Peel and his Police Act of 1828 that there was a nationwide system of policing. These early policemen were initially referred to informally as 'peelers' before the nickname 'bobby' took over.

Photo Courtesy The Open University and Metropolitan Police Authority

11.13: A 'Peeler' from the 1850s

BIG BEN

For a convincing demonstration of the fact that sound waves travel far more slowly than radio waves, lurk across the Thames from the Houses of Parliament with a portable radio one evening. Tune in to Radio 4 for the ten o'clock news introduced by the chimes of Big Ben and you will find that you hear the actual chimes from the clock one or two seconds after you hear them through the radio. Someone so surprised at the persistence of this very noticeable time lag raised the question with the BBC to find out the reason. Had the BBC chimes perhaps been pre-recorded and were merely broadcast at (roughly) the appropriate moment? The response was "certainly not". In 1923 a microphone was installed in the tower close to the bell and the chimes are transmitted directly from that.

The name Big Ben is often used to refer to the clock – or even the clock tower – of the Houses of Parliament, but strictly speaking it is the name of the hour bell alone and does not even include the bells responsible for the familiar 'ding dong' quarter chimes. Big Ben has been reminding Londoners of the relentless passage of time since 1859. Its sombre sound marking the beginning of the two minutes silence on Remembrance Day has become an integral part of the nation's tribute to those who died in war.

Both clock and bell proved extremely reliable once the teething problems were over. Even the bombing of London during the Second World War was unable to stop the clock, although it has suffered the very occasional lapse. The 1963 New Year was rung in a few minutes late because heavy snow on the hands had slowed it down, and it did become a little irritable during the hot weather in 2005. The only major problem was in 1976/7 when Big Ben was unable to strike for nine months because the chiming mechanism had broken down: news broadcasts were driven to rely on the time signal pips alone. In 2007 the chimes again stopped for a few weeks for maintenance purposes, but the clock itself continued to tell the time.

This image of reliability contrasts dramatically with Big Ben's early history that began with the unfortunate side effects of modernising an archaic system of recording financial transactions. Since the thirteenth century officials of the Exchequer at the old Palace of Westminster had been keeping important financial records on tally sticks, examples of which can still be seen at the Bank of England Museum. When money was paid into the Exchequer a stick was notched to record the amount of the deposit, each notch representing a certain round sum such as one pound, ten pounds, one hundred pounds and so on, larger notches being used to indicate larger amounts. The notched stick was then split in half lengthways with half of every notch appearing on each half of the stick, both parties to the transaction then keeping one half of the stick as a permanent record. The system worked well as proof of payment and also prevented fraud since it would show up any attempt by either party to change the notches. But it was cumbersome and the sticks were often quite long, particularly when recording the sort of sums involved in the Crown's finances. Eventually in 1826 the Exchequer changed to more modern methods and by 1834 tally sticks were a thing of the past and officials at the Palace had a big clear out. Out of date tally sticks were used to stoke the boilers, which were overwhelmed and the Palace was almost completely destroyed by fire.

Parliament set up a commission to organise the rebuilding and architects were invited to submit their proposals. The winning design included a clock tower complete with clock, chimes and a fourteen ton hour bell, far heavier than any other bell that had at that time been cast in Britain. There were fierce arguments over who should design and make the clock and to settle the issue the Astronomer Royal was appointed to prepare a specification for the clock that could then be put out to tender. Parliament also appointed the barrister Edmund Beckett Denison (later Baron Grimthorpe), who had an interest in horology, to help assess the applications. The specification was daunting, requiring amongst other things that the clock was to be accurate to within one second per day. Clockmakers at the time were sceptical that such accuracy could be achieved in a clock of the necessary size and Denison ended up designing it himself. By now the building of the tower was well advanced and the original plans had been amended with the result that the clock, at last under construction, was no longer going to fit into the clock tower. The contract had to be renegotiated and the clock modified. Again there followed further delays – and delays in this context are measured in years, not months. At last a new Commissioner of Works, Sir Benjamin Hall, was appointed in 1855 and he clearly brought the necessary administrative skills that had so far been lacking.

Courtesy Whitechapel Bell Foundry

11.14: Arrival of the new bell at the clock tower, new Palace of Westminster

Denison had thrown himself into the design of the clock with enthusiasm and now turned his attention to the bell, on which he also had strong views. He specified both its shape and the composition of the metal to be used, in both cases departing from tradition. The bell was first cast in 1856 by a bell-founder in the North East of England. It was shipped to London and then drawn by sixteen horses through the streets to Westminster, to the cheering of huge crowds. During its final testing the striking hammer (the weight of which had been specified by Denison) unfortunately split the bell in two and the Whitechapel Bell Foundry was given the task of recasting it. It took a week for the old bell to be broken up into pieces small enough to fit into the furnaces. The metal, when molten, was then poured into a new mould and an idea of the size of the task can be gleaned from the fact that twenty days were needed for it to cool down and solidify. Various practical problems arose over hanging the bell, giving rise to arguments between the architect and Denison as to which of them was responsible for the problems, but the job was at last accomplished.

There remained the small matter of the clock's minute hands of which there were four, one for each face. It turned out that they were far too heavy for the clock's mechanism to cope with and again arguments raged, the architect and Denison each blaming the other. New, comparatively lightweight hands (a mere two hundredweight instead of twenty-five) were fitted and at last the clock went into action. The bells rang out from the top of the new clock tower for the first time in the summer of 1859.

More problems were to come. In September the newly installed bell cracked so a lighter bell-hammer had to be fitted and the bell was rotated to prevent the hammer from striking the damaged part. The immediate problem was solved but again there were furious arguments, this time about the cause of the crack. The view of the Whitechapel Bell Foundry was that the composition of the bell-metal that Denison had insisted on, in opposition to the Foundry's expert advice, was not the most suitable. The Foundry also considered that the bell had been badly hung and that Denison had insisted on a bell-hammer that was too heavy, again against their advice. Denison blamed the architect for the hanging of the bell and also claimed that it had been badly cast and the defects disguised with filler. The Foundry owner sued Denison for libel but as Denison was not allowed to take a sample of metal from the bell for analysis, he was unable to prove that there was any truth in his argument and so lost the case. A second libel case was brought against him several years later after he had made further accusations against the Whitechapel Bell Foundry, and again he lost.

It is customary for bells of exceptional importance to be given a name. Hence York Cathedral has Great Peter and there are several bell towers housing a Great Tom. But Big Ben is different. It was never officially named and it is not exactly known how it acquired its soubriquet. Some sources suggest that it may have been named after Ben Caunt, a well-known heavyweight boxer of the time popularly known as Big Ben. The more likely candidate is Sir Benjamin Hall (1802-1867) (later Lord Llanover), a man renowned for his size, who had done so much to get the project completed and whose name is inscribed on the bell itself.

HANSARD

Like Big Ben, Hansard is a Parliamentary icon with something of a murky past. It is now the official verbatim record of all Parliamentary debates, although unparliamentary language or behaviour may be covered by merely a discreet bracketed reference such as 'disturbance'. It is held in high regard, with reports being published on the day following the relevant debate.

Originally the business of Parliament was considered to be secret. Reporting Parliamentary debates was a breach of Parliamentary privilege for which the perpetrator could be fined. Even in those days, however, Parliament needed an official printer to document the outcome of its debates and in 1800 one Luke Hansard, who had been involved in the official printing of debates for many years, took over the running of the business.

Public interest in what its elected representatives were up to had led to the publication of many unofficial reports of Parliamentary debates. Initially these were thinly disguised as accounts from fictional clubs or places, such as 'Report of the Senate of Lilliputia'(vi), or 'Proceedings of the Lower Room of the Robin Hood Society'(vii). In 1770 John Wilkes began to publish reports openly, quoting words and naming the speaker, as part of a political campaign to establish the right to do so. In effect he succeeded and Parliament gave up defending its secrecy even though it still claimed that publication remained a breach of privilege.

Before long the political journalist William Cobbett was organising the first regular, but still unofficial, series of reports called "Parliamentary Debates". Cobbett was also an outspoken extreme radical. When he published a pamphlet denouncing the flogging of British soldiers after a minor mutiny over unfair deductions from pay he was convicted of seditious libel and sent to prison. A similar fate was suffered by his printer, Thomas Curson Hansard (1776 – 1833), who was the son of Luke Hansard and who had set up his own independent publishing business after working in his father's firm for some years.

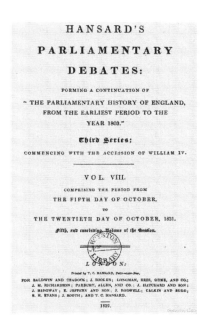

11.15: A title page from Hansard, 1832

Cobbett was ruined and had to sell up. His business of 'Parliamentary Debates' was bought by his printer Hansard, under whose direction it did so well that Hansard decided to rename the reports after himself. When Hansard died the business remained within the family until his son sold it to a company under the control of one Horatio Bottomley, a flamboyant character with a mistaken confidence in his own business acumen. Bottomley was subsequently imprisoned for fraud. The company failed and Parliament tried out several other printers, but none could do the job successfully. In

1909 Parliament decided to take on the task itself and The Official Report was born but, because people still kept on referring to the reports as Hansard, the old name was readopted in 1943. So well established had the name become that the Parliaments of both Canada and Australia also adopted it for their own Parliamentary reports, although the publishers of both those reports are completely independent.

CLERIHEW

St. Paul's School for boys in London, the school that regularly comes at or near the top in the league tables for A level results, had a pupil whose talents lay more in languages than in science. Like any other school it will have had many such pupils but this particular one, Edmund Clerihew Bentley (1875 – 1956), made a name for himself – primarily as a result of not listening during science lessons. He passed the time by making up amusing rhymes, hardly to be described as fine poetry, in a format that had not been previously explored and that subsequently became known as a 'clerihew'. A clerihew is a poem in the sense that it consists of two rhyming couplets, but the length of each line is extremely flexible. It usually begins with the name of a person and is falsely biographical. One of Bentley's first efforts whilst still at school clearly indicates a mind wandering during chemistry:

> Sir Humphrey Davy
> Abominated gravy.
> He lived in the odium
> Of having discovered sodium.(viii)

After leaving school Bentley studied classics and then law before going into journalism. He also wrote a few successful detective stories that had a considerable influence on later writers of the genre. But he carried on producing amusing verse and published several books of clerihews. The first one was called Biography for Beginners and was illustrated by his school friend G. K. Chesterton. Reading some of them now it is all too easy to imagine how, once the idea of the rhymes had taken hold, concentration on more serious issues must have taken increasing amounts of self-discipline:

> Sir Christopher Wren
> Said "I am going to dine with some men.
> If anyone calls
> Say I am designing St. Paul's".(ix)

> John Stuart Mill,
> By a supreme act of will,
> Overcame his natural bonhomie
> And wrote 'Principles of Political Economy'.(x)

TAWDRY

It does seem rather unfair on St. Audrey, daughter of the king of East Anglia and more formally known as St. Etheldreda (c.630 – 679), that a corrupted version of her name should end up as a description of cheap, flashy jewellery.

Courtesy NYPL

11.16: Late 19thC depiction of Saint Æthelthryth (Etheldreda, or Audrey)

The Isle of Ely (in those days it really was an island, surrounded by wet fenland not drained until the seventeenth century) was given to Etheldreda/Audrey as a dowry on the occasion of her first marriage. Later she remarried. Legend would have us believe that neither marriage was consummated and, in order to maintain the status quo, she ran away to become a nun. Whatever the truth, in 673 she founded a monastery for both monks and nuns at Ely on the site of the present cathedral. She gave the Isle of Ely to the monastery as an endowment and spent the rest of her life as Abbess there, in prayer and contemplation.

Etheldreda/Audrey died of a tumour of the neck and, although sources differ as to whether or not this was caused by the plague, she believed that it was sent by God as a punishment because she had loved necklaces when a young woman. Every year her death used to be commemorated in Ely with the great medieval St. Audrey's fair at which it was customary for young men to buy small gifts for their sweethearts, such items becoming referred to subsequently as 'tawdry' in reference to the fair.

PINCHBECK

In semantic terms Christopher Pinchbeck (1670 – 1732) has a great deal in common with St. Audrey. Strictly speaking pinchbeck was, and still is, a hardwearing and high quality metal alloy made of roughly five parts of copper to one of zinc. It looks impressively like gold and that accounts for both its initial success and its subsequent linguistic transformation to the tawdry.

The alloy was discovered by Pinchbeck and the metal actually made by him was of a greatly superior quality to later imitations. He used it not only for clocks and watches but also for a variety of other things including snuffboxes, buckles, buttons, sword hilts, whip handles and spurs. Less wealthy purchasers keen to keep up appearances were glad to buy imitation gold that could be passed off as the real thing. But there was also a market for pinchbeck amongst the nobility and gentry themselves, because when travelling they faced the risk of robbers or highwaymen and found it wise not to carry anything too valuable. They bought pinchbeck expressly for the purpose. More recently gold plate, and the use of less pure gold alloy such as nine carat gold, has taken the place of pinchbeck, leaving imitation gold decidedly down market.

Courtesy oldbailey@shef.ac.uk

11.17: 'An exact representation of Maclane the Highwayman robbing Lord Eglington'

AS RICH AS CROESUS

Even during his lifetime the name of Croesus (c. 595 BC – c. 546 BC), king of Lydia, was used to describe someone of exceptional wealth. In those days gold was to be found in abundance in Lydia (part of modern day Turkey) and it is believed that that country was the first ever to mint coins from metal. By the time Croesus came to the throne the use of coins was well established and had already spread to Greece.

There is no doubt that Croesus was a real person, but his history oscillates between truth and legend. He came to the throne in about 560 BC after the death of his father and after defeating his half-brother, whom he then had put to death – as one did in those days – in order to protect his own claim to the throne. Croesus' sumptuous court at Sardis attracted not only the rich and famous but also scholars and philosophers. The Athenian law-maker and poet, Solon, paid it a visit and it is said that Croesus, secure in the satisfaction brought by his enormous wealth, asked Solon to name the happiest man of all time. Solon did not produce the expected reply, suggesting three comparatively unknown candidates instead of Croesus himself. When asked why, Solon's response was that for as long as Croesus was still alive no-one could know what the gods might still have in store for him.

Photo © Classical Numismatic Group, Inc.

11.18: Obverse and reverse of a gold coin from Lydia, minted in the early 6th Century BC

During Croesus' reign the power of the Persians under Cyrus the Great built up to such a level that Croesus thought it wise to join battle whilst he still had a good chance of victory. He consulted the oracle at Delphi as to the best course of action and received the answer that, should he send an army against the Persians, he would destroy a great empire. Taking this at face value and not appreciating its ambiguity, Croesus was delighted. He gave generously to the god Apollo by way of thanks and sallied forth. When his efforts resulted in stalemate he retreated to Sardis and began to disband his forces with the intention of resuming battle in the forthcoming spring, in accordance with the contemporary tactics of war. But the Persians pursued him, defeated what was left of his troops, and entered Sardis.

A funeral pyre was built for Croesus, either by Cyrus or possibly by Croesus himself in order to avoid being captured. After it was lit Croesus was heard to cry out the name of Solon, in despairing recognition of the Athenian's wisdom on the subject of happiness. Cyrus, when the reason for Croesus' words had been explained, realised that Croesus was used to moving amongst men of learning and decided to spare him, but by then the flames had taken hold. It is said that Croesus, seeing Cyrus's change of heart, called to Apollo for help and Apollo promptly sent a great rainstorm to quench the fire.

Photo courtesy User AtilimGunesBaydin/Wikimedia Commons

11.19: Ceremonial court of the bath-gymnasium complex at the archaeological site of Sardis, Turkey

Meanwhile the victorious army was ransacking Sardis. Cyrus drew Croesus' attention to this, commenting to him that his city was being looted, whereupon Croesus replied that Sardis was no longer his and that the troops were in fact helping themselves to the wealth of what was now Cyrus' own city. Cyrus seems to have been impressed as subsequently he gave Croesus a place at his court.

YARBOROUGH

Avid players of bridge or whist are all too aware that it is possible to pick up a hand of thirteen cards and find that it contains no court cards: in fact it seems to occur with distressing regularity. But to pick up a Yarborough, a hand that does not even have any tens in it either, is extraordinary, even for a player consistently dogged by bad luck. Statisticians have calculated the chances as 1,827 to 1.

Such an unusually wretched hand is named after one of the Earls of Yarborough, but precisely which one is a moot point. The most popular candidate is Charles Anderson Worsley Pelham (1809 – 1862), once the Member of Parliament for part of Lincolnshire, who became the second Earl of Yarborough. However, some of those who cite him also give 1897 as the year of his death, in which case they either have the wrong year or the wrong Earl.

**11.20:
A Yarborough**

The relevant Yarborough, whichever one it was, was a gambling man. He used to bet with other players at odds of a thousand to one that they would not pick up a hand that contained no cards above a nine. Obviously he nearly always won, but many players were happy to risk a single pound for the chance of winning a thousand. Apparently he did eventually lose once, shortly before his death.

Bridge developed from the much older English game of whist, references to which can be found at least as far back as the sixteenth century. Although whist began as a game played by those of lower social standing, by the eighteenth century it had become extremely fashionable. It was not until the 1890s that bridge came on the scene, probably from the Near East and initially in a form called Russian whist or 'Biritch', which may account for the modern name. In whist the trump suit is decided by either cutting the pack or adopting the suit of the last card to have been dealt. Bridge introduced the idea of choice for the trump suit. Within a very short space of time an early form of bridge called 'bridge whist' had become popular which permitted the dealer or his partner to choose trumps. Auction bridge developed from this, in which all four players bid for the right to choose trumps. Auction bridge also introduced the idea of choosing to have no trumps at all. By

1929 a different scoring system had been introduced and the game evolved into contract bridge, the game played by millions across the world.

QUEENSBERRY RULES

John Sholto Douglas (1844 – 1900), 8th (or 9th) Marquis of Queensberry, was what is politely called a colourful character. He was a proclaimed atheist and, although he did sit in the House of Lords as a representative Scottish peer, the second time he was nominated to do so he was prevented from taking his seat because he refused to take the customary religious oath of allegiance. Nor was he a successful family man: both his marriages ended in failure, which was unusual in Victorian Britain. Gambling and sporting activities were more to his taste.

The 8th (or 9th) Marquis is mainly remembered for the Queensberry Rules regulating boxing. Before these rules were adopted there was only bare-knuckle fighting or pugilism. Various efforts had been made to reduce the severity of injuries inflicted in the sport, the hazards of which are well illustrated by the basic nature of the rules introduced in the eighteenth century. These declared that an opponent could not be held below the waist, that once he was down a man must not be hit and if he was unable to resume fighting after a thirty second recovery time his opponent was declared the winner. These rules did little to prevent the fixing of fights and for many years the sport deserved its bad reputation.

Gradually things began to improve and in 1839 the London Prize Ring rules were introduced. These provided for a (square) ring surrounded by ropes. Kicking, biting and head butting were banned. There was a scratch mark in the centre of the ring and if after thirty seconds a man who was down was unable to return to the mark to resume fighting, he was declared 'not up to scratch' – a phrase which emerged from the world of boxing into general use – and his opponent won.

Fighting had always belonged in a strange world where low-class professional fighters mixed with gentlemen, aristocratic or even royal enthusiasts of the sport, who sometimes took lessons from bare-knuckle champions to improve their own fighting technique. Despite the new rules some fights were still little more than brawls and it was felt that in order to gain the interest – and consequent financial support – of the upper classes further regulation was needed. A new set of rules was drafted and Queensberry agreed to lend his name to them, the aristocratic connection bringing the sport a measure of social respectability. The key features of the change were that padded gloves were to be worn, fighting was to take place in a series of rounds each lasting only three minutes, wrestling was banned and any fighter who was down had only ten seconds to be ready before his opponent was declared the winner. The new rules favoured the skilled fighter and after a little time they gained general acceptance.

THE BATTLE between CRIB and MOLINEAUX fought at Thistleton Gap in the County of Rutland Sept.r 28.th 1811 ran for 600 Guineas. It was terminated in 11 rounds, fought in 20 minutes in which Crib was Victorious, Molineux was turned off senseless, with a broken Jaw. Crit was but slightly hurt.

Courtesy NYPL

11.21: 'The battle between Crib and Molineaux'
fought in the County of Rutland, September 28th 1811, for 600 guineas

It was this same Marquis of Queensberry whose son, Lord Alfred Douglas ('Bosie'), had a notorious relationship with

382

Oscar Wilde. Queensberry publicly accused Wilde of sodomy and Wilde brought a court action for libel. Bosie was not called as a witness but in view of the evidence to be given against Wilde from other men with whom he had had sexual relations, Wilde dropped the case. This led to his arrest, trial and subsequent imprisonment: Bosie's poem that ended with the famous words "the Love that dare not speak its name"(xi), was used in evidence against Wilde. In those days homosexuality was a criminal offence and there was no law protecting consenting adults in private.

Was John Sholto Douglas the eighth or the ninth Marquis? Both numbers are widely quoted, the confusion arising from the identity of marquis number three. James, the eldest son of marquis number two, was dangerously insane but under the feudal law existing at the time was automatically heir to the family titles and estate. James was always kept under close supervision but at the age of ten, when nearly everyone was out celebrating the Act of Union between England and Scotland, he escaped from his rooms. He went down to the kitchen to find something to eat. All he found down there was an unfortunate kitchen boy, so James roasted him on a spit and had begun his meal before the rest of the household returned. In order to disinherit James the second marquis had to obtain a charter of novodamus, under which the right to ownership of the family estate was regranted to him on new terms that expressly excluded the problematic James. But the title of marquis was apparently omitted from the document. Thus, when his father died James was technically the third marquis – although with no property rights – until his own death a few years later. Apparently he was never addressed as the third marquis but his younger brother, who had inherited the family estate, was. This younger brother should properly have been called the fourth marquis but he appears to have adopted the title as soon as he came into the rest of his inheritance, either assuming he really was the third marquis or perhaps in an effort to prevent awkward questions about the existence of his troubled older brother.

MESMERISE

Imagine a rabbit, caught in the headlights of a car travelling towards it at night on a country lane. It stands as if mesmerised, dashing to safety only at the last minute when the car is almost upon it. Another rabbit, mesmerised by the behaviour of an approaching fox, is not so lucky. It remains rooted to the spot, unable to move until Mr. Fox is near enough to catch his dinner. Although it seems that the origin of mesmerism ought to be the result of scientific research on rabbits, it actually has nothing to do with our furry friends. The word began as a reference to the work of the Austrian doctor Franz (formerly Friedrich) Anton Mesmer (1734 – 1815) who for some years ran a popular and lucrative medical practice.

Mesmer had had some initial difficulty with career choices. He began by studying philosophy but changed to theology and then tried law, but eventually came down in favour of medicine. His special interest was in something he called animal gravitation, the influence of heavenly bodies on the human body. He argued that just as gravity produces tides in the sea, so it also has a similar effect on invisible fluids found in the atmosphere, with a consequent effect on the balance of bodily fluids. In those days that did not sound quite as strange as it does now.

He developed his theory further after attending a number of successful exorcisms carried out using a form of early hypnosis by the catholic priest Johann Gassner, now regarded by many as the father of modern hypnosis. Mesmer was impressed with Gassner's results but not convinced that exorcism worked by casting out the devil. He looked for a more scientific explanation and concluded that Gassner's success resulted from invisible fluids created by the magnetic field round the metal crucifix held over those subjected to the procedure. He propounded a new theory of 'animal magnetism' by which magnets could be used to effect medical cures.

384

For ten years or so Mesmer's theory seemed to work well and he enjoyed great popularity. He applied magnets to patients' bodies and held clinics at which groups of patients, sitting round a vat of dilute acid and holding on to the several iron bars protruding from it, were induced to fall into a trance. The reason for his success had little to do with magnets and more to do with hypnosis. Indeed it was not long before he dispensed with the magnets, using what he believed to be the healing magnetic power in his own hands to produce cures. He was also undoubtedly helped by the fact that, following marriage to a woman of comfortable financial means, he had become a respected member of society, hobnobbing with such well-known characters as Mozart and Haydn.

**11.22:
'Completely
mesmerised'**

*Courtesy Liam
Quin, Canada*

Traditional medical treatments of the time tended to be painful so the competition provided by Mesmer's revolutionary approach was a matter of considerable concern to conventional doctors, who were upset by the popularity of his methods. The crunch came with his treatment of a talented young musician who had been blind from childhood and who had close social connections to the Austrian court. Eye specialists could find no reason for her blindness, but after being treated by Mesmer she began to see again. Unfortunately she then lost her ability to play the piano and her enraged parents took her away before Mesmer had completed his treatment. She went blind again and Mesmer was vilified both by the Austrian medical establishment and those of influence in court circles. Accused of magic, his disgrace was such that he had to leave Austria.

Mesmer moved to Paris and went about establishing acceptance for his unorthodox treatment there. He never produced scientific proof of his theories, simply regarding his approach as 'natural': since illness was caused by a blockage in the invisible fluids flowing through the body his treatment, by using the flow of fluids within his own body to reinforce those of his patient, could restore harmony. Many were convinced and he trained other physicians in the use of his methods allowing them, on payment of a large fee (Mesmer was a born businessman), to use his name in connection with their own medical practices. Success followed success but again, as Mesmer's popularity with the public grew, so his relations with those in the scientific and medical world deteriorated. Eventually the King set up a commission to investigate Mesmer's claims. Its report was disastrous. It held that the so-called 'cures' existed only in the imagination of Mesmer's patients. Mesmer was discredited and retired from public life, dying in obscurity some thirty years later.

BOWDLERISE

How dare anyone interfere with Shakespeare's words? This is Shakespeare we are talking about here, the greatest playwright of all time. Cut out the rude and blasphemous bits? Typical Victorian strait-laced, two-faced values!

Such a diatribe summarises the modern attitude to the Bowdlers' book 'The Family Shakspeare' and their censoring of his text has resulted in the creation of the word 'bowdlerise', referring not merely to censorship, but to unnecessary censorship.

There are several misconceptions concerning The Family Shakspeare, one of which is the date of the book. It was in fact published before Victoria was even born. Another is the widely used statement that the book was edited by Thomas

Bowdler (1754 – 1825) and first published in 1818. Comparatively recently it was discovered that it was his sister Henrietta Maria Bowdler (1754 – 1830) who was solely responsible for the first edition. That edition was published in 1807 with no mention of her, or of any other editor's, name. In those days no respectable woman, let alone an unmarried one, could admit to deleting what were regarded as obscenities and blasphemy from a text when the whole point of the deletions was that such wording was considered unsuitable to be read by women and children. To edit the text she would not only have to have read the text in full, but also have understood the offending references. And make no mistake about it – Henrietta was the ultimate in respectability. When dancers appeared on stage during an operatic performance, she apparently always kept her eyes shut the whole time as she found it "so indelicate she could not bear to look"(xii).

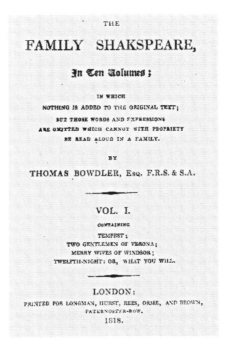

Courtesy Tim Riley

11.23: Title page of the 1818 edition of Bowdler's 'The Family Shakspeare'

387

Henrietta and her brother were born into a highly religious family. Numerous relatives – parents, siblings and nephews – wrote a variety of published essays, papers and books on religious topics. She herself wrote sermons (also published anonymously). Her brother Thomas qualified as a doctor but seems hardly to have practised, devoting himself instead to church societies, charities and inspection of prisons, as well as involving himself in The Family Shakspeare and a similarly expurgated but rather less successful version of Gibbon's Decline and Fall of the Roman Empire.

The publication of a 'respectable' version of Shakespeare's plays was inspired by the best of intentions and derived from the frequent reading of the plays to Henrietta and Thomas by their father to them in the evenings. It was only some years later Thomas realised that his father had omitted wording deemed by him to be unsuitable for children's ears. Thomas must have felt such consideration had been justified since his expressed reason for publishing The Family Shakespeare was to allow less talented parents, who might find it difficult to make appropriate omissions without interrupting the flow of the text, to read Shakespeare aloud at home secure in the knowledge that they would not unintentionally subject their families to possible religious or sexual corruption.

The book was a product of its time, when there was a growing feeling that women should be genteel and that children should be sheltered. In her preface to the 1807 edition Henrietta writes that Shakespeare's plays, though instructive, "contain much that is vulgar, and much that is indelicate"(xiii) and expresses her intention to produce a text "unmixed with anything that can raise a blush on the cheeks of modesty"(xiv).

It is easy now to regard the Bowdlers' work as ridiculously prudish and there was even some contemporary criticism, but many welcomed the work and 'The Family Shakespeare' was highly successful, remaining in print for over a hundred years. Even then its influence lived on and as recently as the 1960s some schools were still using texts of the plays edited to exclude sections considered unsuitable. Nor did they have the monopoly of picking and choosing Shakespeare's text – theatrical productions have frequently thought fit, for whatever reason, to omit scenes or parts of scenes, as is evidenced by annotations in archived prompt copies.

COMSTOCKERY

11.24: Symbol of the New York Society for the Suppression of Vice

In the same way that the Bowdlers' work inspired strong feelings in the UK, so for similar reasons did that of Anthony Comstock (1844 – 1915) in the US. In his determination to protect the morals of the public Comstock set up the New York Society for the Suppression of Vice. He persuaded Congress to pass what became known as the Comstock Law, banning the delivery or transportation (rather than the publication) of material that was 'obscene, lewd or lascivious', an approach that had presumably resulted from his position of Postal Inspector in the postal service. He also had a substantial influence in implementing the new law, and its effect was considerable. Transportation of information about birth control contravened it, and it was apparently even used to prevent anatomy textbooks for medical students being sent by post. Tons of literature regarded as obscene was burnt.

It appears that the word Comstockery actually first appeared in the New York Times in 1895. However, it is often said to have been coined in 1905 as a pejorative term by an irate George Bernard Shaw when efforts were made to prevent the showing in New York of his play 'Mrs. Warren's Profession', which concerns the relationship between a middle aged brothel owner and her highly educated daughter. Comstock and his Society had brought a court action to prohibit its showing, but lost the case. It is said that all publicity is good publicity so perhaps it was only to be expected that tickets for the production were completely sold out.

SWEET FANNY ADAMS

The phrase 'Sweet Fanny Adams', now rather old-fashioned, means 'nothing at all'. It is often believed to have originated merely as a euphemism for a vulgar expression that conveys the same meaning, a saying that uses her two initials in place of two words that the reader can no doubt supply in full. Such a belief is mistaken: the euphemism developed from subsequent usage.

The true origin of the phrase is grim. The story begins in Alton, Hampshire one fine summer morning. Eight year old Fanny Adams (1859 – 1867) set off up the lane from her house in the company of her friend Minnie and younger sister Lizzie. The group was stopped by a respectably dressed young man who gave them some ha'pennies and, telling the other two to go to the shops to buy some sweets, asked Fanny to go with him.

Later in the afternoon when it was realised that Fanny had not returned, her mother and a neighbour went along the lane to look for her. They happened to meet the same man coming back down it. He told the women his name was Frederick Baker and explained that he was a local solicitor's clerk. He agreed that he had seen the girls and given them some money but denied seeing any of them since then. By early evening

390

Fanny had still not reappeared and a search party of neighbours went out to look for her. Most of her dismembered body was discovered in numerous pieces scattered about in a nearby hopfield. Other body parts turned up in the vicinity some time later and her eyes were eventually found in the local river.

Minnie Warner. [COPYRIGHT.] Lizzie Adams.

Courtesy Curtis Museum

11.25: Minnie and Lizzie, beside Fanny Adam's headstone

"Sacred to the memory of Fanny Adams aged 8 years and 4 months,
who was cruelly murdered on Saturday Aug'st 24th 1867.
Fear not them which kill the body but are not able to kill the soul but rather
fear him which is able to destroy both soul and body in hell (Matthew ch10
v28)"

Baker was questioned by the police and although his clothes were splattered with blood he denied all knowledge of the murder. Within two days he was arrested: the police had

391

found his diary and the entry for Saturday read "Killed a young girl. It was fine and hot."(xv)

Baker maintained throughout his trial that he was innocent. The evidence showed that there was a great deal of mental instability in his family and the judge advised the jury that they should consider whether to find Baker not guilty by reason of insanity. The jury clearly did not feel it incumbent upon them to think about it for very long because it took them a mere fifteen minutes to find him guilty of murder. Baker had the unenviable distinction of being the last person to be hanged in public at Winchester prison and some five thousand people turned out on Christmas Eve to watch it. A gravestone in memory of Fanny and her tragic death was paid for by public subscription and is still to be found in the churchyard near her home.

That is the tale of Fanny Adams, but it took the warped sense of humour of the Royal Navy to introduce her name into the dictionary. Very shortly after Fanny had died, tinned mutton was introduced into the official rations. The seamen took the view that this unrecognisable meat must be part of the remains of poor Fanny and so christened it Sweet Fanny Adams. The tinned meat was not popular and the slang naval phrase gradually spread to other forms of unappetising stew, then gained wider use and became extended to its present meaning, no doubt helped by the convenient euphemism it provided.

TEDDY BEAR

It was not until the 1890s that stuffed toy bears first appeared on the market. They were made in Germany and were usually referred to as 'bruins'. There was no indication then that the bear was destined to gain the status that it holds today. The current name of 'teddy bear' comes from President Theodore ('Teddy') Roosevelt (1858 – 1919) who was born in New York into a family descended from the original Dutch settlers. He was therefore technically a Knickerbocker (see Chapter One).

As a young man Roosevelt began his career in politics but when his wife died after childbirth – a tragedy that coincided with the death of his mother from typhoid fever on the same day – he turned for solace to the outdoor life and cattle ranching. Two years later he remarried and went back into politics, eventually becoming governor of the state of New York, vice president and, after the assassination of the incumbent, president.

Roosevelt was a keen hunter and naturalist and it was these interests that led to the connection of his name with toy bears. In 1902, shortly after he had become president, he was invited by the Governor of Mississippi to take part in a bear hunt. There was a political aspect to this sporting event since the Governor was up for re-election, standing against an old-fashioned white supremacist – slavery had been abolished comparatively recently and entrenched attitudes took a long time to die. Presidential support for the Governor could be expected to attract votes, and in particular the black vote, since Roosevelt had recently entertained a prominent black leader to dinner at the White House – provoking vitriolic criticism in the press.

The Governor's hunting party duly set up camp and went off on the trail of a bear. After some hours it appeared that the dogs had lost the scent, so most of the party (including the President) went back to camp. The remaining hunters still in the field continued the search and finally cornered the bear. Taking the view that the President should be the one to have the honour of administering the coup de grace, they tied it to a tree to prevent it from running off and called for the rest of the party to return. The bear, a large old black one, had been severely injured when defending itself from the attacking dogs. The President decided that it was hardly sporting to shoot the animal in these circumstances and refused to do so, asking that someone should simply put it out of its misery. The incident was reported in the press and a cartoon appeared in the Washington Post, inaccurately illustrating the situation with a small, somewhat cuddly, bear and the caption "Drawing the line in Mississippi", which may have been a veiled reference to the President's disapproval of the lynching of black Americans in the Southern states.

Courtesy Estelle & Melvin Gelman Library, George Washington University

11.26: Clifford Berryman's cartoon in The Washington Post of President Theodore Roosevelt's bear hunting trip in Mississippi

Following publication of the cartoon the president's name became inextricably linked to toy bears but exactly why is not absolutely clear. Some say a New York toy maker began making bears and obtained permission from the president to call them 'Teddy's bears'. Others maintain that the name arose when toy bears imported from Germany were used to decorate the dining tables at an important presidential function. Perhaps both tales could be correct.

Bears aside, the President's interests were wide-ranging. He was an early conservationist, being responsible for the creation of millions of acres of national forests, parks and nature reserves. But not all his ideas were successful. His project to introduce a simplified spelling system, for example, was a disaster. He had directed that official documentation was to be published using his new spelling rules, but this caused such annoyance that he was forced to backtrack. Some of his proposed simplifications such as 'crost', 'deprest' or 'fantom' indeed look rather strange but other words were ahead of their time: those such as 'color', 'center' and 'catalog' are now accepted as normal American spelling.

MICKEY FINN

Nowadays girls drinking in nightclubs, particularly in the company of casual acquaintances, are advised to keep a close eye on their drinks. In particular they are warned about the so-called 'date rape' drug Rohypnol®. This is regarded as a comparatively recent hazard, but *plus ça change, plus c'est la même chose* ...

Mickey Finn was the proprietor of The Lone Star Saloon and Palm Garden Restaurant in Chicago from 1896 until it was shut down by the police in 1903. Despite its grandiose title this was not the sort of establishment the ordinary law abiding citizen would wish to patronise. Newspaper articles published following its closure refer to a record of appalling crimes made possible through the discreet addition to customers' drinks of a drug similar to chloroform, thought to be chloral hydrate. A drink treated with Finn's 'knock-out drops' rendered the consumer unconscious, whereupon he was carried to a room at the back, robbed of anything valuable, and dumped in a nearby street. When he finally came round the victim would be unable to remember anything about what had happened.

As with many slang words no contemporary written record of the phrase has been found and a possible alternative meaning for a Mickey Finn is a laxative or an emetic, quietly slipped into the drink of someone who was unpleasantly drunk in order to encourage him to leave the bar in a hurry. This is more in keeping with the phrase's appearance in the report of a Chicago court case some fifteen years after Finn's saloon had been closed(xvi). It was used then to refer to an emetic added to customers' food at a restaurant by waiters conducting a campaign to require the leaving of tips.

The case reports do not, of course, explain the origin of the phrase. The most widely quoted source for that is a book published in 1940, allegedly based on the word of a prostitute who had worked in Finn's saloon(xvii). She linked the phrase to the saloon, to the year 1903 and to the 'knock-out' meaning. Although the events had taken place nearly forty years before the book was published, nothing other than the lapse of time has been found to cast doubt on the tale's authenticity and it is widely quoted as the most probable version of events.

CODSWALLOP

This wonderfully appealing word is colloquial and so dictionaries have been slow in waking up to its existence. It is accepted that the word existed well before its currently recorded earliest use, which was by Sid James in 1959 during an episode of the BBC television series 'Hancock's Half Hour'. Because by its very nature the word is spoken rather than written it is difficult to find proof of earlier usage.

One rather academic suggestion is that it is derived from the Anglo-Saxon meaning of cod, being a bag, linked to wallop, which in some dialects apparently means chatter. A more likely origin, embraced as such by the authoritative Brewer(xviii) but for which there is as yet no definite proof, is that the word was an unflattering reference to the invention of a certain Mr. Hiram Codd (1838 – 1887). Codd was born in Bury-St.-Edmunds and worked in the non-alcoholic fizzy drinks business. In those days bottles were stoppered using corks and the problem was how to prevent the fizz in the drink from proving too powerful for the cork. During storage corks shrink slightly as they begin to dry out and this decreases their efficacy, to the point where eventually the fizz gains the upper hand and the cork flies out of the bottle, rapidly followed by most of the drink. The most advanced solution to this problem before Mr. Codd came on the scene had been the Hamilton bottle, using an idea that was elegant in its sheer simplicity. It had a pointed base that effectively prevented it from standing upright, so it had to be stored lying down and the continual contact of the cork with the contents of the bottle kept the cork moist. The problem with that was that the bottles had a nasty tendency to roll off the shelf.

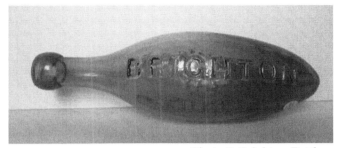

Photo © Brighton Bottles

11.27: Hamilton bottle

The principles relevant to the storage of fizzy drinks were turned upside down, both literally and metaphorically, by the Codd bottle. Codd was no scientist and one can only marvel at his ingenuity and at the skill of the glass-blowers who put his idea into effect. His complex design incorporated various features in the neck of each bottle, plus one marble and a ring-shaped rubber washer. The first of these features was that the rim at the top of the bottle was narrower than the neck below it and there was a groove immediately below the inside of the rim to accommodate a washer. The marble had to be positioned in the neck of the bottle whilst the bottle was being made because, although it had to be small enough to move freely up and down the neck, the marble also had to be too large to come out through the narrow rim at the top. Then there was a platform with a hole in the centre, positioned at the base of the neck of the bottle to prevent the marble falling down to the bottom. Finally, there was a ledge of glass in the shape of an inverted curve on one side of the inside neck of the bottle that caught the marble as the drink was being poured out, in order to prevent it obstructing the flow.

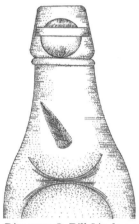

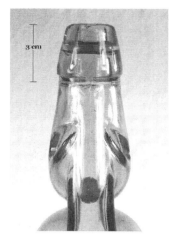

Diagram © Bill Lindsey   *Photo © Bill Lindsey*

11.28: Codd's Ball Stopper

So much for the structure: now for the physics. When the bottle was inverted during filling the marble rested against the rim, cushioned by the washer. A small shake of the bottle whilst still in its inverted position released some of the fizz, which increased the pressure inside the bottle and so pushed the marble firmly down against the rim, the washer between the two providing an airtight seal. When the bottle was returned to an upright position the pressure inside it ensured that the marble remained securely in place. To open the drink all that was necessary was to press the marble in to release the pressure. The marble then dropped down to its platform and the drink could be poured out. The beauty of this system was that the bottle could be recycled and refilled and a corkscrew was no longer needed for opening it.

This cheap and effective way of stoppering fizzy drinks was widely adopted by the whole industry within a very short space of time and continued in use until about 1930. Similar patents were taken out and there is a multiplicity of bottles of various designs and colours. One even used an oval shaped

398

marble to discourage small boys from breaking empty bottles in order to add to their marble collections. Collecting the bottles themselves is now a thriving hobby, the most valued of all being the rare cobalt blue – the cost of which apparently runs into four figures.

It seems a shame that Codd's name is now seldom associated with his highly successful achievement but instead features mainly as part of the derogatory phrase 'a load of old codswallop'. And why the wallop? Somewhat surprisingly, this is not a reference to any need to wallop the marble in order to open the drink – gentle pressure was apparently all that was necessary. Wallop used to be a slang word for beer. Brewer's(xviii) suggestion for the possible etymology of codswallop is that weak beer of poor quality was likened by disapproving drinkers to the products of the burgeoning fizzy drinks trade and referred to as Codd's wallop. There is, however, a lapse of nearly ninety years between Codd's invention and the first recorded appearance of the word, so the etymology does remain open to doubt.

APPENDIX 1 – FOOTNOTES

CHAPTER 1: CLOTHING, ACCESSORIES and TEXTILES
(i)   *Trilby* by George du Maurier, 1895.

(ii)   *Martin Chuzzlewit* by Charles Dickens, 1844.

(iii)   *The Man on the Flying Trapeze*, words by George Leybourne, 1868.

(iv)   *1066 and All That* by W. Sellar and R.J. Yeatman, 1930 (my underlining).

(v)   *How to get on in Society* by John Betjeman (Oxford Dictionary of Quotations 4th edition 1992).

CHAPTER 2: FOOD and DRINK
(i)   The various references to 'Larousse' in this chapter are to *The Concise Larousse Gastronomique,* 1999.

(ii), (iii) & (iv) Ministry of Food, 1939-1945.

(v)   *Kettner's Book of the Table* by E.S. Dallas, 1877.

(vi)   *Essex County Rolls*, 1592.

(vii)   *The Winter's Tale*, IV: IV - "Gloves as sweet as damask roses"; *Much Ado About Nothing*, III:IV - "These gloves … are an excellent perfume".

(viii)   *Life a la Henri: Being the Memoirs of Henri Charpentier*, by Henri Charpentier and Boyden Sparkes, 1934.

(ix)   *Terrace Tested Recipes*, compiled by the ladies of Terrace Congregational Church, 2nd edition. Published Wellington, 1927 (Oxford English Dictionary, 1982).

(x)   *Davis Dainty Dishes*, 1927, 6th edition, published by Davis Gelatine New Zealand Ltd. (Oxford English Dictionary, 1982).

(xi)   *Practical Home Cookery, Chats and Recipes* by K. McKay, 1929. (Oxford English Dictionary, 1982).

(xii)   *Rangiora Mother's Union Cookery Book,* 1933 (from "George Negus Tonight", ABC Television Australia interview with Prof. Helen Leach, broadcast 30 Aug 2004).

(xiii)   *The Valetudinarians Bath Guide* by Philip Thicknesse, 1780.

(xiv)   *Brewer's Dictionary of Phrase & Fable* 16th edition, 1999.

CHAPTER 3: VEHICLES and TRAVEL
(i)   *The Times, 14 Nov 1849.*

(ii)   *Brewer's Dictionary of Phrase & Fable* 16th edition, 1999.

(iii)   *The Bible, Genesis* 24: 60.

(iv)   Words spoken by Neville Chamberlain, 30 Sept 1938.

CHAPTER 4: MEASUREMENT
(i)   http://en.wikipedia.org/wiki/Gregorian_calendar, accessed 31.1.12.

(ii)   *The Life of William Thomson, Baron Kelvin of Largs*, by Silvanus P. Thompson, 1910.

(iii)   Verse by 'Wilhelma' published in *Photography* and quoted in *Electrical Review*, 17 Apr 1896.

(iv)   *Life of Davy* by Dr. J.A.Paris, quoting a letter written to him by Faraday dated 23 Dec 1829.

(v) *The Times,* letter from Faraday dated 7 July 1855.

(vi) *Faraday: The Life,* by James Hamilton, 2002.

(vii) Believed to have been coined by Sir Charles Bowen QC when junior counsel in the Tichborne case (1871-4) (*Brewer's Dictionary of Phrase & Fable* 16th Edition, 1999). [See 'titchy' at page 351.]

(viii) *Dynamic Fields and Waves (The Physical World series).* Editor Andrew Norton et al, ISBN 0-7503-0721-8.

(ix) *Laboratory notebook of Alexander Graham Bell, 10 March 1876.* From American Treasures of the Library of Congress Exhibition, http://www.loc.gov/exhibits/treasures/trr002.html, accessed 3 Sept 2012.

(x) *Famous Scots – Alexander Graham Bell (1847-1922),* http://www.rampantscotland.com/famous/blfambell.htm, accessed 27.3.12.

(xi) *Information Fact sheet No. 6,* published by the Met Office, 2010.

(xii) *Earthquakes* by Bruce A. Bolt, 1988: Modified Mercalli Intensity Scale.

(xiii) *An interview with Charles F. Richter,* Earthquake Information Bulletin 1971 Vol. 3, No. 4.

CHAPTER 5: MEDICAL

(i) *Observations on an Ethnic Classification of Idiots* by J. Langdon H. Down, London Hospital Reports, 3:259-262, 1866.

(ii) *Encyclopaedia Britannica* (Anatomy, Gross), 1973 4th edition, published William Benton.

(iii) *The American Journal of Human Genetics* 45:169-175 1989, quoting an address to the New York Neurological Society by George Huntington, 1909.

(iv) *Munchausen's Syndrome* by R. Asher, The Lancet, 1951 i:339-341.

(v) *A Counterblaste to Tobacco* by King James I of England, 1604.

(vi) *Cautions Against the Immoderate Use of Snuff* by Dr. John Hill, 1761.

(vii) *Smoking and Carcinoma of the Lung* by R. Doll & A.B. Hill, British Medical Journal 1950 2: 739.

(viii) *Treason Act 1351* c. 2 25 Edw 3 Stat 5.

(ix) *An Essay on the Shaking Palsy* by James Parkinson, 1817.

(x) *Annales Xantenses,* 857 as quoted in '*Ergot and Ergotism: A Monograph*' by George Barger, 1931.

(xi) *A Dictionary of the English Language* by Samuel Johnson, 1755.

(xii) Comment by Mrs. R. DePuy, as quoted by Zimmer, http://www.fundinguniverse.com/company-histories/Zimmer-Holdings-Inc-Company-History.html, accessed 13.3.12.

CHAPTER 6: BEHAVIOUR

(i) Quoted by Julian Huxley in SEAC (Calcutta) 27 Feb 1944 (*Oxford Dictionary of Quotations* 4th edition 1992).

(ii) *Oxford Dictionary of National Biography.*

(iii) *Spooner* by Sir William Hayter, 1977 (Oxford Dictionary of Quotations 4th edition 1992).

(iv) *Oxford Dictionary of National Biography.*

(v) *Daily Telegraph 11 Mar 2006:* obituary of John Profumo,.

(vi) *Biographical Encyclopedia of Texas,* 1880. By courtesy of University of North Texas Libraries, Denton, Texas.

(vii) *The Hooligan Nights* by Clarence Rook, 1899.

(viii) *The Official Sloane Ranger Handbook: The First Guide to What Really Matters in Life* (Harpers & Queen) by Ann Barr & Peter York, 1982.

(ix)   *Johnson's Lives of the English Poets* by Samuel Johnson, 1797.

(x)   *To Charlotte Pulteney* by Ambrose Philips, 1724.

(xi)   *Poems on Several Occasions* by Henry Carey, 3rd edition, 1729.

(xii) *La Cocarde Tricolore* by T & H Cogniard, 1835 (first performed 19 Mar 1831).

(xiii) *Macdermott's War Song* by G.W. Hunt, 1877.

(xiv) *Psychopathia Sexualis* by R. von Krafft-Ebing, 1886.

(xv)   *Strange Fruit* by Lewis Allan (Abel Meeropol), 1937. Performed by Billie Holiday in 1939.

(xvi) Compact dated 22 Sept 1780, signed by Lynch and others, http://www.search.com/reference/William_Lynch, accessed 31.3.12.

(xvii) Act of Indemnity 1782, *The Statutes at Large of Virginia (1809-1823)* vol. 11, ed. William Waller Hening, quoted by *The American National Biography*, 1999.

(xviii) Joseph Addison, *The Spectator* 1712, No. 509, quoted in *Annals of Cambridge* by Charles Henry Cooper, 1865.

(xix) John Milton, from *A Banquet of Jests. Or A Collection of Court, Camp, Colledge, Citie, Country, Iests*, 1640.

(xx)   Will of Thomas Hobson. PRO, PROB 11/159, q.17 (*Oxford Dictionary of National Biography*).

CHAPTER 7: PLANTS

(i)   *Catalogus arborum, fruticum ac plantarum tam indigenarum, quam exoticarum, in horto Iohannis Gerardis* by John Gerard, 1599.

CHAPTER 8: CREATURES

(i)   *Legends of the Bocas, Trinidad* by A.D. Russell, 1922.

(ii)   *A History of British Birds*, by William Yarrell, 1843.

(iii) *Samuel Pepys' Diary*, entry for Friday 25 May 1660.

CHAPTER 10: MILITARY

(i)   *Brown Bess* by Rudyard Kipling, 1911.

(ii)   *The Star Spangled Banner* by Francis Scott Key, 1814.

(iii) *Every Day's a Holiday* (1937 film).

(iv)   *Peel me a Grape* by Mae West, 1975.

CHAPTER 11: MISCELLANEOUS

(i)   *BBC press release 20 Jan 2006* re BBC/Oxford English Dictionary Wordhunt.

(ii)   *Brewer's Dictionary of Phrase & Fable* 16th edition, 1999.

(iii) *The Daily Telegraph*, February/March 1882.

(iv)   Eyewitness account of Sir Charles Lyttelton, http://www.everything2.com/index.pl?node=Jack%20Ketch, accessed 23.9.12.

(v)   *The Apologie of John Ketch, Esq., the executioner of London, in Vindication of Himself as to the Execution of the Late Lord Russel on July 21, 1683.* By Jack Ketch, 1683.

(vi) & (vii) *Story of Hansard*, Commonwealth Hansard Editors Association, http://www.commonwealth-hansard.org/chea_story.asp, accessed 23.9.12.

(viii), (ix) & (x) *Biography for Beginners* by Edmund Clerihew Bentley, 1905.

(xi)   *Two Loves* by Lord Alfred Douglas, 1896.

(xii) Quoted from *The Gentlemen's Magazine 1830* in *Dr. Bowdler's Legacy: A History of Expurgated Books in England and America* by Noel Perrin, 1969.

(xiii) & (xiv) Quoted in *The Bowdlers and their Family Shakespeare* by Colin
        Franklin, The Book Collector 49 (2000).
(xv)   *Diary* of Frederick Baker, entry 24 Aug 1867.
(xvi)   *Chicago Daily Tribune, 25 June 1918.*
(xvii) *Gem of the Prairie: An Informal History of the Chicago Underworld* by Herbert
        Asbury, 1940.
(xviii) *Brewer's Dictionary of Phrase & Fable* 16th edition, 1999.

APPENDIX 2 – REFERENCES for ILLUSTRATIONS

For terms of licences see the following websites:
CC BY_SA 3.0: http://creativecommons.org/licenses/by-sa/3.0/deed.en
CC BY-SA 2.5: http://creativecommons.org/licenses/by-sa/2.5/deed.en
CC BY-SA 2.0: http://creativecommons.org/licenses/by-sa/2.0/deed.en
CC BY-SA 1.0: http://creativecommons.org/licenses/by-sa/1.0/deed.en
CC BY 3.0: http://creativecommons.org/licenses/by/3.0/deed.en

CHAPTER 1: CLOTHING, ACCESSORIES and TEXTILES

1.1: 'Bloomer' dress of the 1850s
Source: http://xroads.virginia.edu/~HYPER/HNS/domwest/mcauley.html. Author: not known. Date: not known. See
http://commons.wikimedia.org/wiki/File:Bloomer.gif, accessed 24.8.12.   Public domain, old.

1.2: 'Diedrich Knickerbocker'
Source: *Diedrich Knickerbocker's A History of New-York from the Beginning of the World to the End of the Dutch Dynasty* (frontispiece) pub. G.P. Putnam, New York. Author: Washington Irving, artist F.O.C. Darley.   Date: 1849. See
http://commons.wikimedia.org/wiki/File:Diedrich_Knickerbocker.jpg, accessed 24.8.12. Public domain, old.

1.3: Pantalone
Source: *Masques et bouffons (comédie italienne)*, pub. Michel Levy Frères, Paris. Author: Maurice Sand. Colour image. Date: 1860. See
http://commons.wikimedia.org/wiki/File:SAND_Maurice_Masques_et_bouffons_06.jpg, accessed 24.8.12. Public domain, old.

1.4: Jules Leotard wearing his leotard
Source and author: not known. Date: before 1870. See
http://commons.wikimedia.org/wiki/File:Jules_Léotard2.jpg, accessed 24.8.12. Public Domain, old.

1.5: Spencer Jacket
Photo ©Marion May Designs UK (http://www.marionmay.co.uk/id38.html). By their kind permission.

1.6: James Brudenell, 7th Earl of Cardigan
Source and author: not known. Date: before 1869. See
http://commons.wikimedia.org/wiki/File:Cardigan.jpg, accessed 24.8.12. Public domain, old.

1.7: Assistant Surgeon of the 11th (Prince Albert's Own) Hussars, 1855
Source: U.S. Library of Congress Prints and Photographs Division, ID cph.3g09124. Photographer: Roger Fenton. Date: c. 1856. See
http://commons.wikimedia.org/wiki/File:Cornet_Wilkin_11th_Hussars.jpg, accessed 24.8.12. Public domain, old.

1.8: Casual 'top' with raglan sleeves
Drawing © C.M. Wiles. By his kind permission.

1.9(a): Traditional child's plimsolls with elasticated top

Source and author: User Alansplodge/Wikimedia Commons. Date: 2 Nov 2011. See http://commons.wikimedia.org/wiki/File:School_plimsolls.jpg, accessed 18.10.12. © User Alansplodge, licence for reuse CC-BY-3.0.

1.9(b): Basketball trainers

Source and Author: Shaun Labluk. Date:18 Feb 2007. See http://commons.wikimedia.org/wiki/File:Converse_Weapons.JPG, accessed 18.10.12. Public domain, by courtesy of Shaun Labluk.

1.10: The Modern Plimsoll Load Line

Source and author: User Welkinridge/Wikimedia Commons. Date: 19 May 2007. See http://commons.wikimedia.org/wiki/File:Load_line.jpg, accessed 24.8.12. © User Welkinridge, licence for reuse CC BY-SA 3.0.

1.11: Wellington Boots worn by the Household Cavalry (other ranks)

Source: www.householdcavalry.info/boots.html, accessed 1.11.11. Photographer: Peter J Ashman. Date: 2010. © Peter J. Ashman. By his kind permission.

1.12: Gamekeepers' Lunch, Holkham, circa 1910

Photo © Holkham Estate, Holkham, Wells-next-the-Sea, Norfolk. By their kind permission.

1.13: Traditional 'Anthony Eden' Felt

Photo © James Lock & Co., Ltd., hatters of St. James's St., London (http://www.lockhatters.co.uk/Homburg-details.aspx, accessed 1.11.11). By their kind permission.

1.14: Stetson from the 1920s

Source and author: User -oo0(Gold Trader)0oo-/Wikimedia Commons. Date: 2009. Colour image. See http://commons.wikimedia.org/wiki/File:Stetson_cowboy_hat_1920s_renovated.jpg, accessed 24.8.12. © User -oo0(Gold Trader)0oo-, licence for reuse: CC BY-SA 3.0.

1.15: 'Boss of the Plains' original design

Source and author: User -oo0(Gold Trader)0oo-/Wikimedia Commons. Date: 2009. Colour image. See http://commons.wikimedia.org/wiki/File:1800s_Boss_of_the_plains_.jpg, accessed 24.8.12. © User-oo0(Gold Trader)0oo-, licence for reuse CC BY-SA 3.0.

1.16: A much used leather Gladstone Bag

Photo © Cameo Auctioneers (http://gracemusiccompany.co.uk/contact-cameo-auctioneers). By their kind permission.

1.17: Maj. Gen. Ambrose E. Burnside, circa 1860

Source: Library of Congress Prints and Photographs Division. Photographer: Mathew B. Brady. Date: 1860-65. See http://commons.wikimedia.org/wiki/File:Ambrose_Burnside2.jpg, accessed 8.8.12. Public domain, old.

1.18: A Modern Doily

Photo © C.M. Wiles. By his kind permission.

CHAPTER 2: FOOD and DRINK

2.1: View of the Strogonov Palace from the Nevsky Prospekt

Source and Author: George Shuklin. Date: 26 June 2008. Colour image, cropped. See http://commons.wikimedia.org/wiki/File:Строгановский_дворец_(1).jpg, accessed 25.8.12. © George Shuklin, licence for reuse CC BY-SA 1.0.

2.2: Government posters from the Second World War
Source: http://www.tynelives.org.uk/war/wife/postall.htm, accessed 28.11.11.
Author: not known. By kind permission of the Imperial War Museums, London and by
courtesy of North Shields Library, North Tyneside.

2.3: Beef cut chart, showing position of the relevant cut, labelled 'tenderloin'
Source and author: User JoeSmack/Wikimedia Commons. Date: 2006. Colour
image. See http://commons.wikimedia.org/wiki/File:BeefCutTenderloin.svg, accessed
25.8.12. Public domain, by courtesy of the author.

2.4: Antoine-Augustin Parmentier
Source and author: not known. Date: before 1814. See
http://commons.wikimedia.org/wiki/File:Parmentier_Antoine_1737-1813.jpg,
accessed 25.8.12. Public domain, old.

2.5: Front page of the newspaper L'Aurore, 13th January 1898
Source: *L'Aurore*. Author: Emile Zola. Date: 13 Jan 1898. See
http://commons.wikimedia.org/wiki/File:J_accuse.jpg, accessed 25.8.12. Public
domain, old.

2.6: Baboon
Source and author: Bjørn Christian Tørrissen, http://bjornfree.com/galleries.html.
Date: 9 Nov 2008. Colour image. See
http://commons.wikimedia.org/wiki/File:Portrait_Of_A_Baboon.jpg, accessed
25.8.12. © Bjørn Christian Tørrissen, licence for reuse CC BY-SA 3.0.

2.7: Anna Pavlova as 'The Dying Swan', St. Petersburg 1905
Source: http://commons.wikimedia.org/wiki/File:AP_Cygne.jpg, accessed 25.8.12.
Author: not known. Date: 1905. Public domain, old.

2.8: Melba toast
Photo © Gastronomy Domine (http://www.gastronomydomine.com/?page_id=2.) By
their kind permission.

2.9: First page of an Act of Parliament passed in 1782 to prevent corruption in Parliamentary elections in Cricklade
Printed by Charles Eyre and William Strahan. Date: 1782. Public domain, old. By
courtesy of the Wiltshire and Swindon Archives, Wiltshire Council.

2.10: Ground floor of Sally Lunn's tea shop in Bath
Source: http://www.sallylunns.co.uk/bathbunswhichiswhich,intro.htm, accessed
22.1.12. Author: not known. Date: old. By courtesy of Sally Lunn's, North Parade
Passage, Bath.

2.11: Self portrait sketch by Princess Victoria of Kent (later Queen Victoria)
© HM Queen Elizabeth II 2012. Supplied by Royal Collection Trust and reproduced by
their kind permission.

2.12: Baking tray for cooking petites Madeleines de Commercy
Source and author: User MrDarcy/Wikimedia Commons. Date: 1 Mar 2006. See
http://commons.wikimedia.org/wiki/File:Madeleinetraysmall.jpg, accessed 27.8.12. ©
User MrDarcy, licence for reuse CC BY-SA 2.5.

2.13: Sachertorte from the Hotel Sacher, Vienna
Source and author: User Simfan34/Wikimedia Commons. Date: 2011. Colour image.
See http://commons.wikimedia.org/wiki/File:Sachertorte2009.JPG, accessed
27.8.12. © User Simfan34, licence for reuse CC BY 3.0.

2.14: Guiseppe Garibaldi, 1861
Source: U.S. Library of Congress, ID ppmsca.08351. Author: Unknown. Date:

c.1861. See http://commons.wikimedia.org/wiki/File:Giuseppe_Garibaldi_1861.jpg, accessed 27.8.12. Public domain, old.

CHAPTER 3: VEHICLES and TRAVEL

3.1: A cart carrying pottery, 1897
Drawing © C.E.Wiles, By kind permission of his estate.

3.2: The Brougham
Source and author: User 'Morburre'/Wikimedia Commons. Date: 8 Oct 2007. Colour image. See http://commons.wikimedia.org/wiki/File:Brougham.jpg, accessed 27.8.12. © User Morburre, licence for reuse CC BY-SA 3.0.

3.3: The Victoria
Photo © Catherine Lassesen, Hestehaven the Horse Garden, see http://www.thehorsegarden.com/carriageservices/weddings.html. By their kind permission.

3.4: The Sherlock Holmes Museum's 1899 Forder Hansom cab
Source: The Sherlock Holmes Museum, http://www.sherlock-holmes.co.uk. By their kind permission.

3.5: Black maria used in the TV series 'Foyle's War', set during World War II
Source: Kent Police Museum, see http://www.kent-police-museum.co.uk/core_pages/archive.shtml, accessed 28.1.12. Author: not known. Date: possibly 2006. By courtesy of the Kent Police Museum Photo Archive.

3.6: Rebecca Rioters
Source: *Illustrated London News*. Author: not known. Date: 11 Feb 1843. See http://commons.wikimedia.org/wiki/File:RebeccaRiots.gif, accessed 30.8.12. Public domain, old.

3.7: Cross Channel ferry from the early 1900s
Drawing © C.M. Wiles. By his kind permission.

3.8: Cluster ballooning
Source: http://www.flickr.com/photos/omnibus/31588081/. Author: User Omnibus on www.flickr.com. Date: 5 Jan 2006. Colour image, cropped. See http://commons.wikimedia.org/wiki/File:Cluster_Ballooning.jpg, accessed 28.8.12. © User Omnibus/Wikimedia Commons, licence for reuse CC BY-SA 2.0.

3.9: UK Government Poster 1915
Source: U.S. Library of Congress Prints and Photographs division, ID cph.3g10972. Author: Publicity Department, Central Recruiting Depot, Whitehall, London. Date: 1915. Colour image. See http://commons.wikimedia.org/wiki/File:It_is_far_better_to_face_the_bullets.jpg, accessed 28.8.12. Public domain, old.

3.10: The Hindenburg catching fire on May 6, 1937
Source: http://www.lakehurst.navy.mil/nlweb/images/1213d.gif. Photographer: Gus Pasquerella. Date: 6 May 1937. See http://upload.wikimedia.org/wikipedia/commons/8/84/Hindenburg_burning.jpg, accessed 28.8.12. Public domain, U.S. Navy.

3.11: 1937 Rolls-Royce Phantom III in Ivory
Photo © Belinda Bailey. By her kind permission, and with permission of the bride and groom.

3.12: Sopwith F1 Camel, single-seat scout, 1917
Photo © Imperial War Museums (Q 67556). By their kind permission.

3.13: Front of the first edition of the Highway Code, 1931
Source and author: *Ministry of Transport*, HMSO. Date: 1931. Colour image. See
http://commons.wikimedia.org/wiki/File:The_Highway_Code_1931.djvu, accessed
30.8.12. Public domain, UK government.

3.14: JCB Backhoe Loader
Source and author: User Gabinho/Wikimedia Commons. Date: 20 Sept 2011. Colour
image. See
http://commons.wikimedia.org/wiki/File:JCB_3CX_Backhoe_Loader_on_outriggers.jp
g, accessed 28.8.12. © User Gabinho, licence for reuse CC BY-SA 3.0.

3.15: Farm trailer, believed to be the first vehicle made by J.C. Bamford
Source and author: Anthony Appleyard at en.wikipedia. Date:1 July 2006. Colour
image. See http://commons.wikimedia.org/wiki/File:Aa_jcb_firstproduct.jpg,
accessed 30.8.12. © Anthony Appleyard/Wikipedia Commons, licence for reuse CC
BY-SA 3.0.

CHAPTER 4: MEASUREMENT

4.1: Medieval ploughmen with oxen
Source: *Manners, Custom and Dress During the Middle Ages and During the
Renaissance Period.* Author: Paul Lacroix, artist not known. Date: 1870 (image
medieval). Public domain, old.

4.2: Interior of a Flemish apothecary's shop
Source: *Illustrated History of Furniture, From the Earliest to the Present Time*, pub.
Truslove & Hanson, London. Author: Frederick Litchfield, artist not known. Date:
1893 (image from an old painting). Public domain, old.

**4.3: Fludd's Illustration of 'X' Philo's thermometer and 'Z' Fludd's
rearrangement of it**
Source: *Philosophia Moysaica.* Author: Robert Fludd. Date: 1638. Public domain, old.
By kind permission of the Wellcome Library, London.

4.4: Memorial plaque at Fahrenheit's burial site in The Hague
Source and author: User Donarreiskoffer/Wikimedia Commons. Date: 6 Sept 2008.
Colour image. See
http://commons.wikimedia.org/wiki/File:Daniel_Gabriel_Fahrenheit,_place_of_burial.
jpg, accessed 2.1.12. © User Donarreiskoffer, licence for reuse CC BY-SA 3.0.

4.5: Celsius' illustration of his thermometer
Source: *Observations about two fixed degrees on a thermometer*, pub. Annals of the
Royal Swedish Academy of Science. Author: Anders Celsius. Date: 1742. See
http://commons.wikimedia.org/wiki/File:Celsius_original_thermometer.gif, accessed
1.2.12. Public domain, old.

**4.6: Opening page of Genesis telling of the creation of the world,
containing a note in the right hand margin 'Before Christ 4004'**
Source: *Scofield edition of the Authorised King James Version of the Bible*, see
http://www.tekauri.com/saints/ accessed 2.1.12. By kind permission of Richard
Spence, Dangerous Saints.

4.7: "Hand mit ringen"
Source: National Aeronautics and Space Administration (NASA). Author: Wilhelm
Roentgen. Date: 22 Dec 1895. See
http://commons.wikimedia.org/wiki/File:First_medical_X-
ray_by_Wilhelm_Röntgen_of_his_wife_Anna_Bertha_Ludwig%27s_hand_-
_18951222.gif, accessed 3.2.12. Public domain, old. By courtesy of NASA.

4.8: From the front page of the Washington Post, May 21, 1921
Source and author: *Washington Post*. Date: 21 May, 1921. See *Radiology* May 2002
vol. 223 no. 2 299-303 at
http://radiology.rsna.org/content/223/2/299/F4.expansion.html, accessed 12.2.12.
Public domain, old. By courtesy of U.S. Library of Congress and of the Radiological
Society of North America.

4.9: Galvani's 'atmospheric discharge detector'
Source: *De viribus electricitatis in motu musculari commentarius*, memoirs of the
Institute of Sciences of Bologna, volume 7. Author: Luigi Galvani. Date: 1791. See
http://www.bo.infn.it/galvani/cultura-estero/latin-america/pannelli/a4.html,
accessed 13.2.12. Public domain, old. By courtesy of the Luigi Galvani Bicentennial
Celebrations Bologna, September-October 1998 organized by the University of Bologna
and the Bologna Academy of Sciences.

**4.10: Illustration of Galvani's twitching frog leg when touched with an
arc made of zinc and copper**
Source: *The science of common things: a familiar explanation of the first principles of
physical science. For schools, families, and young students*, pub. Ivison, Phinney,
Blakeman. Author: David Ames Wells. Date: 1859. See
http://en.wikipedia.org/wiki/File:Galvani-frogs-legs-electricity.jpg, accessed 15.4.12.
Public domain, old.

4.11: A voltaic pile – Alessandro Volta's electric battery
Source and author: User GuidoB/Wikimedia Commons. Date: 1 May 2005. Colour
image, label '10' deleted. See
http://commons.wikimedia.org/wiki/File:VoltaBattery.JPG, accessed 2.9.12. © User
GuidoB, licence for reuse CC BY 3.0.

4.12: Common torpedo fish
Source and author: Roberto Pillon,
http://fishbase.org/photos/thumbnailssummary.php?ID=2062#. Date: 6 Dec 2010.
Colour image. See
http://upload.wikimedia.org/wikipedia/commons/1/1a/Torpedo_torpedo_corsica4.jp
g, accessed 13.2.12. © Roberto Pillon, licence for reuse CC BY 3.0.

4.13: Sketch of a steam engine designed by Boulton & Watt, 1784
Source: *A History of the Growth of the Steam Engine*, pub. New York. Author: Robert
Henry Thurston. Date: 1878. See
ttp://commons.wikimedia.org/wiki/File:SteamEngine_Boulton%26Watt_1784.jpg,
accessed 13.2.12. Public domain, old.

4.14: Portrait of André-Marie Ampère
Source: *Practical Physics*. Authors: Millikan and Gale. Date: 1920 copy of an older
image. Public domain, old. By courtesy of California Digital Library, University of
California

4.15: Series E £20 note featuring Faraday
Note: legal requirements for copying bank notes fulfilled.

4.16: Cartoon published in Punch, 1855
Source: *Punch*. Author: not known. Date: 21 July 1855. See
http://www.victorianweb.org/periodicals/punch/19.html, accessed 13.2.12.
Public domain, old. By courtesy of The Victorian Web.

**4.17: The magnetic field of a bar magnet revealed by iron filings on a
piece of paper placed over the magnet**
Source: *Practical Physics*, published The MacMillan Co., USA. Author: Newton Henry
Black, Harvey N. Davis. Date: 1913. See

http://commons.wikimedia.org/wiki/File:Magnet0873.png, accessed 2.9.12.
Public domain, old.

4.18: Saturn eclipsing the sun, seen from behind, from the Cassini orbiter

Source: http://photojournal.jpl.nasa.gov/catalog/PIA08329 (actual file
http://photojournal.jpl.nasa.gov/4ures/PIA08329_42.jpg). Author: NASA/JPL/Space
Science Institute. Date: 15th Sept 2006. Colour image. See
http://commons.wikimedia.org/wiki/File:Saturn_eclipse_exaggerated.jpg, accessed
2.9.12. Public domain, {{PD-USGov}}. By courtesy of NASA.

4.19: Bronze bust of Tesla sculpted by R. Farrington Sharp, as presented to educational institutions

www.ntesla.org/, accessed 20.2.12. By their kind permission. The description reads
"NIKOLA TESLA 1856-1943 American Inventor. His name marks an epoch. In a
single burst of invention he created the polyphase alternating current system of
motors and generators that powers our world. He gave us every essential of radio, and
laid the foundation for much of today's technology."

4.20: The back of a radio, showing frequencies in megahertz

© C.M. Wiles. By his kind permission

4.21: Bell's first drawings of his telephone, 1876

Source: *The Alexander Graham Bell Family Papers.* Author: Alexander Bell.
Date:1876. See http://memory.loc.gov/cgi-
bin/ampage?collId=magbell&fileName=273/27300105/bellpage.db&recNum=0. By
courtesy of U.S. Library of Congress, Manuscript Division.

4.22: Gray's notebook entry that led to his caveat

Source: http://repo-
nt.tcc.virginia.edu/classes/tcc315/resources/alm/telephone/exhibits/gray.html.
Date:14 Feb 1876. See http://en.wikipedia.org/wiki/File:Gray-telephone-caveat.gif.
By courtesy of Michael E. Gorman, School of Engineering and Applied Science,
University of Virginia.

4.23: Copy of a drawing filed with Meucci's caveat demonstrating his invention

Source: *Scientific American Supplement, No. 520.* Author: Nestori. Date: 19 Dec 1885.
Public domain, old.

4.24: Dobson's ozone spectrophotometer, 1968 model

Source: *Applied Optics Vol 7 No 3 page 388: Forty Years' Research on Atmospheric
Ozone at Oxford: a History.* Date: March 1968. Author: G.M.B.Dobson. © Optical
Society of America. By their kind permission.

4.25: FA-18 Hornet breaks the sound barrier

Source: http://www.news.navy.mil/view_single.asp?id=1445, Photo number: 990707-
N-6483G-001. Author: U.S. Navy photo by Ensign John Gay. Date: 7 July 1999.
Colour image. See http://commons.wikimedia.org/wiki/File:FA-
18_Hornet_breaking_sound_barrier_(7_July_1999).jpg, accessed 4.9.12. Public
domain, U.S. Navy.

4.26: Opening page of Sir Isaac Newton's own first edition copy of his Principia with his handwritten corrections for the second edition

Source: *Philosophiae Naturalis Principia Mathematica*, property of the Wren Library,
Trinity College, Cambridge. Author: I. Newton. Date: 1687. By kind permission of
the Master and Fellows of Trinity College, Cambridge.

4.27: Diagram of a mercury barometer illustrating the space (vacuum) at the top

School Science Lessons, UNPhysics2. By kind permission of the School of Education, University of Queensland, Australia.

4.28 & 4.29: Contemporary drawing of Guericke's Magdeburg experiment in 1656

Source: *Mechanica Hydraulico-pneumatica, Appendix.* Author: Gaspar Schott. Date:1657. Image cropped. See http://commons.wikimedia.org/wiki/File:Magdeburger-Halbkugeln.jpg, accessed 4.9.12. Public domain, old.

4.30: Zones used by the UK shipping forecast

Source and author: User Emoscopes/Wikimedia Commons. Date:21 Apr 2007. Colour image. See http://commons.wikimedia.org/wiki/File:UK_shipping_forecast_zones.png, accessed 4.9.12. © User Emoscopes, licence for reuse CC BY-SA 3.0.

4.31: Drawing of a frigate

Source and author:. Date:2009. See http://commons.wikimedia.org/wiki/File:Frigate_(PSF).png, accessed 4.9.12. Public domain, by courtesy of Pearson Scott Foresman.

4.32: Earthquake in Italy, 5th Century BC, as drawn by Lycosthenes in 1557

Source: *La Nature* No. 13 (30 Aug 1873), reproducing a plate from *Prodigiorum ac ostentorum chronicon.* Author: Conrad Lycosthenes. Date: 1557. See http://commons.wikimedia.org/wiki/File:Lycosthène.jpg, accessed 4.9.12. Public domain, old.

CHAPTER 5: MEDICAL

5.1: Successful Caesarian section performed by indigenous healers in Uganda 1879

Source: *Notes on Labour in Central Africa*, pub. Edinburgh Medical Journal, vol 20. Author: R.W. Felkin. Date: 20 Apr 1884. Public domain, old. By courtesy of U.S. National Library of Medicine.

5.2: A man on pedalled roller skates, 1910

Source: George Grantham Bain Collection, U.S. Library of Congress. Author: George Grantham Bain. Date:8 Nov 1910. Public domain, old. By courtesy of U.S. Library of Congress.

5.3: 'An old crone': the Newbury witch

"A Most Certain, Strange, and true Difcovery of a VVitch", front page of a pamphlet printed by John Hammond, 1643. By kind permission of University of Glasgow Library, Special Collections.

5.4: Adult Hands (a) showing normal creases and (b) showing a Simian crease

Source and author: User Wurdbendur/Wikimedia Commons. Dates: 10.2.2008 and 11.2.2008. Colour images. See http://commons.wikimedia.org/wiki/File:Normal_creases_adult.jpg and http://en.wikipedia.org/wiki/File:Single_transverse_palmar_crease_adult.jpg, both accessed 7.9.12. © User Wurdbendur, licence for reuse CC BY-SA 3.0.

5.5: Domestic goat
Source: *Exploring Nature Educational Resource: Farm Animals, Goat.* See
http://www.exploringnature.org/db/detail.php?dbID=6&detID=90. © Sheri Amsel.
By her kind permission.

5.6: Frontispiece of Bartholomaei Eustachii's Romanae Archetypae Tabulae Anatomicae, published 1783
Source: *Romanae Archetypae Tabulae Anatomicae.* Author: Bartholomaei Eustachii.
Date: 1783. See
http://www.nlm.nih.gov/exhibition/historicalanatomies/eustachi_home.html,
accessed 10.3.12. Public domain, old. By courtesy of U.S. National Library of
Medicine.

5.7: George Huntington with his pony and trap
Source and author: not known. Date: pre-1917. Sepia image. Public domain, old. By
courtesy of Ria van Hes (www.allesoverhuntington.nl, accessed 16.7.12).

5.8: Mid 16thC portrayal of Aztec ritual human sacrifice
Source: *Codex Magliabechiano* (page 141, folio 70r), facsimile edition, pub.
Akademische Druck- u. Verlagsanstalt (ADEVA), Graz 1970. Public domain, old.
Facsimile image © ADEVA. By their kind permission.

5.9: Baron von Münchausen riding on a cannon ball
Source: Распе. Мюнхаузенъ. С.-Петербургъ. Изданіе книгопродавца Ф. А. Битепажа. Author:
August von Wille. Date: 1872. Colour image. See
http://commons.wikimedia.org/wiki/File:Münchhausen-AWille.jpg, accessed 7.9.12.
Public domain, old.

5.10: Engraving of a man smoking, 1595
Source: *Tabaco* (a pamphlet). Author: Anthony Chute. Date: 1595. See
http://commons.wikimedia.org/wiki/File:Chute_tobacco.JPG, accessed 7.9.12.
Public domain, old.

5.11: Paralysis agitans: the posture and gait of a man with Parkinson's disease
Source: *A Manual of Diseases of the Nervous System,* vol 2 page 591 (2nd edition), pub.
J. & A. Churchill Ltd., London. Author: W.R. Gowers. Date: 1888. Public domain,
old. By courtesy of C.M.Wiles.

5.12: The hand of a 25 year old male showing Raynaud's phenomenon
Source and author: User Tcal/Wikimedia Commons. Date:6 Oct 2008. Colour image.
See http://commons.wikimedia.org/wiki/File:Raynaud%27s_Syndrome.jpg, accessed
7.9.12. © User Tcal, licence for reuse CC BY-SA 3.0.

5.13: An ear of rye showing the growth of sclerotia (the fruiting structures of the fungus claviceps purpurea) containing ergot alkaloids
Source: *Köhler's Medizinal-Pflanzen.* Author: Hermann Kohler. Date: 1887. Colour
image. See http://commons.wikimedia.org/wiki/File:Claviceps_purpurea_-_Köhler–
s_Medizinal-Pflanzen-185.jpg, accessed 7.9.12. Public domain, old.

5.14: Angiograms showing the flow of blood to the hand in a recent case of ergotism: (a) before treatment and (b) after treatment
Source: *Ergotism With Ischemia In All Four Extremities: A Case Report* (pub. Korean
Neurological Association's Journal of Clinical Neurology, Vol 2. page 281 fig 2, see
http://synapse.koreamed.org/Synapse/Data/PDFData/0145JCN/jcn-2-279.pdf,
accessed 16.3.12. Authors: Seok-Young Jeong, M.D., Eui-Seong Lim, M.D., Byoung-
Soo Shin, M.D., Man-Wook Seo, M.D., Young-Hyun Kim, M.D., Hyo-Sung Kwak,
M.D.*, Gyung-Ho Chung*, M.D., Seul-Ki Jeong, M.D. (*Department of Neurology and
Diagnostic Radiology, Chonbuk National University Medical School, Jeonju, South

Korea). Date: Dec 2006. By kind permission of the Korean Neurological Association's Journal of Clinical Neurology.

5.15: Front page of *Le Pays Illustré* from December 1893, with sketch of a patient's attack on Dr. Tourette
Source: *Le Pays Illustré*. Author: not known, author of digital image http://baillement.com/lettres/tourette.html#la%20thèse. Date: 1893. See http://en.wikipedia.org/wiki/File:Petit-illustre-gdlt.gif, accessed 16.3.12. By courtesy of Dr. Olivier Walusinski.

5.16: Dancing girls
Drawing © C.M. Wiles. By his kind permission.

CHAPTER 6: BEHAVIOUR

6.1: The White Rabbit
Source: *Alice in Wonderland*. Author: Lewis Carroll, artist John Tenniel. Date: 1865. See http://commons.wikimedia.org/wiki/File:Alice_par_John_Tenniel_02.png, accessed 17.3.12. Public domain, old.

6.2: Caricature of Dr. WA Spooner MA
Source: *Vanity Fair* (from http://www.antiquemapsandprints.com/scansj/j-20476.jpg). Author: Leslie Ward. Date: 21 Apr 1898. Colour image. See http://commons.wikimedia.org/wiki/File:William_Archibald_Spooner_Vanity_Fair_1898-04-21.jpg, accessed 14.9.12. Public domain, old. By courtesy of Bill and Julie Bennett, http://stores.ebay.com/juliesantiqueprints?refid=store.

6.3: Cliveden House, Berkshire, from the lawn
Source and author: User Daderot/Wikimedia Commons. Date: 10 June 2005. Colour image. See http://commons.wikimedia.org/wiki/File:Cliveden,_June_2005.JPG, accessed 14.9.12. © User Daderot, licence for reuse CC BY-SA 3.0.

6.4: Tenanted properties à la Rachman
Drawing © C.M. Wiles. By his kind permission.

6.5: The Alamo Mission in San Antonio ('The Alamo') today
Source and author: User ←Baseball Bugs *What's up, Doc?* carrots→/Wikimedia Commons. Date: 15 Aug 2010. Colour image. See http://commons.wikimedia.org/wiki/File:Alamo_rain.JPG, accessed 14.9.12. Public domain, by courtesy of the author.

6.6: 'Brothel creepers'
Source and author: User Alchemica/Wikimedia Commons, retouched by User Il Passeggero/Wikimedia Commons. Date: 5 Nov 2009. Colour image. See http://commons.wikimedia.org/wiki/File:Creepers_shoes_White.jpg, accessed 14.9.12. © User Alchemica and User Il Passeggero, licence for reuse CC BY-SA 3.0.

6.7: The D.A. (Duck's arse hairstyle)
Source and author: User Charlesfrederickworth/Wikimedia Commons. Date: 28 July 2011. See http://commons.wikimedia.org/wiki/File:Ducktail.jpg , accessed 14.9.12. © User Charlesfrederickworth, licence for reuse CC BY-SA 3.0.

6.8: Green Wellies with a boot remover
Photo © C.M.Wiles. By his kind permission.

6.9: The title page of Volume 1 of Sloane's flora and fauna of the West Indies, first published in 1707
Source: *A Voyage to the Islands of Madera, Barbados, Nieves, St. Christopher's and Jamaica*. Author: Hans Sloane. Date: 1725. See http://www.biodiversitylibrary.org/item/11242#, accessed 15.9.12. Public domain,

old. By courtesy of the Biodiversity Heritage Library and Missouri Botanical Garden, Peter H. Raven Library.

6.10: John Duns Scotus as painted by Justus van Gent in the 15th Century
Source: Research Group John Duns Scotus, Utrecht, Netherlands at http://www.dunsscotus.nl/index_en.htm. Author: Justus van Gent. Date: 15th Century. Public domain, old. By courtesy of Research Group John Duns Scotus.

6.11: In disgrace
Drawing © C.M. Wiles. By his kind permission.

6.12: A groat from the reign of William IV (diameter 1.5 cm)
Photo © C.M. Wiles. By his kind permission.

6.13: Title page of the Dunciad (2nd edition, 1929)
Source: *Dunciad Variorum*. Author: Alexander Pope. Date: 1729. Colour image. See http://en.wikipedia.org/wiki/File:Pope_dunciad_variorum_1729.jpg, accessed 23.3.12. Original image public domain, old. Copy image by kind permission of the Hay Library, Brown University, Providence, RI, USA.

6.14: 'Un martinet' (modern)
Source and author: User Shattonbury/Wikimedia Commons. Date: 8 Dec 2004. Colour image. See http://commons.wikimedia.org/wiki/File:Martinet.jpg, accessed 23.3.12. © User Shattonbury, licence for reuse CC BY-SA 1.0.

6.15: The emerald green Lytta vesicatoria (spanish fly, or blister beetle)
Source and author: User Franco christophe/Wikimedia Commons. Date: May 2007. Colour image. See http://commons.wikimedia.org/wiki/File:Lytta-vesicatoria.jpg, accessed 14.9.12. © User Franco christophe, licence for reuse CC BY-SA 3.0.

6.16: Vincennes Prison: the château today
Source and author: User Selbymay/Wikimedia Commons. Date: 21 Feb 2012. Colour image. See http://commons.wikimedia.org/wiki/File:Vincennes_-_Chateau_02.jpg, accessed 8.12.12. © User Selbymay, licence for reuse CC BY-SA 3.0.

6.17: Cartoon threatening that the Ku Klux Klan would lynch carpetbaggers, 1868
Source: Independent Monitor, Tuscaloosa, Alabama. Author: not known. Date: 1868. See http://commons.wikimedia.org/wiki/File:Kkk-carpetbagger-cartoon.jpg, accessed 14.9.12. Public domain, old.

6.18: One of the Piombi prison cells, Doge's Palace
Source and author: Ignazio Marconi, see http://www.viaggiaresempre.it/fotogallery47cItaliaVeneziaPalazzoDucale.html, accessed 26 Mar 2012. © Ignazio Marconi. By his kind permission.

6.19: Duchcov (Dux) castle in Duchcov, Bohemia
Source and author: User Zacatecnik/Wikimedia Commons. Date: 7.10.07. Colour image. See http://commons.wikimedia.org/wiki/File:Front_side_of_Duchcov_castle_in_Czech_Republic.jpg, accessed 14.9.12. © User Zacatecnik, licence for reuse CC BY-SA 3.0.

6.20: The Italian States in 1494
Source and author: User MapMaster/Wikimedia Commons. Date: 2007. Colour image. See http://commons.wikimedia.org/wiki/File:Italy_1494_v2.png, accessed 14.9.12. © User MapMaster, licence for reuse CC BY-SA 3.0.

6.21: Cartoon of 'The Gerry-Mander' from the Boston Centinel, 1812
Source: *Boston Centinel*. Author: Elkanah Tisdale. Date: 26h Mar 1812. See http://commons.wikimedia.org/wiki/File:The_Gerry-Mander_Edit.png, accessed 15,9.12. Public domain, old.

6.22: Troops escorting volunteer labourers to Lord Erne's estate, 1880
Source: *The Graphic*. Author: not known. Date: 20 Nov 1880. See
http://www.maggieblanck.com/Mayopages/Boycott.html, accessed 26.3.12. By
courtesy of Maggie Land Blanck.

6.23: Early 19th Century engraving showing frame-breaking in progress
Source: *Luddites* (Nottinghamshire Heritage Gateway). Author: Prof. John Beckett,
artist unknown. Date of image: early 1800s. See
http://www.nottsheritagegateway.org.uk/people/luddites.htm, accessed 27.6.12.
Public domain, old. By courtesy of Nottinghamshire Heritage Gateway project team.

6.24: Hobson's conduit, Cambridge 2006
Source and author: User Mammal4/Wikipedia. Date:2006. Colour image. See
http://en.wikipedia.org/wiki/File:Hobson%27sconduit3.JPG, accessed 27.3.12. ©
User Mammal4, licence for reuse CC BY-SA 3.0.

CHAPTER 7: PLANTS

7.1: Route of Tournefort's Research Journeys
Source and author: Valérie Chansigaud (User Valérie75/Wikimedia Commons). Date:
2 Nov 2007. Colour image. See
http://commons.wikimedia.org/wiki/File:Travels_Tournefort.svg, accessed 15.9.12. ©
Valérie Chansigaud, licence for reuse CC BY-SA 3.0.

7.2: Portrait of the French monk Charles Plumier
Source: http://upload.wikimedia.org/wikipedia/en/2/28/Plumier_Charles.jpg.
Author: not known. Date: not known. See
http://commons.wikimedia.org/wiki/File:Plumier_Charles.jpg, accessed 15.9.12.
Public domain, old.

7.3: Cinchona officinalis, harvested quinine bark
Source and author: User H. Zell/ Wikimedia Commons. Date: 3 Oct 2009. Colour
image. See http://commons.wikimedia.org/wiki/File:Cinchona_officinalis_001.JPG,
accessed 15.9.12. © User H. Zell, licence for reuse CC BY-SA 3.0.

7.4: Bromeliads growing on telephone lines in Bolivia
Source: Flickr. Author: User Cody H/Wikimedia Commons. Date: 2 July 2007.
Colour image, cropped. See
http://commons.wikimedia.org/wiki/File:Tillandsia_sp._telephone_line_(codiferous).jp
g, accessed 15.9.12. © User Cody H, licence for reuse CC BY-SA 2.0.

7.5: Dahlia coccinea, parent of all European 'single' dahlias
Source: *The Botanical Magazine, Vol 20*. Author: Sydenham Edwards, artist Sansum.
Date: 1804. Colour image. See http://commons.wikimedia.org/wiki/File:Scarlet-
flowered_dahlia.jpg, accessed 15.9.12. Public domain, old.

7.6: 'Solomon's Glory, or the Rival Mistresses'
Source: U.S. Library of Congress Prints and Photographs Division Washington, D.C.
20540 USA http://hdl.loc.gov/loc.pnp/cph.3c03093. Author: Not known. Date: 29
Aug 1749. See
http://commons.wikimedia.org/wiki/File:William_augustus_duke_of_cumberland_sol
omons_glory.jpg, accessed 15.9.12. Public domain, old. By courtesy of U.S. Library of
Congress.

7.7: Tradescant's House, South Lambeth, c. 1878
Source: *London, Old and New, vol 6*. Authors: Thornbury and Walford, artist 'WF',
from Pennant. Date: 1878. Sepia image, wood engraving. See

http://commons.wikimedia.org/wiki/File:Tradescant%27s_House,_South_Lambeth.p
ng, accessed 15.9.12. Public domain, old.

7.8: Tahiti: a black sand beach

Source and author: User Fred/ Wikimedia Commons. Date: 2006. Colour image. See
http://commons.wikimedia.org/wiki/File:Plage.sable.noir.Tahiti.JPG, accessed
20.9.12. © User Fred, licence for reuse CC BY-SA 3.0.

7.9: Cannabis sativa from Fuchs' *De Historia Stirpium Commentarii Insignes*

Source: *De historia stirpium commentarii insignes*. Author: Leonhart Fuchs. Date:
1542. See http://images.wellcome.ac.uk/indexplus/image/L0063951.html, accessed
4 Oct 2012. By kind permission of the Wellcome Library, London

7.10: The Illustrators of Fuchs' *De Historia Stirpium Commentarii Insignes*

Source: *De historia stirpium commentarii insignes*. Author: Leonhart Fuchs. Date:
1543. See http://special.lib.gla.ac.uk/exhibns/month/oct2002.html. By kind
permission of University of Glasgow Library, Special Collections.

7.11: Joel Roberts Poinsett, 15th U. S. Secretary of War

Source: U.S. Library of Congress, Prints and Photographs division,
http://www.loc.gov/pictures/item/2003656274/, rep no. LC-USZ62-23834,
accessed 12.1.13. Author: Charles Fenderich. Date: Not known. Public domain, old.
By courtesy of U.S. Library of Congress.

7.12: Canker on the trunk of a birch tree

Source and author: User MarkusHagenlocher/Wikimedia Commons. Date: 19 Mar
2006. Colour image. See   http://commons.wikimedia.org/wiki/File:Baumkrebs-
Birke.jpg, accessed 20.9.12. © Markus Hagenlocher, licence for reuse CC BY-SA 3.0.

7.13: Bones of the prehistoric giant ground sloth from a paper published by Wistar in 1799

Source: *A Description of the Bones Deposited, by the President, in the Museum of the
Society, and Represented in the Annexed Plates*, pp. 526-531, pub. Transactions of the
American Philosophical Society. Author: Caspar Wistar. Date: 1799. Colour image.
See
http://commons.wikimedia.org/wiki/File:Megalonyx_CasparWistar_claw_Griffe1799.j
pg, accessed 20.9.12. Public domain, old.

7.14: Magnolia grandiflora at the Jardin des Plantes at Nantes, planted in 1807

Source and author: User Pymouss44/Wikimedia Commons. Date: 14 Mar 2008.
Colour image. See
http://commons.wikimedia.org/wiki/File:Jardin_des_plantes_Nantes-
Magnolia_Hectot.jpg, accessed 20.9.12. © User Pymouss44, licence for reuse CC BY-
SA 3.0.

7.15: Cone of a Coast Douglas Fir grown from a seed collected by David Douglas

Source and author: User MPF/Wikimedia Commons. Date: 2005. Colour image. See
http://commons.wikimedia.org/wiki/File:Pseudotsuga_menziesii_cone.jpg, accessed
20.9.12. © User MPF, licence for reuse CC BY-SA 3.0.

7.16: Sequoya's syllabary

Source and author: User Robfergusonjr/Wikimedia Commons. Date: 13 May 3009.
See http://commons.wikimedia.org/wiki/File:Sequoyah_Arranged_Syllabary_.png,
accessed 20.9.12. Public domain, by courtesy of the author.

7.17: Bramley apples
Source and author: Marcin Floryan. Date: 25 Oct 2006. Colour image. See
http://commons.wikimedia.org/wiki/File:Brimley_Apples.jpg, accessed 20.9.12. ©
Marcin Floryan, licence for reuse CC BY-SA 2.5.
7.18: Cox's orange pippins – before and after
Photo © C.M. Wiles. By his kind permission.
7.19: Granny Smiths
Photo © C.M. Wiles. By his kind permission.
7.20: A sentry on duty at Buckingham Palace
Source: http://www.publicdomainpictures.net/view-
image.php?image=7785&picture=buckingham-palace-guard. Author: Petr Kratochvil.
Date: 27 Oct 2011. Colour image. See
http://commons.wikimedia.org/wiki/File:Buckingham-palace-guard-
11279634947G5ru.jpg, accessed 20.9.12. Public domain, by courtesy of the author.
7.21: Filbert nails
Photo © J.E. Baldwin. By his kind permission.

CHAPTER 8: CREATURES
8.1: Portrait of a Maori man with tattoos, c.1770
Source: *A journal of a voyage to the South Seas*, plate 16, pub. London. Author:
Sydney Parkinson. Date: c.1769, pub. 1784. Colour image. See
http://commons.wikimedia.org/wiki/File:MaoriChief1784.jpg, accessed 20.9.12.
Public domain, old.
8.2: Przewalski's horse
Source and author: Joe Ravi. Date: 17 Sept 2011. Colour image. See
http://commons.wikimedia.org/wiki/File:Portrait_of_Przewalski%27s_Horse.jpg,
accessed 22.9.12. © Joe Ravi, licence for reuse CC-BY-SA 3.0.
8.3: Jesus Christ lizard, or brown basilisk
Photo © Terrance Wright. See
http://www.jjaudubongallery.com/Costa%20Rica/animals.html, accessed 19.7.12.
By his kind permission.
8.4: 'Wild Swan' engraved by Thomas Bewick c.1804
Source: *History of British Birds vol II.* Author: *Thomas Bewick*, printed by Edw.
Walker. Date: 1826. See
http://www.sharecom.ca/bewick/waterbirds/frwb1826.html, accessed 27.10.11. By
kind permission of the Art Gallery of Alberta Collection, gift of Mr. David E. Lemon,
Vancouver, 1990.
8.5: Temminck's stint
Source and author: Andreas Trepte, www.photo-natur.de. Date: 5 June 2011. Colour
image. See http://commons.wikimedia.org/wiki/File:Temmincks_Stint.jpg, accessed
23.9.12. © Andreas Trepte, licence for reuse CC BY-SA 2.5.
8.6 The Rev. John Russell: frontispiece from *Memoir of the Rev. John Russell and his Out-of-Door life* by E.W.L.Davies
Source: *Memoir of the Rev. John Russell and his Out-of-Door life* (frontispiece), pub.
Chatto & Windus, London. Author: E.W.L.Davies, artist N.H.J. Baird. Date: 1902.
Public domain, old.
8.7: Barry, exhausted (pre 1923)
Source: Panabasis archive, 4 Feb 2007 at
http://www.janusmuseum.org/panabasis/feb07.htm, accessed 3.4.12. Author: not

known. Date: pre 1923. Sepia image. By kind permission of the Janus Museum, Washington Grove, Maryland, U.S.A.

8.8: Heroic Barry (post 1923)
Source: Naturhistorisches (Natural History) Museum, Bern, Switzerland. Author: not known. Date: post 1923. See
http://www.nmbe.ch/entdecken/ausstellungen/dauerausstellung/barry, accessed 4.4.12. Photo © Naturhistorisches Museum Bern. By their kind permission.

8.9: Dobermann Pinscher, 1909
Source: *Nordisk familjebok*. Author: Heinrich Sperling. Date: 1909. See
http://commons.wikimedia.org/wiki/File:Doberman_Pinscher_Portrait.jpg, accessed 23.9.12. Public domain, old. By courtesy of Projekt Runeberg,
http://runeberg.org/nfbk/0687.html.

8.10: Cavalier King Charles Spaniel
Source and author: Andrew Eatock (Darilance Cavalier King Charles Spaniels). Date: 13 June 2009. Colour image. See
http://commons.wikimedia.org/wiki/File:CarterBIS.Tiki.13.6.09.jpg, accessed 23.9.12. © Darilance Cavalier King Charles Spaniels (www.darilance.com), licence for reuse CC BY-SA 3.0.

CHAPTER 9: INVENTIONS and DISCOVERIES

9.1: Early mechanical orrery by Gilkerson
Source and author: Armagh Observatory, Northern Ireland (image slightly cropped). See http://www.arm.ac.uk/orrery/, accessed 6.4.12. By kind permission of Armagh Observatory.

9.2: Petri dish, without its lid
Source and Author: User Polimerek/Wikimedia Commons. Date: 2005. Colour image. See http://commons.wikimedia.org/wiki/File:Szalka_petriego.jpg. accessed 23.9.12. © User Polimerek, licence for reuse CC BY-SA 3.0.

9.3: Waves emitted by a source moving from right to left
Source and author: User Tkarcher/Wikimedia Commons. Date: 2 Jan 2006. Colour image. See
http://commons.wikimedia.org/wiki/File:Doppler_effect_diagrammatic.png, accessed 23.9.12. Public domain, by courtesy of the author.

9.4: Sketch of the steam locomotive used in the Buys-Ballot experiment
© Royal Netherlands Meteorological Institute (KNMI). See
http://www.knmi.nl/cms/content/64698/het_muzikale_doppler_experiment_van_buys_ballot, accessed 9.4.12. By their kind permission.

9.5: Swan neck flask of similar shape to that used by Louis Pasteur
Source and author: User YassineMrabet/Wikimedia Commons. Date:16 Jan 2007. Colour image. See http://commons.wikimedia.org/wiki/File:Coldecygne.svg, accessed 23.9.12. © User YassineMrabet, licence for reuse CC BY-SA 3.0

9.6: Silk moth cocoons in a jar
Source and author: Krish Dulal. Date:2011. Colour image, cropped. See
http://commons.wikimedia.org/wiki/File:Cocoon.jpg, accessed 23.9.12. © Krish Dulal, licence for reuse CC BY-SA 3.0.

9.7: Silhouette of the author
Photo © C.M. Wiles. By his kind permission.

9.8: 'The Artist's Studio', possibly the first daguerreotype made by Daguerre, 1837

Source: Société française de photographie. Author: Louis Daguerre. Date: 1837. See http://commons.wikimedia.org/wiki/File:Daguerreotype_Daguerre_Atelier_1837.jpg, accessed 9.4.12. Public domain, old.

9.9: Corn Exchange Clock, Bristol

Source and author: Rod Ward (Rodw at en.wikipedia). Date: 20th Apr 2007. Colour image, cropped. See http://commons.wikimedia.org/wiki/File:Exchangeclock.JPG, accessed 23.9.12. Public domain, by courtesy of Rod Ward.

9.10: Replica of The Halifax Gibbet at Gibbet Street, Halifax

Source: geograph.org.uk. Author: Paul Glazzard. Date: 26 Feb 2007. Colour image, cropped. See http://commons.wikimedia.org/wiki/File:The_Halifax_Gibbet_-_geograph.org.uk_-_350422.jpg, accessed 23.9.12. © Paul Glazzard, licence for reuse CC BY-SA 2.0.

9.11: Birthplace of Louis Braille

Source and author: User Kou07kou/Wikimedia Commons. Date: 26 Feb 2009. Colour image. See http://commons.wikimedia.org/wiki/File:Braille_house04.JPG, accessed 11.4.12. © User Kou07kou, licence for reuse CC BY-SA 3.0.

9.12: B-flat curved soprano, E-flat alto and B-flat tenor saxophones

Source and author: User Ommeh at en.wikipedia. Date: 4 Nov 2007. Colour image. See http://commons.wikimedia.org/wiki/File:CurvedSopranoAltoTenorSaxophoneComparison.jpg, accessed 11.4.12. Public domain, by courtesy of the author.

9.13: Sousaphones in a Santa Claus parade, USA

Source and author: User Glogger/Wikimedia Commons. Date: 18 Nov 2007. Colour image. See http://commons.wikimedia.org/wiki/File:Santaclaus2007_Sousaphones_dsc120.jpg, accessed 23.9.12. © User Glogger, licence for reuse CC BY-SA 3.0.

9.14: The original Ferris wheel, built for the Chicago World's Fair 1893

Source: The New York Times. Author: Not known. Date: 1893. See http://commons.wikimedia.org/wiki/File:Ferris-wheel.jpg, accessed 23.9.12. Public domain, old. By courtesy of The New York Times Photo archives.

9.15: Electric vacuum cleaner by Electric Suction Sweeper Company, circa 1908

Source and author: User Daderot/Wikimedia Commons. Date: 18 Jan 2011. Colour image (of exhibit in National Museum of American History, Washington, DC, USA). See .http://commons.wikimedia.org/wiki/File:NMAH_DC_-_IMG_8859.JPG, accessed 11.4.12. Public domain, by courtesy of the author.

9.16: A Hurricane Mk I (R4118) that fought in the Battle of Britain

Source and author: Adrian Pingstone (User Arpingstone/Wikimedia Commons). Date: July 2008. Colour image. See http://commons.wikimedia.org/wiki/File:Hurricane_mk1_r4118_fairford_arp.jpg, accessed 23.9.12. Public domain, by courtesy of the author.

CHAPTER 10: MILITARY

10.1: Sten Mk II submachine gun

Source and author: Grzegorz Pietrzak (User Vindicator/Wikimedia COmmons). Date: 9 Sept 2007. Colour image (of exhibit in The White Eagle Museum, Skarżysko-Kamienna). See

http://commons.wikimedia.org/wiki/File:Pistolet_maszynowy_STEN,_Muzeum_Orła_B
iałego.jpg, accessed 23.9.12. © Grzegorz Pietrzak, licence for reuse CC BY-SA 3.0.

10.2: Short Magazine Lee Enfield Mk I (1903)

Source: Armémuseum (Swedish Army Museum) through the Digital Museum
(http://www.digitaltmuseum.se). Author: Armémuseum (The Swedish Army
Museum). Colour image. See
http://commons.wikimedia.org/wiki/File:Short_Magazine_Lee-Enfield_Mk_1_(1903)_-
_UK_-_cal_303_British_-_Armémuseum.jpg, accessed 23.9.12. Public domain, by
courtesy of Swedish Army Museum.

10.3: Thompson submachine gun, stored in a violin case

Source and author: C. Corleis. Date: 15 Apr 2007. Colour image. See
http://commons.wikimedia.org/wiki/File:Thompson_in_violin_case.jpg, accessed
23.9.12. © C. Corleis, licence for reuse CC BY-SA 3.0.

10.4: The Paris Gun 1914-1918

Source and author: not known. Date: presumed before Nov 1918. See
http://commons.wikimedia.org/wiki/File:Parisgun2.jpg, accessed 23.9.12.
Public domain, old.

10.5: Diagram of a shrapnel round (as used in World War I)

Source and author: Pearson Scott Foresman, see
U.S.Ahttp://commons.wikimedia.org/wiki/File:Shrapnel_(PSF).png, accessed 23.9.12.
Date: 2007. Public domain, by courtesy of the author.

**10.6: The Battle of Baltimore garrison flag on display at the Star
Spangled Banner Centennial, Baltimore, 1914**

Source: National Star-Spangled Banner Centennial, Baltimore, Maryland, Official
programme. Author: Not known. Date: Sept 6 to 13, 1914. Sepia image. See
http://commons.wikimedia.org/wiki/File:Fort_McHenry_flag.jpg, accessed 17.4.12.
Public domain, old.

**10.7: Molotov cocktail as produced by the Finnish alcohol monopoly
ALKO 1939–1940, with a storm match for a fuse**

Source and author: User Ohto Kokko/Wikimedia Commons. Date: 2006. Colour
image. See http://commons.wikimedia.org/wiki/File:Molotovin_cocktail.jpg, accessed
23.9.12. © User Ohto Kokko, licence for reuse CC BY-SA 3.0.

10.8: An unexploded 'Molotov Bread Basket' incendiary bomb

Source:
http://www.sodatkuvina.cjb.net/images/Talvisota/Rintama/cwdata/4001MolotovinL
eip%E4kori.html. Author: unknown. Date:1939/40. See
http://commons.wikimedia.org/wiki/File:Molotov_bread_basket.jpg, accessed
23.9.12. Public domain, old (Finland).

10.9: Nissen hut near Old Romney, Kent

Photo © Mark Duncan. See
http://www.geograph.org.uk/photo/463076, accessed 20.4.12. Colour image,
cropped. Licence for reuse CC BY-SA 2.0.

10.10: Badge of Sam Browne's Cavalry (12th Frontier Force)

Source and author: User Beloochee/Wikimedia Commons. Date Feb 2011. Colour
image. See http://commons.wikimedia.org/wiki/File:12th_Cavalry_(FF)_badge.jpg,
accessed 23.9.12. Public domain, by courtesy of the author.

10.11: Landing pier at Southwold with a Bailey Bridge beyond

Photo © Belinda Bailey. By her kind permission

CHAPTER 11: MISCELLANEOUS

11.1: Burton's factory in Burmantofts, Leeds, now used as a warehouse
Source and author: User Chemical Engineer/Wikimedia Commons. Date: 9 Apr 2009. Colour image, cropped. See
http://commons.wikimedia.org/wiki/File:BurtonsLS9.jpg, accessed 24.9.12. Public domain, by courtesy of the author.

11.2: Flying Fortress aeroplane 'gone for a burton'
Source: Flickr http://www.flickr.com/photos/30674396@N00/2540483543. Author: Taro Taylor. Date: 4 Jan 2008. Sepia image. See
http://commons.wikimedia.org/wiki/Image:WWII_Plane_Crash.jpg?uselang=it, accessed 24.9.12. © Taro Taylor, licence for reuse CC BY 2.0.

11.3: 'The Beggar's Petition' - a cartoon from 1872 of the Tichborne Claimant
Source: Rex Nan Kivell Collection (The Tichborne trial original drawings, photographs and caricatures collection), National Library of Australia, pic-an6647805-8. Author: unknown. Date: 1872. Public domain, old. By courtesy of National Library of Australia.

11.4: Jumbo's arrival in America, 1883
Source: NYPL (New York Public Library) picture collection. See
http://digitalgallery.nypl.org/nypldigital/dgkeysearchresult.cfm?keyword=jumbo&submit.x=3&submit.y=10, accessed 4.5.12. Author: not known. Date: 1883. Sepia image. Public domain, old. By courtesy of NYPL.

11.5: Heading of an anti-Catholic pamphlet from the 17th or early 18th Century
Source: political pamphlet. Author: unknown. Date: 17th or early 18th Century. See
http://commons.wikimedia.org/wiki/File:GunpowderPlot.jpg, accessed 2.10.12. Public domain, old.

11.6: Two ignited Catherine wheels, spinning
Source and author: User BigRiz/Wikipedia. Date: 2008. Colour image. See
http://en.wikipedia.org/wiki/File:Groundfireworks-burning.jpg, accessed 25.9.12. Public domain, by courtesy of the author.

11.7: Early 20thC depiction of the breaking wheel as used during the Middle Ages
Source: *Petit Larousse*. Author: Pierre Larousse, uploader User Dixie/Wikimedia Commons. Date: 1912. See
http://commons.wikimedia.org/wiki/File:Lamanie_kolem_L_001xx.jpg, accessed 25.9.12. Public domain, old. By courtesy of User Dixie.

11.8: Ring of St. Catherine, as given to pilgrims visiting Mount Sinai
Source and author: User Testus/Wikimedia Commons. Date: 29 Mar 2008. Sepia image. See http://commons.wikimedia.org/wiki/File:Ring_Sinaya.jpg, accessed 25.9.12. © User Testus, licence for reuse CC BY 3.0.

11.9: China bourdaloue with lid
©Topic-Topos, le patrimoine des communes de France, http://fr.topic-topos.com/bourdaloue-vitre. By kind permission of Topic-Topos.

11.10: Tyburn tree, or the 'Three Legged Mare', about 1680
Source: National Archives, Kew. Author: not known. Date: c.1680. See
http://www.nationalarchives.gov.uk/education/candp/punishment/g06/g06cs1s2.htm#, accessed 8.5.12. By courtesy of National Archives, Kew.

11.11: Plaque set into the pavement on the traffic island at Marble Arch
Source and author: User Rioverde/Wikipedia. Date: 19 June 2010. Colour image.
See http://en.wikipedia.org/wiki/File:TyburnStone.jpg, accessed 8.5.12. Public
domain, by courtesy of the author.

**11.12: Contemporary playing card depicting Jack Ketch beheading the
Duke of Monmouth on Tower Hill**
Source: EN.Wikipedia. Author: not known, author of digital image User Raymond
Palmer/Wikimedia Commons. Date: 1685. See
http://commons.wikimedia.org/wiki/File:Monmouth%27s_Execution.gif, accessed
25.9.12. Public domain, old.

11.13: A 'Peeler', from the 1850s
Source: The Metropolitan Police Authority. Author: not known. Date: early 1850s.
See http://www.open.ac.uk/Arts/history-from-police-
archives/Met6Kt/MetHistory/mhDocsOppPeeler.html. Accessed 16.5.12.
Public domain, old. By courtesy of The Open University and Metropolitan Police
Authority.

**11.14: Arrival of the new bell at the clock tower, new Palace of
Westminster**
Source: *Illustrated London News*. Author: not known. Date: 5th June 1858. See
http://www.whitechapelbellfoundry.co.uk/newsv.htm, accessed 26.9.12. Public
domain, old. By courtesy of the Whitechapel Bell Foundry.

11.15: A title page from Hansard, 1832
Source and author: Hansard. Date: 1832. See
http://en.wikipedia.org/wiki/File:Hansard-1832.jpg, accessed 5.10.12. Public
domain, old.

**11.16: Late 19thC depiction of Saint Æthelthryth (Etheldreda, or
Audrey)**
Source: *Little Pictorial Lives of the Saints*, ed. John Gilmary Shea, pub. Benziger
Brothers. Author: not known. Date: 1894. See
http://archive.org/details/littlepictorial00shea, accessed 26.9.12.
Public domain, old. By courtesy of New York Public Library.

**11.17: 'An exact representation of Maclane the Highwayman robbing
Lord Eglington'**
Source: The Old Bailey Proceedings Online, 1674-1913 (www.oldbaileyonline.org,
version 7.0, 24 Mar 2012). Author: not known. Date: 1750. See.
http://www.oldbaileyonline.org/static/images/highwayman.jpg, accessed 17.5.12.
Public domain, old. By courtesy of oldbailey@shef.ac.uk.

**11.18: Obverse and reverse of a gold coin from Lydia, minted in the
early 6th Century BC**
Source and author: Classical Numismatic Group, Inc. See
http://www.cngcoins.comhttp://commons.wikimedia.org/wiki/File:BMC_06.jpg,
accessed 26.9.12. Colour image. © Classical Numismatic Group, Inc., licence for
reuse CC BY 3.0.

**11.19: Ceremonial court of the bath-gymnasium complex at the
archaeological site of Sardis, Turkey**
Source: en/wikipedia. Author: User AtilimGunesBaydin/Wikimedia Commons. Date:
1 Feb 2003. Colour image, cropped. See
http://commons.wikimedia.org/wiki/File:SardisGymnasium1February2003.JPG,
accessed 26.9.12. Public domain, by courtesy of the author.

11.20: A Yarborough

Photo © C.M. Wiles. By his kind permission.

11.21: 'The battle between Crib and Molineaux'

Source: NYPL (New York Public Library) Digital Gallery, digital ID: 1240380, record ID: 592695. Author: Unknown. Date: 3 Oct 1811, depicted date 28 Sept 1811. See http://digitalgallery.nypl.org/nypldigital/dgkeysearchdetail.cfm?strucID=592695&imageID=1240380, accessed 26.9.12. Public domain old. By courtesy of NYPL.

11.22: 'Completely mesmerised'

Source: *Safe Counsel: Searchlights on Health: Light on Dark Corners.* Authors: B.G. Jefferis and J.L. Nichols, artist W. Bertram. Date: 1896. See http://www.fromoldbooks.org/Jefferis-SearchlightsOnHealth/pages/504-completely-mesmerized/, accessed 23.5.12. Public domain, old. By courtesy of Liam Quin, Canada

11.23: Title page of the 1818 edition of Bowdler's *The Family Shakspeare*

Source: *The Family Shakspeare.* Author: Thomas Bowdler (uploader Tim Riley). Date: 1818. See http://en.wikipedia.org/wiki/File:Bowdler-title-page.png, accessed 23.5.12. Public domain, old.

11.24: Symbol of the New York Society for the Suppression of Vice

Source: http://commons.wikimedia.org/wiki/File:NewYorkSocietyForTheSuppressionOfVice.jpg, (from http://www.drugwar.com/inquisition.shtm) accessed 26.9.12. Author: not known, uploader User Apeloverage/en.wikipedia. Date: before 1894. Public domain, old.

11.25: Minnie and Lizzie, beside Fanny Adam's headstone   Source: Curtis Museum (see http://www3.hants.gov.uk/curtis-museum/alton-history/fanny-adams.htm, accessed 24.5.12). Author: not known. Date: about 1867. Public domain, old. By courtesy of the Curtis Museum, Alton, Hants.

11.26: Clifford Berryman's cartoon in The Washington Post of President Theodore Roosevelt's bear hunting trip in Mississippi

Source: *The Washington Post, 16th Nov 1902.* Artist: Clifford Berryman. Date: Nov 1902. Sepia image. See http://commons.wikimedia.org/wiki/File:TheodoreRooseveltTeddyBear.jpg, accessed 26.9.12. Public domain, old.

11.27: Hamilton bottle

Source: http://www.brightonbottles.com/brightonglass.htm, accessed 26.5.12. Author: Brighton Bottles (image cropped). © Brighton Bottles. By their kind permission.

11.28: Codd's Ball Stopper (a) diagram and (b) photograph

Source and author: Historic Glass Bottle Identification & Information Website, Society for Historical Archaeology at http://www.sha.org/bottle/index.htm. © Bill Lindsey. By his kind permission.

INDEX

426